The Courageous Classroom

Ms. Shully - Art

Ms. Shelly - Art

The Courageous Classroom

Creating a Culture of Safety for Students to Learn and Thrive

Dr. Janet Taylor, MD, MPH
Jed Dearybury, MAT, NBCT

JB JOSSEY-BASS™
A Wiley Brand

Published by Jossey-Bass
A Wiley Brand
111 River Street, Hoboken NJ 07030
www.josseybass.com

Jossey-Bass books and products are available through most bookstores. To contact Jossey-Bass directly call our Customer Care Department within the U.S. at 800-956-7739, outside the U.S. at 317-572-3986, or fax 317-572-4002.

Wiley also publishes its books in a variety of electronic formats and by print-on-demand. Some material included with standard print versions of this book may not be included in e-books or in print-on-demand. For more information about Wiley products, visit www.wiley.com.

Library of Congress Cataloging-in-Publication Data is Available:

ISBN 9781119700722 (Paperback)
ISBN 9781119700715 (ePDF)
ISBN 9781119700708 (ePub)

Cover design: PAUL MCCARTHY
Cover art: © JACEK KITA | GETTY IMAGES

FIRST EDITION

SKY10027497 060921

*Dedicated to my mother Joan Neal Taylor,
an educator and my first teacher.*

—Dr. Janet Taylor

*Dedicated to my mother Lynn,
the most courageous person I know.*

—Jed Dearybury

Contents

About the Authors

Dr. Janet Taylor is a community psychiatrist in Sarasota, Florida, working with individuals who are criminal justice involved and have mental illness. She also has a private practice. The practice of community mental health is extremely rewarding to Dr. Janet, because "being on the frontline with individuals and their families battling the emotional and economic impact of Mental Illness is where I can make a difference." She attended the University of Louisville in Louisville, Kentucky, for undergraduate and medical school. An internship in internal medicine at the Miriam Hospital-Brown University followed. Her psychiatric residency was completed at New York Medical College-Westchester Medical Center. She received a Master of Public Health in Health Promotion/Disease Prevention from Columbia University. Her medical experience is also international. While living in Vancouver, British Columbia, she practiced Community Psychiatry at Greater Vancouver Mental Health. During that time, Dr. Janet developed an interest in life coaching and became a certified professional coach through the Coaches Training Institute. She is a frequently invited speaker on the subjects of minority health, self-care, stress management, parenting, and work-life balance. She is a frequent contributor to CBS "This Morning," and NBC "The Today Show" and ABC "Good Morning America" on issues of motherhood, parenting, and mental health. Dr. Janet is also regularly featured on CNN and MSNBC. Dr. Janet is a frequent speaker on the impact of Racial Trauma and Racism, Antiracism, and Conscious Allyship.

Jed Dearybury began his education career in 2001. During his 13-year early-childhood classroom tenure, Jed received numerous awards. He was featured in GQ Magazine as Male Leader of the Year, met President Obama as the South Carolina honoree of the Presidential Award for Excellence in Math and Science Teaching, and was named as a top five finalist for South Carolina Teacher of the Year because of his passion, love, and success in education. Since leaving the second-grade classroom in 2015, he has been leading professional development across the country, as well as training the next generation of educators through his work and teaching in higher education, teaching children's literature, creativity and play for early childhood, and fine arts in the elementary classroom. In August 2019, he started his own education consulting business, mrdearybury.com LLC, where he is the director of Creativity and Innovation. He published his first book, *The Playful Classroom: The Power of Play for All Ages*, co-written with Dr. Julie P. Jones, in June of 2020, thus adding author and illustrator to his list of educational credits. *Courageous Classroom* is his second book. His mission: Equip, Encourage, Empower the teaching profession using creativity, laughter, and hands-on fun!

Foreword

When student and teacher meet with a shared respect, magic happens. Mythical things happen. Over the past 20 years I have worked with urban youth through the telling, discussion, and analysis of mythological stories. We provide a safe space, a *temenos*, where youth feel comfortable being and becoming who they are meant to become. The goal is to have them become the hero/heroine in their own stories. Our process helps make real the idea that they will need heroic character traits to get through life; traits such as perseverance, humility, resourcefulness, and willingness to make necessary sacrifices for something larger than themselves. And, they will need courage to continue despite the odds not being in their favor.

Janet Taylor has been a champion of our methods, and of all teachers who seek to educate in ways that meet the needs of the youth, instead of the needs of adults who insist on sterile measurements. She observed our sessions, and she reported to her audience on what she witnessed. She lifted up our method of telling myth to the beat of a djembe drum, stopping at critical points in the myth, and asking the youth what resonates with them – no right or wrong answers. A key to our process is that as educators, we share intimate parts of our history, about times when we found ourselves facing dilemmas similar to those that the myth depicts, and similar to those that the youth face. As adults, we have found the courage to shed tears in front of our youth, and they in turn have found the courage to shed tears in front of us.

In myth the hero often cries, and as we tell our youth, "It is okay to cry." As a man, I model that it is okay for boys to cry. We create an environment of trust and mutual respect. It is beyond amazing what youth share in our circles. Part of the amazement is because we realize we have a symbiotic relationship. We know we are learning just as much from the students as they are from us. Another key aspect of our process is the importance of listening and keeping an open mind. It is this level of wonder that Janet and Jed are advocating with their book.

Dedicated teachers have a challenging and stressful job. Most are looking for methods that will bring success to student and teacher alike. I have personally held back tears watching some teachers and administrators take advantage of authority in the name of rigid policy that does not serve the students. When this happens, we lose another youth with vast potential. In myth, the hero/heroine never accomplishes their tasks alone. They always have some sort of assistance from a guide and mentor. They are given tools and advice to overcome obstacles before them. When education works best, teachers are allowed to serve this role in the lives of students. Students feel free to come to them with hopes, dreams, and fears. Teachers must uncover both the gifts and wounds of their students, often while having to revisit past fears of their own.

As adults, we often project our own fears and past experiences onto present situations. Adults who work with youth need tools that will allow us to look into the mirror of our own souls and heal our own wounds, prior to working with youth. It takes courage to be an educator. It takes patience. It takes a belief in oneself and a belief in the student. This book allows both the teacher and student to garner the courage to become the heroes/heroines in their own stories.

Kwame Scruggs, PhD

Founder and Director

Alchemy, Inc.

Introduction

There is no courage without fear.

What is fear? Fear is an emotional experience in reaction to a situation perceived as threatening, unsafe, or dangerous. Although it is often perceived as negative, fear is a response that has evolved to help us both survive and reproduce as a species. When we experience fear, we have three kinds of responses: behavioral, physiological, and emotional. The behavioral response might be to attack (fight), run away (flight), or immobilize ourselves (freeze). Physiological responses include elevated heart rate, perspiration, or a trembly voice. The emotional response typically includes feelings of anger or sadness. Freezing can include hiding or "shutting down" emotionally. Most of us know how we feel and can recall a time when we were very afraid. Many of us have recurrent fears or specific phobias, or even what we still may be afraid of or have a phobia about but why? What happens to the brain and our body when we hear a sound, see something that frightens us, smell a noxious agent, or are touched by something unexpected?

To understand how fear impacts our body, we first need to understand some basics of the brain. The brain has two different kinds of tasks that it must balance. On the one hand, it must keep our body running, making sure our metabolism is humming along. On the other hand, it must process information from our environment to make sure we are not under threat. The brain has an evolutionary drive to balance our metabolic functioning with information processing and fear responses (Woods and Khierbeck 2017). Since survival is a foundational evolutionary concern, the hypothalamus, responsible for fear-related emotional behaviors in animals and humans, is one of the oldest structures, deeply located in the brain (Hasan et al. 2019). It is responsible for fear-related emotional behaviors in animals and humans. It has evolved over time as have newer structures like the amygdala and medial prefrontal cortex. The amygdala is a hub in the brain for the expression and processing of threat and fear. When it receives cues – it receives visual, olfactory, auditory, and gustatory – it sends output to the prefrontal motor cortex (decision-making, mindful self-regulation) and the brainstem for behavioral and physiological output (freezing, fight, or flight). In other words, it tells our whole body whether we need to freeze, fight, or flee.

Fear and its associated behaviors have developed over millions of years so that we as humans could get through the day by listening, using our other senses, and being aware that danger was close, using our brain to adapt to threatening, dangerous situations. To survive, fear acquisition or fear learning had to happen quickly. There were no do-overs when the prehistoric wooly mammoth had you in his clutches. After one exposure to danger, humans and animals can form long-lasting fear memories and have the capacity to predict danger (Schiller et al. 2008). Fear learning is "rapid and resistant to modification" (Schiller et al. 2008) with the realization that constantly returning to dangerous situations is not advantageous to survival. The ability to flexibly analyze and adjust behavior is critical in unpredictable, changing environments. We are no longer living side-by-side with prehistoric predators, but we still maintain these evolutionary adaptations that influence how we respond to our environment, like school classrooms and within the four walls of home.

Our brain can be conditioned to automatically fear something: if we know a particular predator wants to make us his lunch, it is in our best interest not to waste valuable time and energy deciding whether we want to stick around and chat with him. However, in more nuanced circumstances – like our present-day world often presents – our brain can also update itself, leading to a concept known as fear safety. Thanks to research carried out in mice, scientists believe that we have a "courage switch" that can shift fear to courage: a mouse that would ordinarily freeze in response to a visual threat, can become bold, fiercely thumping its tail (Huberman 2018). A similar structure exists in humans.

Fear might be evolutionarily adaptive, but so too is courage.

Courage, the process of addressing your own fear to achieve a specific purpose, is not just something that can be learned, it is learning itself. Defined as "the act or experience of one that learns," learning also means "the modification of a behavioral tendency by experience" (Merriam-Webster n.d.).

Fear is a learned association between at least two things that are meant to be adaptive for us in an effort for minimizing exposure to danger. Rather than having to constantly expend energy to relearn what is dangerous or safe, we preserve fear memories and fear learning. However, our brain has the capacity for fear extinction and fear reversal, which allows us to gain cognitive control over our fears. In other words, your brain wants to keep you safe but not afraid. You can use emotional awareness and self-regulation to calm yourself and unlearn fear, using breathing techniques and having a courageous mindset.

What is the difference between a classroom governed by fear and a courageous classroom? While a fearful classroom is focused on student ability, a courageous classroom prioritizes learning for and from the students who are valued for their potential. And what makes that difference? The teacher. As noted psychologist,

Carol Dweck writes, "Every student has something to teach me" (Dweck 2014/2015). The underlying principle of a courageous classroom is belief in the capacity for students and teachers to be courageous in their learning and teaching.

Dr. Janet's Story

This book is a collaboration between two professionals with different experiences with and viewpoints on education. I (Dr. Janet) am not a teacher but a psychiatrist who usually sees kids who are not progressing in school and/or who have mental health issues impacting their ability to focus, learn information, or get along with their peers. As they grapple with underlying trauma, I am motivated by a desire to assist them as they face their own reality. My voice in this book is evidence-based, providing the neuroscience of fear and courage while sharing my own personal stories of finding my own courage. As the mother of four daughters, I respect teachers who, while raising their own families, skillfully and selflessly taught mine.

Jed's Story

As Dr. Janet's co-author, I (Jed) bring my almost-two-decade-long experience as a teacher and a direct voice of my own trauma, in the manner of a *speaking wound*, "the trauma born by an Other that speaks to the wound of the healer" (Dutro and Bien 2014). I share raw accounts of the difficulties of many of my students to illustrate the challenging experiences of trauma and fear that students and teachers bring into the classroom. These stories are the heart and soul of this book. They are told in a personal narrative format. I am more of a story teller than a researcher, so the tone of the book may feel a bit different when I chime in. The students I write about are the ones who above all need(ed) a culture of safety within their classroom walls. The retelling of their stories is multi-purpose. One, to let other teachers know they are not alone in the work. We all have students with lots of trauma that we must talk about so we can figure out how to help them best. Two, talking about the needs of our students helps us to identify the strategies we need for assisting and teaching them. Three, talking about the effects of their trauma on their learning helps us to see where our own education fell short in preparing us for this profession. As a point of caution here, some of the stories may create deep grief for you. You may cry, you may cuss. You may even get mad at me because I didn't handle the situation like I should have. I admit, I wish I could have a rerun with some of these students as I have learned more now than I knew then. Some of the stories may be triggers for you as you process and navigate the waters of your own childhood trauma. Lord knows I have had my fair share: sexually, physically, mentally abused by my father; being gay in the Bible Belt South; and attending a Southern Baptist college while being gay and enduring two years of conversion therapy so I'd "turn straight" and Jesus would love me. These are just a few of the details of my own traumatic past. They alone could be a whole book. I digress.

Through research and relationships, this book will answer the question of how teachers can thrive and learn in spaces where, at times, both parties may experience stress, distress, fear, and anxiety from both internal and external sources. There are moments when the work may read like a college lecture and others where a therapist is talking to a client on the couch in the consulting room. The hope is that we provide advice about how to harness our neurobiological understanding of fear, and help educators and students realize how to push fear aside both inside and outside classrooms. We believe it will show you how to tap into your own potential for healthy psychological functioning and intellectual growth as an individual, and within your institutional culture, by learning how to establish and maintain Courageous Classrooms and promote a growth mindset. Fear and adversity can disrupt the environment of optimal learning. Classrooms and schools that promote a culture of safety, creativity, resilience, and mindfulness will serve as a needed intervention strategy for students and teachers.

Today's teachers are "in the arena," the words that President Theodore Roosevelt used in his 1910 speech (Sweeney 2020, p. 32), stating:

> It is not the critic who counts; not the man who points how the strong man stumbles, or where the doer of deeds could have done them better. The credit belongs to the man who is actually in the arena, whose face is marred by dust and sweat and blood; who strives valiantly; who errs, who comes short again and again, because there is no effort without shortcoming; but who does actually strive to do the deeds; who knows great enthusiasm, the great devotions; who spends himself in a worthy cause; who at best knows in the end the triumph of high achievement, and who at the worst, if he fails, at least fails while daring greatly, so that his place shall never be with those cold and timid souls who neither know victory nor defeat.

Our teachers have to make decisions every day in the face of fear, whether it's their own past history and experience of trauma or the events that emerge from within the classroom. As Sir Edmund Hillary stated, "Fear can help you extend what you believed your capacity was." That happens when instead of acting out of fear, one acts from a place of opportunity, a chance to stretch and learn while utilizing courage.

No one – outside immediate family – has greater impact on students than a teacher. Who doesn't remember the one teacher who pushed them, challenged them, held them accountable, or triggered a fierce and terrific feeling within their being, ready to be unleashed?

As a community psychiatrist, Dr. Janet is asked to assess and treat students who may have mental health issues. As an educator, I (Jed) frequently find myself being asked to do the job of a community psychiatrist – Janet's job – yet the professional training I have received to assess and treat students that have mental health issues is minimal at best. As you will read, instead, I draw on my own traumatic childhood experiences to help students who have experienced trauma. I know that I am not alone in my lack of access to appropriate training and resources. Every day overtaxed and under-supported administrators and educators across the country wake up trying to maximize their own potential, live their calling, and serve their communities. Who is helping them? What training do they receive? What are college EDU programs doing to ready their students for classrooms full of the effects of fear and trauma? They are the ones who can lift our students up – or allow them to slip out of reach. With the odds stacked against them, the latter is more common than the former.

This book argues that we can meet the fears of our time with courage. Fear and courage have a relationship. Whether fear manifests itself as caution, apprehension, or flat-out terror; whether we feel fear internally or exhibit outward symptoms (trembling, sweating, or a shaky voice), courage allows us to meet those fears. The word "courage" has its root in the Latin word *cor* meaning heart, as "the seat of feeling." Author Brené Brown writes "Courage is a heart word . . . In its earliest forms, the word courage meant 'to speak one's mind by telling all one's heart'" (Brown 2007, p. x).

Educators enter the teaching profession with great hope, empathy, and the determination to make a difference. Each teacher has a theory about learning and how children develop, learn, and manage their academic achievements. Lev Vygotsky was no exception. As a Russian psychologist and educator, whose brilliant theories about the process of children's learning and development were lost for almost a half a century after he was banned by an oppressive Russia in 1934, his ideas are applicable to *Courageous Classrooms*.

Vygotsky did not believe that how children learn was based on their genetic history, ethnicity, or socioeconomic class. He believed in the critical role of adults as mediators, "that is, the engagement of children in age-appropriate activities, in the context of which adults promote the development in children of new motives and teach them new tools of thinking, problems solving and self-regulation" (Karpov 2014, p. 9). Good teachers know this and reach across stereotypes and bias to connect to their students. Parents know this and try to model and teach accordingly.

Zaretta Hammond, a former English teacher and sought-after speaker on issues of equity, literacy, and culturally responsive teaching writes of Vygotsky and his sociocultural nature of learning that students develop agency and independence when they're in spaces that promote connecting with others through conversation and have the freedom to give voice to the narration of their own lives. *Courageous Classrooms* endorse that theory because we argue for classrooms that promote psychological safety, openness, an awareness of children's developmental stages, the importance of building educational capacity through emotional regulation, and the management of emotions in the service of safety, listening, and shared empathy.

To live courageously, we must build our inner resources. We must adopt a mindset based on our own self-awareness of what's happening in our lives at every moment, one focused on thriving not just surviving and rooted in successful adaptation to challenges instead of impulsive reactions. Our brain is wired for a courageous mindset, but it must be initiated by flipping on the switch of creative, curious thought.

What to Expect in This Book

The goal of *Courageous Classrooms* is to help both students and teachers interact in ways that promote a courage-based mindset, develop a positive adaptation to trauma and fear, and realize that courage in the face of fear within classrooms is a necessary choice. This book will utilize three principles to illustrate three truths for students and teachers:

1. the power of story and narrative for self-awareness;
2. the role of educators as *encouragers* of students; and
3. the importance of a courageous mindset.

The framework for the book is:

- Teachers and students have stress, fearful experiences, and trauma.
- Fear and trauma inhibit learning and contribute to anxiety-linked conditions.

- Courageous classrooms promote healthy learning related to resolving conflict, eliminating bullying, and maximizing potential.
- A fear response can be modified by fear extinction, fear reversal, and cognitive regulation of fear by attending to it (thoughts), regulating it (visual imagery), and choosing courage (persevering through fear).

Teachers who are encouragers (embodying and instilling more courage) provide appropriate encouragement to their students as an important mechanism in response to pain and to facilitate their growth and learning. They provide *value* in the interaction with their acceptance, attention, and affirmations; *insight* by being sensitive to a student's present emotional level and sharing that insight with the student; and *challenge* students to build on past learnings about how they successfully handled a situation, to keep trying as they think, grow, and take positive actions. Teachers who are encouragers also constantly re-evaluate their own skills with the goal of building courageous classrooms and their own self-efficacy.

At the heart of this work is a belief that teaching needs to be done with empathy, compassion, understanding, and love. It is written with the sincere wish that educators continue to work fearlessly, because the welfare, education, and safety of their students is their primary concern. Teachers wear many hats, including those of counselor, disciplinarian, role model, and a friendly shoulder to lean on. Managing their students, empowering them, and keeping them safe in the classroom and halls of the school while doing their primary job as educators is not easy. Teachers are on the frontline, weathering the storm of student fears while managing their own in times of stress, anxiety, and conflict. The courage of educators is a beacon of light that we need to continue to shine brightly for students, and *Courageous Classrooms* will promote creativity, communication, compassion, confidence, freedom, connectedness, and courage over fear. Read and join the movement of courageous classrooms. Start a conversation.

Chapter 1
The Brain's Fear System

Fear Is Normal

Fear is a normal part of psychological development for infants and children and critical to our survival across the lifespan. At every developmental stage, conquering fear allows children to grow, take risks, be adventurous, remain open to possibilities, and stay curious. Traversing through life is dependent upon the brain identifying patterns of familiar associations that may signal a dangerous outcome versus safety, and the ability to update those associations as our circumstances change. Fear is the associated learning of memories and the emotional and internal response generated by them. As we grow and develop throughout our lives, fear learning (distinguishing between what's safe and/or dangerous) and the ability to overcome or adapt to fear (fear extinction) by diminishing, reversing, or cognitively controlling fear as our circumstances change, is important to our survival, growth, and learning.

Infants learn early from their caregivers the necessary cues of who may be a threat and who is safe and who needs to be kept around. Infants learn early how to recognize and remember their caregiver by how they are touched, what they hear, smell, and can see (Debiec and Sullivan 2017). The quality and characteristics of those interactions shape infant behavior and physiologic response early on. Psychologist John Bowlby theorized that an attachment relationship to at least one primary caregiver is the most important aspect of social and emotional learning for a child. Attachment learning begins at birth and so does the learning of fear.

Caregivers can trigger a fear response in infants and children through social referencing. Social referencing refers to how a child uses caregiver cues to evaluate certain situations, like when a stranger comes close. Studies show that infants are very sensitive to a caregiver's emotional state, including fear and anxiety and readily pick up on it. From birth, we are primed to both attach for safety to our caregivers, learn about fear from them, and practice behavior that promotes our survival. Students utilize the same cues from teachers.

As children get older, what they fear may change. While younger children might fear the dark or scary monsters, older kids will shift to current events, like Covid-19, car accidents, or a family member being hurt. Our kids are always paying attention to what we discuss as adults and they sense what we are afraid of. Too much unmonitored time watching the news or being on social media without the context of feeling safe by having a discussion with their parents or teachers may increase children's fears by contributing to uncertainty and feeling unprotected.

Children will process fear depending on their age, the intensity and duration of exposure to a threat or image, and context. As adults do, children will use a variety of coping behaviors when dealing with a fearful event. Children may want to cuddle more or be clingy, try to take control of the situation by asking questions to understand, or cry and disengage. They reach for reassurance or safety by turning to a familiar face or favorite stuffed animal – all normal responses.

Although fear has been described by some researchers as a "childish emotion" that must be repressed in order to be considered mature, fear is not an emotion: it's a sensory and an evolutionary response that generates emotions. Fear is a brain and body phenomenon that connects our internal and external experiences to keep us safe. When a mother scares her child by screaming at him to not run out into traffic, the combination of being startled by her voice and actions will generate a fear memory (utilizing his senses, inner feelings, and being startled) that will be retained and direct him to look both ways when crossing the street. Now jump back thousands of years, and replace "traffic" with a hungry lion, and fear response begins to make a lot of sense.

Fear Keeps Us Alive

Avoiding being eaten by predators is an early evolutionary task of animals and humans. Basic survival is one of the most cogent demands in the ecosystem. The neurophysiology of both our body and brain for survival has been engineered and adapted over time for one reason . . . *staying alive*. Charles Darwin, a biologist and geologist known for his writings about our human struggle for existence through natural selection, said, "Organisms unable to adapt to the demands of their environment will fail to pass on their genes and fall as casualties in the 'war on nature'" (Darwin 1871).

Human beings are tasked with being smarter than their predators while managing the demands of eating, sleeping, procreating, and avoiding being resource depleted. Lines are drawn as we constantly monitor whether we can safely eat, live, and sleep. Imagine your brain on a Zoom conference call that never stops: there's cross talk and background noise, distractions abound, feelings arise – anxiety, excitement, boredom, anger, frustration – you want to exit, but your brain never hits "leave the meeting." Our brain has the ability to uniquely focus, allowing us to respond to different environments, and circumstances whether they are non-threatening or life-endangering, 24/7.

Fear can result from the presence of a real threat that may be in your face or miles away. The level of danger that you feel is anchored in how close it is and how great the potential is for it to get closer. If you have had the experience of listening to weather forecasts that start as a threat, advance to a warning, and leap to blaring sirens instructing you to take immediate cover, then chances are you have experienced the physiological symptoms of fear: increased heart rate, rapid breathing, sweaty hands, and a sinking feeling in your gut. At the same time, your brain is processing the depth of danger and sending biochemical messages throughout your body.

In that same situation of an ominous weather forecast, anxiety may present when you hear the initial forecast, and will depend on both your experience with bad storms, or watching others' bad experiences with storms, or simply having a personality that worries about natural disasters. Anxiety can occur with remote, unusual, or abstract triggers that usually aren't related to a direct threat. Anxiety can occur in conditions that are safe, but lead to *what if* thoughts triggering brain and body unrest.

Both anxiety and fear can lead to avoidance behavior, and involve emotions that can invade our sense of well-being. It's important to understand that even with fear and anxiety we have time to think, assess the threat, determine if we need to run or fight or relax and stay put. The key point here is when you feel fearful, notice your anxiety . . . take a breath. When our brain perceives a threat, it actively will work for our safety and survival.

To survive, animals and humans must know how to recognize and respond to a threat. Our preferred state is to be in a safe, secure place. When we are chilled and stress free, we are in balance and can focus on finding food, relaxing with friends or family, engaging in romantic pursuits, and teaching or learning with a clear head. If the risk of a threat appears, is felt but not detectable and there is no obvious danger yet, we may be wary but are still good. In the presence of a detectable threat or predator, all systems are "go" and either we freeze, run away, or fight. As presumed prey, our singular goal is to escape and fight only if we have to; the predator's goal is to capture and consume.

When there is a smell, sound, glance, taste, or perception of danger, our brain adapts to multi-sensory mode. Fear is not produced from only one brain region but is a network of brain structures that coordinate responses (see Appendix A). The amygdala, an almond shaped structure located in the temporal lobe is one of those.

The amygdala is a part of the brain's ancient neural circuits and part of the limbic system and receives inputs from our senses. The limbic system supports emotion, behavior, long-term memory, and input from our senses. It influences how we respond to stress and the stress response by its interaction with other brain systems like the endocrine system and autonomic nervous system. The amygdala plays a role in fear expression, fear learning, and fear extinction. Emotional, behavioral, and physiological responses to fear are all mediated by the amygdala (Gozzi et al. 2010). The amygdala has multiple nuclei that function to enhance fear and messaging to engage the stress response in the brainstem or to engage the prefrontal cortex for behavioral control and resilience coping (Sinha et al. 2016). Sitting next to the amygdala lies one of the oldest brain structures; the hypothalamus. It relays fear-related information to the amygdala and prefrontal cortex and is a critical structure for learning, memory, and fear behavior (Hasan et al. 2019). Oxytocin, a neuropeptide produced by the hypothalamus and released by the pituitary gland, plays a role in the behavioral response to fear, specifically freezing as an expression of fear (see Appendix B). It's commonly known as a bonding hormone after childbirth and may explain why women when stressed will "tend and befriend" bringing others close by in response to threat.

The hippocampus is a brain structure that arches over the amygdala and hypothalamus. It is a part of the limbic system and regulates motivation, emotion, learning, and memory. Fear is associated memories and the hippocampus stores long-term memories, making them harder to forget. People who have PTSD, OCD, or depression may have dysregulated limbic systems that make fear extinction or lessening the trauma of memories much harder.

Fear, whether learned or acquired, triggers a fear response. The fear response triggers adaptive behaviors including activating the amygdala and the autonomic nervous system through the vagal nerve and the Hypothalamic-Pituitary-Adrenal (HPA) axis that controls the stress reaction or stress response. The stress response is generated by any potential or real threat or stress and triggers the HPA to release cortisol throughout the body. As a result, the brain and body focus resources on survival: release fats and glucose into the bloodstream for energy; increase the heart rate; inhibit digestion; suppress the immune system; and slow down reproductive hormones. Acute stressors, if resolved, allow the body to recover but chronic stress contributes to cardiovascular disease, anxiety, depression, diabetes, and impairments in learning and memory. When stressors are removed, both brain, body and psychological impairments can be reversed.

The prefrontal cortex, a part of the cerebral cortex covering the frontal lobe allows us to understand, process, and behave in a way that integrates our fear and stress into thinking and behaviors to regulate our stress and fear response. Our prefrontal cortex has two lobes: the dorsolateral prefrontal cortex and the medial prefrontal cortex that play a big role in coping, resilience, memory, and how we think about our circumstances that can help overcome, learn from, and extinguish fear. Using our cognitive thoughts to reframe and reappraise, listening and watching how others process fear and tapping into our courage to persevere through fear begins and ends in our brain.

Our brain wants us to be safe but not afraid. We have the cognitive tools to switch from fear to courage and adapt to fearful circumstances.

In a classroom setting with high levels of anxiety or stress, you can see how learning may be impacted based on the outside environment and internal perception. Our ancestors were masters at changing environments and solving problems under unique and new circumstances to allow us to survive and thrive. Students and educators can utilize the same advantage with awareness and training, if we use our head and heart.

Another evolutionary asset that is on our side is our tendency to form close bonds. As we said above, our fear-learning unfolds over the course of our life in relation to our caregivers. After a baby is born, its brain is dependent on sensory stimuli to grow, adapt, and change structure and functioning. The length of time for this development is longer in humans and necessary for social bonding. The human brain takes the longest for maturation and is impacted by structural factors like environment, stressors, economic resources, genetics, and social stability. Humans' extended infancy and childhood mean we have a multitude of influences on brain and body development. At birth, our brains are 30% of the size they will grow to as we mature into adults. By the age of three, the brain is 80% of adult size, and 90% by the age of five. That means childhood influences, exposures, and resources from birth to five can have a long-lasting impact on brain functioning.

Fear Becomes Courage

Our mind is fear-based because our primitive, lizard brain wants to control our reality and keep us safe. When we are faced with a situation that makes us confused, on guard or afraid, our lizard brain takes over. Although fear itself is not an emotion, it can push us into a river of feelings. However, we have the power to control fear and use our physical and mental response to a fearful situation to our advantage by engaging our wizard brain, which is responsible for executive functioning, in other words, "thinking about thinking."

When we are traumatized or have a terror event, our brain combines all of our sensory material, thoughts, feelings, beliefs, and creates a semantic memory (events and facts). Semantic memory imprints on the brain like indelible ink; it never goes away. Since we can't erase a semantic memory, we can use our courage to face our fears and create a new more powerful memory that incorporates our purpose, strength, resilience, and healthy coping skills to overcome events that happen in our life.

Keanon Lowe did just that.

On a crisp, but gray spring day in Northeast Portland, ex-pro football star Keanon Lowe calmly drove his dented red Cherokee to work at Parkrose High School not too far from his modest home. As he bit into his apple and gulped his coffee his mind undoubtedly was on his part-time job as the school security guard, but also, on his double-coaching duties as the head coach of the football and track teams. Keanon had two jobs at Parkrose. Neither were easy nor left him financially comfortable, but he chose to be there because, for him, being a positive role model for teenagers was invaluable.

Parkrose High is not unlike other city schools across the nation. Almost three-quarters of the diverse student body at Parkrose qualify for a free lunch because of their families' financial status. The grim brick on the outside in no way reflects the emotions and relationships – positive and negative – swirling inside. Keanon came to the school to make a difference after losing a childhood buddy to a devastating drug overdose. He brought to the job his life experience and knowledge of sport and competition. Lowe says of the school, "I've always known that Parkrose, they didn't win at anything . . . it's a small forgotten school." He continues, "That's what attracted me to the place" (Bishop 2019).

Growing up a stone's throw away from Parkrose in a suburb eight miles away, Lowe was raised by a single mother. Taking responsibility for his siblings at a young age, he had a great ethic and set an example for others. As a college star at the University of Oregon he played fearlessly, undersized but very determined on special teams, both defensive and offensive, a testament to his skill. His teammates and coaches describe him as unselfish but tough, as well-known as much as a leader as he was a player. Keanon Lowe was a first-year coach at Parkrose when he got a call to escort a depressed student from another building to the guidance officer. Leaving his cramped office that he shared with another security guard, he willingly complied.

Walking on the concrete walkway bordered by sparse grass, he joked with students as he passed them. The sun had come out in full force and felt good. As he reached the classroom where the students were learning about government, he heard screams bounce off the cement hallway walls. The shrill screams were soon replaced by the sounds of a human stampede of panicked students rushing out of their class because one of their classmates had a weapon, a shotgun partly sticking out from under his black trench coat.

That student was the same one that Keanon Lowe had been tasked to get. Awkwardly face to face, the black metal of the long gun served as a blistering ruler; the distance between them measured by the shotgun squarely placed in the upset student's trembling hands. Looking directly into the teenager's eyes, Lowe saw confusion, anger, desperation, and tears. As the distressed young man suddenly lifted the shotgun to turn it on himself, the remaining students ran for their lives.

Lowe could have too.

He did not.

Keanon Lowe made the decision to grab the shotgun from the young man. At the time, Lowe was unaware that the student, upset over a failed romantic relationship, had recently been diagnosed with depression. They wrestled around the classroom, clanging on blackboards, and ended up in the hallway banging against the metal lockers. Miraculously, Lowe was able to grab the shotgun while keeping the young man in a strong grip. Lowe breathlessly tossed the shotgun to another teacher while screaming at him to call 911.

Putting the young man on the floor while waiting for the police to come, the student was agitated and upset, tearfully shouting, "Nobody cares about me!"

Keanon Lowe did the unthinkable.

He looked into his eyes and said, "I care about you." Lowe continued saying, "I do bro, That's why I'm here, I got you buddy." As the police swarmed in and took the student into custody, Lowe was spared. The student was arrested and later released to a hospital for mental health treatment.

Fear. Keanon Lowe used courage and caring to transform his fear into the energy of compassion.

Fear and Trauma Affect Learning

According to the Trauma and Learning Policy Initiative (TLPI), a collaboration of Massachusetts Advocates for Children and Harvard Law School,

> trauma resulting from overwhelming experiences has the power to disturb a student's development of foundations for learning. It can undermine the development of language and communication skills, thwart the establishment of a coherent sense of self,

compromise the ability to attend to classroom tasks and instructions, interfere with the ability to organize and remember new information, and hinder the grasping of cause-and-effect relationships – all of which are necessary to process information effectively. Trauma can also interfere with the capacity for creative play, which is one of the ways children learn how to cope with the problems of everyday life.

Not only is academic performance hindered, but classroom behavior and peer to peer relationships are negatively impacted as well.

The trauma of childhood abuse can have long-term effects that continue to shape your sense of self and the world around you in adulthood. Often, one of the most tragic consequences of such trauma is its impact on your interpersonal relationships; by disrupting healthy development in your formative years, childhood abuse can deeply compromise your ability to form and maintain the healthy bonds that nurture us throughout our lives.

Childhood trauma is a dangerous or frightening event that a child between the ages of infancy and 18 years of age experiences personally or witnesses. Three hours in a hallway with a textbook over your head while not knowing if a tornado is going to destroy your school at any given moment, possibly injuring you or taking your life is most certainly a traumatic event for anyone, especially a child who is away from their parents as it all happens. It makes me wish that districts had just cancelled schools that day.

In the 1950s during the early stages of the Cold War, when the threat of nuclear bombs in the United States had its citizens in a panic, across the country school children would scurry under desks for duck-and-cover drills just like the tornado safety procedure mentioned above. Years later, surveys of children from this revealed that almost 60% of them still had nightmares about atomic bombs (Pinkser 2019). During the 1980s and 1990s reports of children being kidnapped dominated the airways and with US parents and their children frequently watching television, a 1987 poll found that the most common fear of children was to be kidnapped (Allen 1998). Paula Fass, a historian at UC Berkeley wrote a book about child abductions, *Kidnapped*. She commented that for most kids, "It didn't seem that there were any protected places" (Pinkser 2019). In reality, the fear of kidnapping by a stranger in 1987 was low, because then like now, on average fewer than 350 people under the age of 21 have been abducted in the United States since 2010, according to the FBI (Reuters Staff 2019).

School shootings today create similar fears and feelings for students and their parents. There is a constant 24-hour exposure to news across a variety of platforms. Smartphones capture terror in real-time and are easily shared in case one missed it. Between actual exposure and drills for a shooter, children report that the majority of US students worry that a shooting could happen at their school, and so do their parents (Graff 2018). In *How the Mind Works*, Steven Pinker writes, "Fear is an emotion of anticipation that is triggered when a situation that is at risk for our safety and or the safety of others is perceived. Emotions serve a variety of functions. Our desires and beliefs are information for our brain." He continues to say that, "Fear is the emotion that motivated our ancestors to cope with the dangers they were likely to face" (Pinker 1999).

As important as fear is, surprisingly, we don't experience it as often as we might think (Whalen 2007). Think of how many times you have literally been "scared to death" not just afraid. It's probably not that many. Our experience has been that when people feel afraid in a situation, they are not always in touch with their own feelings of fear and may act defensively or angrily. For example, when we see a young person who is frequently agitating others and engaging in behavior that some would consider as aggressive or taunting, we see pain. Our first inclination is not to label, judge, or punish the behavior but to question, "What is driving it?"

Fear as a Teacher

The need to look beneath aggressive behavior and understand the underlying motives became apparent when I (Janet) was working as a part-time psychiatrist at Rikers Island and assigned to work with male juveniles. Rikers, at the time, was the largest jail in the United States. It spans almost 414 acres between the boroughs of Queens and Brooklyn.

Stopping at the first of many checkpoints is an intimidating process. You are held captive by a non-smiling officer, and asked for proof of identification, including an up-to-date car registration. Small talk is usually not reciprocated and any attempts at banal chatter is usually met with stone cold silence. I attended a thoroughly chilling orientation about how to think and act while a visitor, working at Rikers Island, making me worry if my presence there was worth it. Honestly there were many days when I wondered why I was. But deep down I knew.

Over my career, I have always worked with folks who have been marginalized. Being at Riker's taught me about the impact of trauma on behavior, and how trauma contributes to feelings of fear, anger, and hopelessness. My role, I would learn, was to unleash the individual potential and freeing power, for individuals involved in criminal justice to acknowledge past trauma and openly speak about their pain. Many of these patients of mine had never disclosed their pain, suffering, and trauma to anyone. Their behavior patterns would be labeled as criminal deviance without adequate understanding of the underlying root causes.

As I was working there part-time, I was assigned to different buildings, never knowing where I would end up for the day. The first time that I worked with the male adolescents, I was floored by how much I connected with each young man. They were mostly Brown and Black and would shift uncomfortably while waiting for our session, warily watching each other. Expecting negative attitudes, they had me at "Yes Ma'am" and "No Ma'am" while politely answering my questions. Their easy willingness to open up and talk was both compelling and heartbreaking. Telling me their life stories helped to make sense of their trauma as their words formed a consistent narrative about youth, abuse, low-resources, and peer pressure. Many were in for violent offenses, and I quickly learned that knowing a charge without knowing their past life experiences was meaningless. My job was to assist them in making sense of their own trauma and for them to relate it to their behavior. *Hurt people hurt people* and most of these young men had suffered emotional and/or physical abuse from someone in, or close to, their own household. Noticing my pain, I'll never forget what one Correction Officer said to me. He told me, "Doc, don't fall for their lies, these little m***********s will smile at you then kill you." His words caught me off guard. I never saw these young men as threats to me; I was too busy trying not to be a threat to them.

The process of walking into Rikers was anxiety provoking. My thoughts would range from a fear of being attacked, (although I was never threatened by an inmate) to what if I beeped on the metal detector and I was arrested. Both my thoughts were irrational but felt real to me. Every time that I went to Rikers, my anxiety lessened because instead of focusing on what could happen, I changed my thoughts to being prepared if something did happen. I prepared for the worst, and actually found myself excited to talk to the inmates and assist them in making sense of their trauma.

When you are able to interpret your fear as excitement, change happens in your brain and your perspective shifts. Here's how. We have cells in our brain named pyramidal cells that are responsible for our guesses and conclusions. They feed our thinking and predictions to the amygdala and can influence our interpretation about the dangerousness of the outside world. The bottom line is this: as we create and narrate our own story, why not make it one of courage and triumph over fear? Being curious, committed to learning, and open to examining our experience lends to shifting from fear to courageousness.

The effects of trauma on children contributes to their inability to self-regulate and have healthy relationships much like it did for my criminal justice involved adolescents. The National Child

Traumatic Stress Network in the United States reports that up to 40% of students have experienced or been witness to traumatic stressors in their lifetime (Brunzell, Waters, and Stokes 2015). Many children are not taught to question their fears in an effort to understand and dismantle them. As a result, they are in constant *react* or battle mode. In school classrooms, fear and trauma may present as disruptive, impulsive, defiant disorder, formally labeled as Attention-Deficit Disorder, Acute Stress Disorder, or even Bipolar Disorder and compromise learning because of frequent suspensions, failed grades, lower expectations, and suboptimal communication between teachers and students. Can you imagine how engaging and powerful these classrooms could be by flipping the switch on their trauma and fears and turning on courage and an enhanced understanding of themselves as adaptive beings?

Fear Is Paralyzing

Today, as I (Jed) type, it is Friday September 11, 2020. Nineteen years from the date that fear, trauma, and anxiety gripped our entire country. I, like most of you reading this, remember exactly where I was the moment our world changed forever on 9/11/2001. I was working at a school as rumors started to buzz around the school that morning about a plane crashing into the World Trade Center. I couldn't fathom what I was hearing. I assumed it was a Cesna or some other small plane that veered off course due to a pilot's medical issue or possibly even a suicide attempt. I was a news junkie and had heard of something like that happening before. I was disappointed I couldn't get to a TV at that moment, and the luxuries of live streaming Internet just weren't a thing in 2001. The only person I knew who would be watching the news at the moment was my dad. He and I had the worst relationship, he was an abusive alcoholic, but he was also a faithful morning TV watcher, so I gave him a call on my red Samsung flip phone. It is funny how you remember details of some things and for the life of you can't remember others. Here is what I remember of that phone call.

Me: Hey Daddy, what's going on in the world? I heard there was a plane crash at the World Trade Center. Is that true?

Dad: Yes, I am watching the news now. (He paused to take a puff of his cigarette.) They are saying it was a passenger plane full of people, but they haven't confirmed it yet. Lots of smoke coming out of one of the towers. (He exhales his own smoke.)

Me: WHAT? Are you kidding me? What in the . . .

Dad: Oh My God SON!!!! Oh my God . . . Oh My God!!! Another plane just flew into the other building!! I JUST SAW IT ON LIVE TV!!!!

Me: What? You must be . . .

Dad: Oh my god! SON! IT'S AWFUL!!!! There was a huge fire-ball!!! WHERE ARE YOU? I THINK WE ARE UNDER ATTACK! (He continued to scream in disbelief.)

The rest of the conversation was a blur. Eventually we hung up, but I have no idea how the call ended. Dad was terrified and his fear came through the phone and shook me to the core. "What should I do?" I thought.

I walked hurriedly into the school from the playground where I was standing to make the call. I went straight to a co-worker's classroom and told her what I had heard from my dad. We were teaching first grade at the time so we tried to remain calm, but we were both incredibly scared. It was almost impossible to stay calm because a group of students from the school were in NYC for their senior trip. Former students, kids of teachers, siblings of our students, part of our community . . . and their destination that morning was supposed to be the towers.

Within moments it seemed everyone in the school knew. The team I worked with at the time did the best they could to keep the news quiet so that the students wouldn't panic, but man was it hard. It got even harder when the principal passed by the rooms around 9:40 to tell us that a plane had hit the Pentagon. I will never forget his face, his tone, his words . . . "PRAY. We are under attack."

I didn't recognize the fear I experienced that day. Our country under attack? By whom? For what? As I have mentioned previously in this book, I had a very violent father who abused my mom and I both. I am also a gay man in the Bible Belt South. I know fear well, but that day . . . it was a whole different fear than I had ever experienced.

I was paralyzed from working. I couldn't think. I couldn't teach. I could hardly even move. I was not in charge of students at the time so I, like the rest of the US, found the nearest TV and began to watch what was happening. I was paralyzed. Fear gripped me so tightly I ceased to function.

As the day moved on and we all realized that we were indeed under attack, the school I worked for at the time decided to dismiss early. It was the right call. No one in the building could function. Parents of the students on the trip to NYC began to come to the school to pull their other kids for the day. Teachers who had kids on the trip were not able to do their work. None of us were. I was so grateful they sent us all home.

I got home and my two roommates, Matt and Luke were there. We all sat around the TV with our eyes so fixed on every detail that the paralyzation I felt at school only worsened. Normally, home is a safe space. A place where the worries of the outside world seem to vanish, but not this day. I called my mom. She invited us over for dinner with the whole family. We needed to be together. It was only later that night after a meal with my loved ones that I felt somewhat better. Then, it started all over as I realized how many thousands of people would never have that moment again because of the day's events.

As I typed this portion of the book, I did some research about survivors of that day. I ran across an interactive timeline that details the day moment by moment. There I heard a recording of Constance Labetti, an Aon Corporation employee on the 99th floor of the South Tower, describe seeing Flight 11 heading toward the North Tower.

I just stood frozen. I didn't move. I couldn't move. I just stood at the window.

Fear is paralyzing.

Fear's Capacity

Everyone is afraid of something. We all have fears. Some big. Some little. Some that could shake us to the core. Mr. Lowe no doubt experienced fear that morning, and the student he met with the gun had fears. In February 2020 on a Thursday morning the weather in Spartanburg, SC, where I (Jed) live, was quite volatile, and fear was almost tangible across the area. Local meteorologists were on television bright and early, warning of potentially hazardous weather approaching. Even a meteorologist from New York City that I follow on Instagram, @reedmcdonough, posted alerts on his social media for dangerous conditions across our region. Based on the confidence the weather forecasters had that severe weather was incoming, I was surprised that schools didn't delay or cancel for the day. "Safety is paramount" was the favorite slogan of one local high school principal. Yet this particular morning, no district in the county opted for a day off. Buses rolled out at their usual time, kids filled the schools up, and the day of learning began.

Around 10am the first tornado siren sounded. It was so odd to hear it blaring early in the day. Tornadoes are not extremely common in the area like they are in the infamous tornado alley of the Midwestern United States, but if we do get them, they come later in the afternoon once the heat of the day has juiced up the atmosphere. I was at home that day, not in a classroom teaching, but my first thought as the wailing alarm continued was, "Poor kids at school. I bet they're terrified."

I always think about the students at school because of the countless tornado drills I endured as both a student and teacher, and because of my niece Sophie. She, like lots of students, (myself included when I was a kid), is terrified of storms. At the first rumble of thunder nearby, she and I always exchange a quick text or brief phone call to ease her fears of what could be headed our way thanks to the thunder that alerts us. She calls me because I am a bit of a weather nerd, and she's convinced that I know where the storms are headed. She's not wrong. I do know. If I weren't an educator I would be on air for The Weather Channel no doubt! I study the weather probably more than any topic other than education. I get my obsession with the weather from my great grandma Maudie. I spent lots of time with her as a kid and she loved all things weather. She even had a little ceramic owl that changed colors based on the barometric pressure. The darker the color, the wetter/snowier the weather. Who knows if it was accurate, but I was obsessed with it. When Maudie passed away, she willed me that little owl. I am looking at it as I type this.

Within minutes of the initial siren sound, my phone began to blow up. The first text . . . Sophie. She was at school with a book over her head. The next one, my oldest niece, Taylor. She took a pic in the hallway in a face down position with an algebra book the only thing between her head and a cinder block wall. Not long after that my teacher friends began to text wanting updates about the storm's path. Word gets around about my weather knowledge thanks to social media. Students across the county were hunkered in place just like the drills had taught them to be, but this was no drill. The storms were loud, full of heavy rain, and indeed a real tornado.

It struck through the heart of town. It passed right over my old school taking down lots of neighborhood trees and power lines. It moved right over or within a mile of at least five or six other schools that I was connected to. The kids were terrified and many teachers were too, as their own kids were battening down in hallways without them. Luckily, no one was seriously injured, but lots of damage was done, more than just physical. Emotional damage occurred that morning as frightened students of all ages hid under their books, fearing the worst. According to my nieces they stayed in position for more than an hour. Not long after the first alarm sounded another went off and a new storm was approaching. The initial hour turned into two, three more hours. Teachers were delivering lunches in the hallways and asking students to eat with one hand and stay covered with the other. I cannot fathom how unnerving it all must have been. It gives me anxiety just to type about it.

Around 1:30pm that day, some three-and-a-half hours after the first alarm, schools began to dismiss early. The amount of debris on the roads scattered all around the county was concerning enough to school officials that they decided to release early so bus drivers would have extra time to navigate the cluttered roads safely before it started to get dark. No need to stay the last hour or two anyway. No learning was going to happen. The fear and trauma of the day had surely closed down all brain receptors.

Fear, while paralyzing, can also present as anger. In threat or protective mode, every ounce of your being puffs up to be louder, larger, and more of a threat to your adversary. The mentality of "I'm going to get you before you get me" results in destructive patterns, lashing out and hurting others without any clear sense or end goal other than to hurt someone. Fear can also make you withdraw inside yourself, hiding at the slightest sound, trying to not be seen or heard, a false sense of safety that appears to work because you are ignored but not being seen, doesn't lessen internal, psychic pain. Unresolved trauma can lead to anxiety, resentment, and sadness filling a space primed for confidence but replaced with anxiety, anger, or a low mood.

We are born with the capacity for fear. Like other emotional responses, fear can be activated by exposure to different stimuli like a moving snake or the black onset of darkness. There is an evolutionary component of fear that goes back to dangerous events, animals, or people that our ancestors had to avoid in order to stay alive. That fear response is sensory and primal.

Keanon Lowe wasn't paralyzed that day. He didn't run away from his student when he felt fear. His lizard brain was not in control. Flight, fight, or freeze was not in command. He ran to the student with the gun. Perhaps, it was Lowe's underlying personality as a compassionate helper, selfless and committed to excellence. Maybe in his training as a competitive athlete, he learned how to push through pain and fear to achieve a goal or outcome. The ability to control and self-regulate fear is an important component of self-awareness. You have to recognize that you are afraid and fearful but still in control. Some see pushing through fear towards heroic action as courage. We expect our firemen, soldiers, and police officers to be brave and achieve extraordinary feats because they trained to be that way.

When Keanon Lowe responded, his life experiences proved his mental and physical toughness. But he didn't respond to his fear with aggression; he responded with compassion. Abigail March, in *The Fear Factor*, writes that some individuals when placed in fearful situations see the fear in their adversary and respond with compassion or altruism. Their amygdala responds with nurturing or caring. Keanon Lowe's actions exemplified both courage and goodness. He did the "good work" that is the goal of many educators entering the field.

The Story of Kimmie

Wherever you are when you get to this portion of the book, take a pause, breathe deeply, and know that the story you are about to read is factual. It is a true account, like all of the stories of my (Jed) students that you will read in this work.

It was about 9:30am on a mid-October morning. Halloween's approaching arrival was looming over the school, and my second graders were borderline chaotic at the mere thought of the impending sugar rush. While I was standing across the room talking with a student about a book, there was a knock at the door. Per the safety protocols for my school, a student peeked out of the rectangular window to let me know who was there and asked if he should open the door. It was the guidance counselor, the principal, and some kid he didn't know. I immediately knew it was a new student. My gut reaction at that moment was, "Nope, don't open the door, our room is full." I feel very vulnerable telling you all that, but if you are an educator and claim you have never let out a deep sigh about a new student arriving mid-year, you are lying. It is not that we don't love our students, but two-and-half months into the year and most classroom routines are clicking along nicely, and a new face can often send ripples through an otherwise calm pond.

I walked to the door and stepped outside to get the news of my new student. The moment my feet entered the hallway, the kid screamed to the top of her lungs, tears flooded her rosy red cheeks, and she took off running down the hall and darted into the bathroom. Stunned and concerned, I looked at my principal with a very confused look. The guidance counselor hurried after her leaving the principal and me alone.

I closed the door to give us privacy because you know the screams of the new kid had alerted every student in the class, and their wandering eyes and nosey ears were straining to see and hear everything they could! Can you blame them? All of us would have done the same thing.

"Cindy," I said, "What in the world is going on? What was that all about?"

"Jed, it's so tragic. It's very complicated. I will tell you more after school, but right now we just need to get her into your room to try to have a normal day."

Thinking back on it . . . the "normal" for this student was *nothing* of the normal we all hope for. Coming to my classroom was anything but normal for her.

The guidance counselor convinced her to walk back to the room fairly quickly, but as she approached for the second time, her tears continued to flood her face, her strawberry hair was matted to the side of her face because of the cry induced runny nose, and her body trembled as she neared.

"Kimmie, this is Mr. Dearybury. He is your teacher, and he's the best," said the guidance counselor. Kimmie wouldn't look at me. She buried her head into her own arms and clung to Paula as if her life depended on it.

The administrative duo started to move her into the room and she stiffened like a board. She was not entering the room. I knelt down to be eye level with her and she screamed again. She became very combative and resisted all movement towards the classroom. She ran away down the hall for the second time.

"She's been abused Jed," the principal said. "Not physically, but sexually."

My heart sank. I had two nieces at the time and the thought of anyone hurting them enraged me. Now, right in front of me was the first student I had ever had, that I knew of, who had been molested. My principal proceeded to tell me the whole story as she was told by a caseworker. Kimmie had been sexually abused by her father. She was removed from the home and placed with her grandparents. She was then sexually abused by her grandfather. She had been removed from all contact with either side of the family and placed two counties away in a foster home. This particular morning that she arrived at my classroom was the first morning she had awakened in a new home with complete strangers shuffling her from place to place. No wonder she screamed, cried, and snotted all over herself. No wonder she ran to hide in the bathroom. Wouldn't you?

I stopped my principal from telling me more. I didn't need to know much more. The only question I had for her . . . "Why in the world would you put her in my class?" I was the only male classroom teacher in the building. Surely she would've felt safer in another space. All the men she had ever known had hurt her and now she had to come see a strange man at school every day? It just didn't make sense to me.

"If anyone can help her, you can, Jed," my principal told me.

I had more than a few doubts in my ability. I had more than a few concerns about my emotional strength to meet the needs of this moment. I had more than one worry about how the arrival of Kimmie would have a ripple effect across the classroom. I had never been trained for this type of trauma. There were no professional development offerings in my district for these kinds of students. All I had was Google. I took a deep breath. I smiled at Kimmie. And eventually, she walked into my room.

Trauma is real. Our students, whether we know every modicum of the details, come to us having had countless experiences that impact their learning. In order to teach these students, we must be informed of what they bring so that we do not add to their pain, but help. No, we are not their saviors. We are their teachers. But, in order to teach, we have to know about the whole child as best we can.

As I reflect back on my time with Kimmie, I ask myself a million questions.

Did I help?
Did I hurt?
Did I do enough?
Did I do too much?
Did I try as hard as I could?
Did I try too hard?
Was I over the top?
Was I under the top?

I am sure that educators reading this will relate to those questions. Our work is a constant circle of "do, reflect, do again, reflect again." It's the nature of who we are and what drives us to be better each day we enter the school building.

She arrived mid-October without notice, and she left the same way in mid- April. I have not seen or heard from her since. The only thing we were told by the Department of Social Services was that she was in a safe place.

What is a safe place for someone like Kimmie? Certainly the absence of sexual abusers. But, what else does a student like Kimmie need to be safe? The basics for human life of course, but she also needs caregivers, educators, and community members who are trauma informed so that they nurture and love her where she is and help her find her way out of the hellish nightmare she had lived in her seven or so years of life.

Kimmie needed a school with a program, organization, or system that was full of trauma-informed teachers who created courageous classrooms with these three key components.

1. Realizes the widespread impact of trauma and understands potential paths for recovery.
2. Recognizes the signs and symptoms of trauma in clients, families, staff, and others involved with the system.
3. Responds by fully integrating knowledge about trauma into policies, procedures, and practices; and seeks to actively resist re-traumatization. (SAMHSA 2012)

As Kimmie's teacher, I fully *realized* the likely negative impact of trauma on her learning. I was well versed in the effects of my own personal trauma, but I had no ideas about how to provide her a path to recovery as her teacher. I certainly *recognized* the symptoms of trauma as she screamed, snotted, and ran away, but what did I know about dealing with those behaviors as a result of the abuse she had suffered and it all being triggered as she stood looking at me, her male teacher? At that moment, I wish I could have *responded* knowledgeably with a procedure or practice that was research based and relevant to the scene playing out in the hallway. Sadly, I wasn't. Now, some decade later, I have learned a lot, but I often wonder what kind of courageous classroom I could have created had I been trauma informed from day one of my educational certification degree rather than 10 years into it.

Reflect for a moment before reading any further.

- Do you feel adequately trained as an educator for a student like Kimmie?
- Did your college coursework guide you to an understanding of this type of trauma and its effect on a student's ability to learn?
- Has your district provided ongoing professional development and guidance for faculty and staff who will serve as caretakers for students like her?
- Has your school administrator ever offered to send you to a conference or seminar where the focus of the work was educating students of trauma?
- Do you own an educational resource other than this book that has influenced your work with students of trauma?

If you are like me, if you are like millions of other teachers, sadly, the answer – to at least one of these questions – is no. That must change. Our students are becoming more and more affected by trauma each year. According to a 2007 study, students report a traumatic event by the age of 16 (Copeland et al. 2007), traumatic events can include but are not limited to:

- psychological, physical, or sexual abuse;
- community or school violence;
- witnessing or experiencing sexual violence;
- natural disasters;
- terrorism;
- commercial sexual exploitation;
- sudden or violent loss of a loved one;
- deployment, loss, or injury of parent due to military service;
- physical or sexual assault; and
- serious accident or life-threatening illness.

When you read the list, thinking about students past, present, and future, it might feel overwhelming to consider how one might engage in teaching a student who has experienced any of these. It is likely that many students have experienced multiple such events. It is incomprehensible that there isn't more training offered to educators given the overwhelming weight of the task of caring for and teaching a child who has dealt with so much. So where do we begin to become a more trauma-informed educator? You are in the right place.

I told you to imagine it was one of yours. It was one of mine. The fear, the trauma, the abuse that Kimmie faced prior to ever setting foot in my classroom will never leave my brain. Her trauma in many ways became my own. It opened my eyes to the horrible things my students faced on a regular basis and led me to action. Before I could help Kimmie, and students like her, I had to face my own traumatic experiences.

Let's Chat

Jed: Dr. Janet, after years of reflection, I still think about Kimmie and her time in my classroom. What are some strategies that you would suggest to teachers like me, who haven't been adequately trained to help students like her?

Dr. Janet: When we are faced with the pain of others, whether it's students or our clients, we want to help. Our own level of experience or perceived competence can make us feel inadequate or under trained and, frankly, fearful. It's important to understand that by being there and holding a space of calm and a desire to understand them, we can observe, listen, and mindfully create a plan for their safety. You can't teach compassion, but we all have the capacity. Being a trauma-informed teacher can be learned. Given the high number of students who have been exposed to trauma, it's a necessary skill. A strategy would be to non-judgmentally assess the situation. Push away the gremlin (inner critic) who tells you, "You can't handle it." Listen to understand what the student needs at the moment, and then familiarize yourself with your school's resources. Avoid using phrases like, "It's going to be alright" or "stop yelling" and ask, "What do you need?" "How can I help?" When calm has resumed, debrief with a colleague or supervisor to learn and share best practices.

Jed: I often hear the phrase "hold space." Can you elaborate a bit more about what that means?

Dr. Janet: Holding the space refers to honoring the interaction and communication between you and another person. Most of the communication is non-verbal and the deepest listening is when no words are spoken but you notice and feel. It means pushing down your anxiety or angst and being fully present, not compelled to answer or solve but simply to be.

Jed: Can you share some examples of non-verbal communication that we may see?

Dr. Janet: I always look for discrepancies. You may see a tearful child who says, "I'm okay" or one who balls up their fists and doesn't make eye contact. The point is not to ignore their presentation by listening to their words but by carefully, critically looking at them and trying to feel what they are giving off. When someone has their arms folded or head down, it's usually a cue that they feel some angst. Try to lead by observing their stance and eye contact – that often speak volumes more than their words.

Fear Is Overcome-able

There's no escaping the scope of the problem students and educators face. Fear is a real part of daily life for the people who learn and teach in our nation's classrooms. It's wired into our brain as part of our evolutionary journey. However, as insurmountable as the problem might seem, we also are wired for the solution – we just have to work together to learn how to access it ourselves, so that we can, in turn, offer it to our students. We can speak to you with such confidence about the power of courage, because we have seen it in action, in ourselves, and in our students.

Your brain is an amazing piece of machinery. Among its incredible abilities is neuroplasticity, the ability of neural networks in the brain to change through growth and reorganization. These changes range from individual neurons making new connections, to systematic adjustments like cortical remapping. In layman's terms, the brain's ability to rewire itself. This super-power enables people who have experienced trauma as kids to overcome it – and get a shot at adulthood.

As miraculous as this rewiring sounds, it cannot be achieved without significant support, including from trauma-informed educators. Without this support, countless students fall through the cracks and become adults who inflict more trauma. We educators are in a unique place. For 180 days we have the opportunity to help "our kids," as many call them, to discover that their trauma is overcome-able. But how? Keep reading.

Tips for the Courageous Classroom

Consider where fear exists in your body, so that you can acknowledge your feelings and thoughts and respond in a healthy and helpful manner.

Learning Principle

Fear exists in our students, teachers, and classrooms. Fear begins in our brain with the amygdala sending messages in our brain circuitry to be aware of potential danger (flight, fight, or freeze). When we have a conscious feeling of fear, our thoughts, emotions, and behavior can be affected, but remember fear is a response that can be overcome. Recognizing fear can create an opportunity to self-regulate by using the following ABCDE method created by Dr. Martin Seligman, the father of positive psychology.

Adversity: Acknowledge and describe your fear including the who, what, when, and where of the situation.

Belief: Write down what you were thinking and saying to yourself in the middle of your fearful situation or adversity.

Consequences: Write down the consequences of what you thought, felt, and did. Be specific, listing all the emotions and reactions that you can identify.

Dispute: Actively challenge an inaccuracy that you now recognize about your beliefs and fear. Try to create a more optimistic and accurate belief about your fear. For example, you may say, "My fear is not completely true because . . ." or "A more accurate way of looking at this situation is . . ."

Energy: Reflect and recognize how disputing your belief changed your energy. Notice what happened to your mood. How did your behavior change? What solutions do you see now that you didn't before?

Chapter 2
Animals and Fear

Animals Can Cause Fear

Almost 11 years ago, I (Janet) set out on the adventure of a lifetime. Traveling to an exotic destination has always been a dream of mine. When offered the opportunity to join a group of my best girlfriends to fly to Brazil and explore, I hurriedly said yes! As a then-married mother of four daughters who said "I do" at the young age of 25 and started having my children at 26, most of my adult life was spent as a wife or mother. So, I quickly seized my chance to get away for 10 days on what promised to be a fun-filled, storytelling, girlfriend sharing excursion to explore the richness of the Amazon jungle and the meaningful spirit-filled beauty of Bahia. You bet, I was in with fun not fear on my mind.

Our itinerary was planned to the finest degree. Arranging travel for women from all over the United States is no simple feat. I am blessed to have friends who are very detail oriented, and seek out unique experiences guaranteed to imprint lasting memories. This trip was no exception. We flew into the State of Rio de Janeiro meeting at the bustling Tom Jobim International Airport where I had my first hot, cheesy, satisfying bite of pao de queijo. For me, it was love at first bite. Excitedly, my friends and I convened and hopped on a small plane to the city of Manaus.

Manaus is the capital and largest city in the Brazilian State of the Amazonas. Although it's the seventh largest city in Brazil, it didn't feel overwhelmingly populated to me. Perhaps that's because I was lost in the nervous but eager chatter of my travel buddies as we anticipated our adventure. We'd all been given a daunting list of how to pack for our excursion. Our bags were to be limited to two each with a definitive weight limit. We were tasked with bringing supplies containing bug repellent, a mosquito net, a durable flashlight, bandannas, sturdy hiking boots, sunscreen, water carriers, and doses of chloroquine and antibiotics. All of us had tales about getting our visas and required shots including Hepatitis A, Typhoid, and Yellow Fever.

We arrived at a quaint area in Manaus and boarded a small van that drove us away towards the Rio Negro, a tributary of the mighty and powerful Amazon River. Our accommodation for the next four days was a brown, older but sturdy boat with a crew of three or four trustworthy attendants who spoke only Portuguese. Luckily, broken Spanish and lots of gesturing helped us all communicate. Our meals were delicious including lots of fresh fish and rice washed down with a cold Brazilian beer. The first day was spent cruising, relaxing, listening to the sounds of birds and the steady, comforting, rhythms of water hitting our craft.

The reason for our three-night four-day cruise on the Solimoes River was to experience the fauna, animals, wildlife, and inhabitants of the Amazon in their own habitat. Clearly, we were the guests. The Solimoes River is a known as the Meetings of the Waters and where the dark, blackwater of the Rio Negro meets the pale, sandy-colored whitewater of the Amazon River. For almost four miles the two rivers are side by side, never mixing, because of their different qualities of speed, water density, and temperature. The Solimoes River is almost 10 degrees Fahrenheit cooler than the Rio Negro.

Our passion for adventure was not to be fulfilled lounging on a boat in the middle of the Solimoes River. During the day, we would venture out to walk on trails looking at birds, meeting native Amazon tribes, and experiencing breathtaking vistas. I will never forget being on a smaller boat heading to fish for piranhas. Yup. I was very nervous. As I turned a slight bend, there was a sudden roar and parallel to our boat, I both saw and heard the mighty Amazon River in all of its magnificence. I could truly admire its beauty only after finding out that we were not going fishing on the Amazon but would stay on our quiet-but-busy river. My relief was palpable.

I am not a fisherman but was easily able to insert cold, cut-up blood dripping, red meat on the sharp hook and wait for the silver, sharp tooth freshwater fish to bite. Before long, we were able to witness a remarkable sight: The bait would draw scores of the "tooth fish" to viciously go for their food, turning the brown water red. Incredibly, I caught the first one and held it at arm's length away until our guides grabbed the 5–6-inch squirmy fish. That night, the cook made piranha soup from our catch. I heard that it was good. I had no desire to try it.

My moment of true fear, probably the most afraid that I've ever been, was later that evening around 10pm. The night sky was black, the air still and we were nervously gathering ourselves and jokingly using our flashlights to see as we boarded a small man-powered boat searching for the prize of the pitch-black night – Caiman alligators. Turning on our flashlights to gingerly board the boat was terrifying. The thin stream of nothingness from our store-bought flashlights was useless. They provided no light. Sounds were intensified by the Amazon, still at night, and every splash made me imagine that a giant anaconda was lurking under our boat and we'd be flipped in a nanosecond. My heart was in my throat and my hands were beginning to sweat. I was so scared. The narrative in my head was *danger, danger, danger*. Resigned to our fate, silence took over and my sense was of a shared narrative of Wait . . . What? Why had this seemed like such a good idea?

In a moment of trusting the process, we were instructed to keep our hands in the boat as our two guides paddled us away from our floating home. Our two guides had two enormous lights that cast beams long, bright, and wide. I didn't see any weapons like a knife or gun, but I imagine they had some sort of protective capability – if necessary. The frightening night began with our first view of an enormous venomous, green tree frog sitting on the bank, whose body oozes toxins to kill predators but is also capable of a venomous spit. We saw long, pale snakes perched in trees that were too close for comfort while hearing the whir and high-pitched screeches of bats in the sky. Monkeys jumped around in the green trees. My fear was slowly replaced by wonder and felt apprehensive gratitude at being able to bear witness to the wondrous intricacy of nature at night.

Suddenly, two red circles appeared on the top of the water. A collective inhale from our group suspended our attention. It was a Caiman on the surface of the brown river. Their red eyes were creepily intoxicating. Caiman alligators are one of the longest surviving species on the planet and have evolved very little over the past 200 million years. Their long bodies get pushed through the water by their powerful tails. They can grow up to 19 feet long and they usually hunt their prey in the water, but black Caiman will go on land to hunt for humans.

The Caiman Alligator eye is "the most advanced on the planet." In function and in size, their eyes are similar to human eyes in that light passes through the lens and onto their retina. Unlike human retinas, which are circular, the Caiman retina is horizontal and can scan a landscape without moving its head. They can also self-adjust their eyes to see short and long distances by having a multi-focal lens. Their eyelids are reinforced and provide a shield against an aggressive attack, and they can also withdraw their eyeballs into their sockets for further protection. Lastly, they have built in goggles, which allow them to see blurrily underwater. The reason that their eyes reflect red to the beam of a strong light is because their retina contains reflective mirrors (microscopic crystal) that make their eyes light up and shine. In the freshwater of the Solimoes, the Caiman eyes pick up the redder wavelengths of light as saltwater has more blue light.

We went out Caiman alligator hunting three nights in a row, and by the third night my fear had genuinely transformed into anticipation and excitement. How does that happen? How can a situation that creates utter dread and terror morph into an event that you look forward to? I learned that facing my challenges allowed me to look at my fear in a different way.

Let's Chat

Jed: Dr. Janet, you wrote at the beginning of your story about the alligator that your fear response actually pushed you into courage. Can you explain how teachers can help students achieve that when facing fears or the experiences of past trauma?

Dr. Janet: When the brain experiences a traumatic or terrifying experience, it remembers. The memory can play out with flashbacks, bodily sensations like anxiety or physical avoidance. The opportunity is to certainly remember and understand but also work on developing a new approach to fear. I'm not saying to ignore what happened, but you can reframe the event as one that you can and will overcome. Every night that I stepped into the canoe to look for animals that terrified me, I felt stronger, because it was my choice to build my internal reserves and demonstrate courage.

Jed: So, continuing to reflect about Kimmie from Chapter 1. . . . Her fear of me and other men was a result of trauma. Should teachers of students with traumatic histories apply that same thinking of reframing when working with those students?

Dr. Janet: Fear is a sensory response to an event or experience, real or imagined. A traumatic experience can result in fear but is based on an actual event that happened to, or was witnessed by, an individual, resulting in psychological and physical reactions that can impair social functioning, and cause anxiety, depression, behavioral changes, and insomnia. The point is this: reframing can be used in trauma to help someone feel safer and rebuild their ability to focus and self-regulate. Most of these techniques require a therapist or therapeutic intervention. However, teachers can be trained to recognize when a student's behavior or academic progress may be disrupted by trauma and interact with the student to minimize their trauma and promote growth and safety.

Jed: Knowing that most techniques require a therapist or therapeutic intervention reminds me that not all schools have access to guidance counselors or mental health experts. For the teachers who feel they double as a therapist for some students, what should they do?

Dr. Janet: Jed, I applaud the many teachers who wear the hat of educator and therapist because of their dedication to their students. However, I would caution them to be mindful of their own level of trauma and real demands because it's a recipe for burnout. My advice is to take a course in trauma-informed teaching and also make yourself aware of outside resources to refer to students and their families.

Animals Survive Because of Fear

The human brain allows us to think, behave, move, feel, and react for our survival, to seek out rewards, and to maintain social groups. Creatures in the animal kingdom are no different. Mammals, birds, reptiles, and insects like bees manifest behaviors to maximize their safety and security. The need to be safe and free from threats or predators extends across the zoologic cycle. Animals overcome stressors, like the need to fight off predators and compete for resources. So do we. So, whether you are in the jungle of the Amazon or in a classroom full of students, we can learn from the animals around us how to manage fear and how to utilize it for survival and building courage.

Nature wants to survive and thrive. To do so it tries to use the smallest amount of energy needed, without damaging itself or its ecosystem. This behavior isn't limited to humans, mammals, or even just animals in general. Plants have also evolved to play this game. Although a plant can't hide, run, bite, or call for help when facing down a predator, plants defend themselves using physical structures. For example, some plants contain small hairs or trichomes that make it very difficult for small insects to attach to them. Certain plants can move while rooted, folding their leaves and slumping forward to avoid destruction. They can release chemicals into the air to deter insects from landing and release bitter toxins that are unpalatable for would-be attackers.

This isn't just science trivia. Nature has a lot to teach us about how best to deal with stressors. Zebrafish have been studied as an example of animals that have been able to successfully avoid predators and also display coping styles, both behavioral and physiological responses that are consistent across time. They have been researched in laboratory studies to evaluate their learning and memory behaviors in relation to fear conditioning. Some fear responses for Zebrafish include bottom dwelling, swimming in tighter, erratic movements, and freezing. To evaluate them, researchers used both wild and laboratory-generated Zebrafish and exposed all of the fish to a neutral environment that they conditioned by inserting into the water an alarm substance (olfactory signal) that is released by the Zebrafish and triggers anti-predatory behaviors through smell. The fish were tested over seven days and the results were consistent with other animals that have the capacity to learn and recall sensory experiences required to survive (Baker and Wong 2019).

Like people, Zebrafish have traits similar to personality profiles, and can be risk prone or risk averse. Risk-averse animals are more sensitive to environmental cues while risk-prone animals rely on past experiences to guide their decision-making and form rapid routines to cope with stress. By using animal models to evaluate responses to stressful events, their behavior can be monitored and measured after exposure to stressors, thus evidence of useful positive coping mechanisms.

Animals and bees in low-resource environments have been observed to see how they respond. Honeybees were agitated in a laboratory by shaking them for 60 seconds, which simulates a predator attack. The findings indicated that honeybees have pessimistic negative thinking when stressed and anxious. After being shaken, they were more focused on looking for signals of another potential attack instead of trying to find food. In other words, the honeybees remained on edge and displayed pessimistic decision-making. They had inward expectations of punishment, greater attention to potential threats, and responded to vague stimuli as if it were a threat (Bateson et al. 2011). Their outward focus comes from a negative internal place, *which is not unlike what happens in children and adults*, when a current environmental state can alter judgment and trigger a pessimistic response because of what you expect to happen. Instead of focusing on a defensive response like honeybees, choose a positive outcome. Other animals found to have pessimistic judgment include rats, sheep, dogs, starlings, and domestic chickens (Bateson et al. 2011).

We also can take lessons from distant cultures, like the Mbuti Pygmies, hunter-gatherers living in the Ituri Forest of the Congo who were studied by Colin Turnbull, one of the most well-known anthropologists of the twentieth century. In rigorous and eloquent prose that humanized the previous, racist and ignorant descriptions, Turnbull conveyed the character, warmth, intelligence, and values of the Mbuti pygmies. He writes fondly of hearing their voices cascade through the dense tropical rainforest. "This cascade of sounds echoes among the giant trees until it seems to come at you from all sides in sheer beauty and truth and goodness, full of the joy of living" (Turnbull 1962, p. 13).

What can we learn from Mbuti Pygmies, hunter-gathers, one the most documented and carefree societies? They live without fear in an unforgiving lush, but cool rainforest in the Northeast corner of the Congo and speak a language that does not include a concept for the word evil. If we can understand the simple underpinnings of life for the Mbuti Pygmies, how their lives are structured to ensure their growth and development, then perhaps we can learn lessons to assist us in managing our lives and living in a carefree harmonious society. For starters, the Mbuti Pygmies sense alarm, but the feelings of dread, suspicion, and anxiety that linger in us here in the developed world, are markedly diminished because the Pygmies' source of security and freedom comes from living in a sacred space. For them, their whole world, the rainforest is sacred. When misfortune happens, they have a glass half-full perspective, choosing to see the occurrence as not a bad thing, but just a lack of goodness. They believe that every day takes care of itself and as a result they are mindfully present.

Children in Mbuti families are raised in an egalitarian style, where both men and women share the duties of raising the children, building home dwellings, searching for food, and pitching in towards communal activities. Net hunting to capture food is done together, with the men and boys on one side and women and girls on the other half, as they combine their nets to trap animals. Disputes or conflict is managed by bringing in a clown that engenders laughter and pokes fun at turmoil. The clown takes on anger or conflict and diffuses it with humor, chuckles, or a funny song and dance. There is little physical violence in the Mbuti community, as a genuine concern for the well-being of all is a deep value. The goodness that they find in each other originates in the rainforest for they see the forest, not people as a protector and life giver. Anticipation of the future is seen as anxiety provoking and they remain deeply rooted in the present (Tuan 1979).

The presence of fear is not unique to humans. It serves as a warning to stay safe or look for danger. However, not everything that triggers a fearful response is necessarily life threatening. Fear can also trigger more awareness or help decipher what is in the unknown. When we face our fears, we can overcome them, developing the wisdom of perspective in the process. Like the Mbuti Pygmies, we can choose to embrace the sacredness of the space that we contain and rely on each other as co-explorers searching for peace and harmony in the everyday journey.

When we look beyond our immediate cultural context and understand how distant cultures and even other species handle fear, we put new tools in our toolkit for coping with all the obstacles modern life might throw in our path. Animals not only provide a possible template for overcoming fear, however, they can also be an integral step in the process, as Jed recounts below.

Animals and Mental Health

Right now Bear and Biscuit are laying on the floor beside me (Jed). It isn't time to eat. They just peed and pooped about an hour ago. It's not even time for their midmorning snack. They just like being near me. Their love is so unconditional that even when I accidentally slammed Bear's tail in the door last year, that very night after a long trip to the emergency vet, he curled up right beside me. What is it about pets that they are just able to love so hard, so deep, so long? It's like nothing can shake them. The feeling between these two Labradors and I is mutual. I cannot imagine life without them. They are the sweetest. Although Bear can be a handful sometimes.

I wasn't always a dog lover. When I was younger my Aunt Cheryl always had dogs. They smelled funny, they licked me, and some of them scared me to death. A few times we had outside dogs as guard dogs since we lived out in the country, but never did I ever want a dog in the house. That changed when we met Biscuit. She is the Labrador of your dreams. She lays around and lets you just snuggle her to pieces. There is something so therapeutic about coming home after a long, stressful day to doggie cuddles. The smell that I used to think stank so bad as a kid has somehow transformed itself into an aroma comparable to the scents of Zen that accompany a spa visit. For real. I love her so much!

In a chapter about animals and fear, we must recognize how animals can also help alleviate fears of humans. The science behind the effects of pets on positive mental health supports my doggie relaxation experience. According to the ADAA (Anxiety and Depression Association of America 2017), a 2016 study explored the role of pets in the social networks of people managing a long-term mental health problem and found that pets provide a sense of security and routine that provides emotional and social support. Studies have also shown that pets facilitate friendships and enhance social support networks. A study conducted by the Human-Animal Bond Research Institute (HABRI) (Wood et al. n.d.) strengthens the case for pets in fighting the ills of fear and poor mental health. Their findings suggest that pet owners are significantly more likely to get to know their neighbors and others in the community than people with no pets. The study went on to say that 40% of pet owners found emotional support through people they met through their pet. How amazing is that? No surprise here for me. I have met countless people in my neighborhood by walking the dog or visiting a pet park.

HABRI is not alone in their research on the effects of animals on the mental health of humans. Institutes such as John Hopkins

University, Harvard Medical School, and the Mayo Clinic have also conducted research to support the positive role of pets in our lives. Jeremy Barron, M.D., medical director of the Beacham Center for Geriatric Medicine at Johns Hopkins has concluded that having pets or even short-term interactions with pets can have a variety of positive impacts on our lives, including:

- reduced stress;
- lower blood pressure;
- increased physical activity;
- boost heart health; and
- eases loneliness and depression (Johns Hopkins Medicine n.d.).

Reading over the list and reflecting on each benefit, it makes you wonder why everyone doesn't have a pet. Who doesn't need less stress, lower blood pressure, and more physical activity? After the social isolation we experienced during the Covid-19 pandemic, we are all in need of a way to ease loneliness and depression in some form.

What about our students? Could they use some of those benefits? They may not need lower blood pressure, as that is usually a concern of adults, but the rest of the benefits mentioned are definitely needed in the lives of our students. There's no way we can know everything they bring with them into our educational environments, but we most certainly can create safe spaces that bring them peace and calm while they are learning.

Animals in the Classroom

The non-profit organization, Pets in the Classroom, founded in 1990 has spent the past 30 years with one mission: To enhance students' educational and personal development through interaction with pets in their classroom. They have conducted research to support their focus. Their vision to get pets in every classroom in the United States and Canada to help educate and develop students is supported by the research of McCullough et al. (2019) in their study titled "Measuring the Social, Behavioral, and Academic Effects of Classroom Pets on Third and Fourth-Grade Students." Their study assessed the social, behavioral, and academic small animals present in third- and fourth-grade classrooms. Small pets included hamsters, gerbils, toads, lizards, fish, turtles, and guinea pigs. While these creatures aren't the cuddly dogs my Biscuit and Bear are, the findings suggest that students significantly benefited in all areas assessed by the study. In their research, they cited a previous study from 2013 that showed students in Australia who had guinea pigs present in their classrooms had an increase in social skills and a decrease in problem behaviors. Their study also cites that the presence of animals in the classroom aids in empathy development.

Makes sense doesn't it? There is a living creature in the midst of the class that is totally dependent on the students for survival. At least, if the teacher sets it up like that, that's how it will be perceived. For a few years, I (Jed) had a bearded dragon in my class. We never really learned its correct gender. We tried to research. Thought we knew. Wasn't sure. Did it really matter? It was a great teachable moment about gender and pronouns. I digress. Back to the dragon.

I applied for a grant sponsored by a national pet store chain. Upon applying, I didn't read the fine print and failed to realize that the grant was only for a small portion of the needs we would have with the pet. Smart move national pet store chain. Give me half of what I need up front so I then spend 20 times that in your store. Brilliant really, but much to my disappointment, I couldn't front the remaining money.

Because I believe in being transparent with my learning, I decided to tell my second graders about it. I told them the same week we were reading a story called "Lemonade for Sale," by Stuart J. Murphy. Maybe it was divine intervention, maybe it was pure luck, but one student piped up after the story was over and said, "Let's raise money for a pet like they raised money in the story!" His one statement was all it took for the unbridled excitement of children to spread across the classroom like a unicorn swiping across the sky. Their ideas started flowing so quickly, I almost couldn't keep up.

I did what any good teacher would do that day. I threw my morning plans in the trash and followed their lead. Yes, yes I did. Student voice and choice opportunities are powerful and courageous tools that all educators who want to create safe space for students to thrive in should have in their bag of tricks. I grabbed some chart paper and a marker and made a list of all their fundraising ideas. I drew out a thermometer/money tracker thingy so I could visually chart their progress. We researched all the animals available with the grant. We(I) added up the expenses for each option. They didn't have the skills to add with decimals yet, but you rest assured I did the math on the board for them to see! I helped them figure up how much each student should try to raise. I called the principal on the class phone and asked for permission, and I emailed the parents and told them about the student-led initiative that had unfolded that morning. I took a deep breath. It was only 10am. Time for recess.

When we got outside, word spread through the other classes that we were getting a pet. Most of the students were telling their friends we were getting a dragon. I still laugh to this day because so much of the class thought that we were getting a real-life fairy-tale, Game of Thrones dragon. As we were researching the choices for us, all it took was the word dragon to appear and bearded dragon was the only choice. "Who wants a guinea pig?" they said. Me. I did. I wanted something cute and cuddly. Although I didn't officially know all of the research mentioned previously at the time I was getting the pet grant, I hoped that a cute and cuddly something would make our classroom a happier place. Sadly, as is often the case in a battle like this one between a grown up and a room full of kids, the kids won. I should have clarified a bit better that we were getting a tiny lizard rather than a fire breathing killer, but for that day at recess, knights, damsels locked in towers, and the evil dragon captor was a theme to be reckoned with.

Over the next few weeks, money for the beardie was brought in daily. More than money though, the stories that came with the dollars and cents were priceless. One kid washed his nana's car. Another weeded his papa's flower bed. One kid went door to door in his neighborhood and another asked a local restaurant if he could help fill empty drinks for the servers. He made $40!!! It was so heartening and honestly a bit surprising that the mere mention of a classroom pet made such an impact on my students.

After a month of fundraising, our thermometer/money tracker thingy reached the total that we needed to secure the dragon, its terrarium, and the needed heat lights. I fronted the money out of my pocket for the first round of crickets. We met our goal on a Friday so I planned to purchase everything we needed over the weekend and have it all set up by Monday. The kids were not having that! "We want to go with you to get it," was all I heard that day.

"Fine, fine, fine," I told them. "I will send an email to your parents inviting you all to meet me at the pet store."

The next day, VERY much to my surprise, 12 of the 18 students in my class, and their parents, arrived at the pet store to help pick out the dragon. The employees were so beside themselves with happiness. It was a rather slow "shopping for pets" day so they spent so much time with my students. They told them all about the animals, how they care for them, what they eat. They told us about gills, and fur, and scales, and cold blooded. They talked about the food chain, the need all living things have for water, and the class favorite . . . all things have to poop! The students were enthralled. We spent about two hours there listening and learning before we finally got to pick out the creature we came for. It was teeny. Smaller than the palm of my hand. Although it was small, the impact it had already made on my classroom was HUGE!

After we thanked the pet store about a million times, I made my way to school to get everything set up. It wasn't easy, but as I look back, the whole experience up to this point had been incredibly worth it. The educational and social benefits experienced by my students from the initial "let's raise money" to purchase were innumerable. Team building, encouragement, math, science, hard work, etc. etc. etc. ALL had come just at the thought of a class pet.

The excitement on Monday morning as students entered the classroom with the dragon for the first time was tangible. I think all we did that day was watch it. Watched it in the water dish, on the fake limb, in the plastic grass, underneath the heat lamp. I got it out and it rode around in my shirt pocket. It just so happened to be picture day. You know it made it into the class photo! Some would say we wasted that day. I however think that our time spent with "Spike" was priceless. Yes, that is the name they came up with. I was hoping for something a bit more creative, but yet again . . . the kids won out.

Without fail, the new wore off as it often does with a pet. How many of you reading this right now bought a dog/cat/fish/hamster for someone you loved but ended up doing all of the caretaking for it? It happens. But, the students' responsibility and love for Spike never changed. They continued to bring in money for crickets and mealworms. If a bulb went out on the heat lamp, there was always a student who stepped up to say, "I will raise that money Mr. D." For the holidays that year they brought Spike presents. At Christmas, a new water dish and some extra crickets. For Valentine's, we made him a special little mailbox on the side of the terrarium for all of the love notes that came in. Spike's presence provided an analogy or teachable moment almost every day.

Spike made us all happier. Happier people almost always have stronger mental health, more focus in their learning, and better social relationships. I had very few behavior problems after Spike's arrival and students who didn't get along prior to the big Monday arrival suddenly became co-workers in caring for our new creature. Even when there was poop all over the inside of the glass home where most of its life occurred, and even when I had to make extra trips for crickets, and even when my finger got bitten by a terrified dragon who didn't like car travel as I took it home over the holiday break, I smiled because of how courageous and responsible my students became as a result of its presence within our learning space.

Tips for the Courageous Classroom

Observe your stress and anxiety, and find healthy and positive ways to manage it.

Learning Principle

Fear is a response that can create feelings of stress. Stress is the body's response to any non-specific demand placed upon it. Stress begins in the brain and sends messages to every organ in the body to either turn up or turn down. It's important to know how your body responds to stress so that you can find ways to balance it. All stress is not bad: there's positive stress that gives your energy and heightens your awareness but dissipates quickly. Toxic stress is unrelenting and dangerous. Your body never shuts off and can lead to cardiovascular disease, anxiety, depression, a weakened immune system, and fatigue.

Anxiety can be a feeling of dread and nervousness and is not always in response to a trigger. It can come out of the blue (a panic attack) and lead to excessive worry, insomnia, and dread.

Both stress and anxiety can impact learning and focus but both can be managed by eliminating the sources of stress (if possible) and mindful self-regulation. Face your sources of stress and take action. Having a plan can eliminate uncertainty and alleviate stress by having direction.

Mindful self-regulation is an example of a learnable skill and active coping. Active coping rewires the brain and down regulates the stress response. Here are steps:

1. Notice that you are feeling something.
2. Identify and label the feeling by saying, "I am feeling _____ because I notice it _____ in my body.
3. Visualize the feeling of anxiety/stress/fear exiting your body, leaving you feeling calmer by using the breathing exercise in point 4.
4. Inhale deeply (counting to four slowly) then exhale out forcefully (counting to four). Repeat this four times and use it as often as you need too.

Teachers
- Get curious about what makes you and your students fearful
- Make yourself aware of your and their responses.
- Take control of your fear response by creating a new meaning of the experience.
- Ask yourself, What did I learn? How did it make me better?
- Get a pet. :)

Chapter 3
Fear Outside School

Trauma Is an Adverse Childhood Experience

Inequality across school, work, healthcare and even play, can reinforce the impact of trauma on a child and their family, creating effects that may last a lifetime. The impact of oppression, racism, and discrimination is amplified when an individual has been exposed to childhood trauma. In *The Deepest Well*, a seminal book about the long-term effects of childhood adversity and the imperative of prevention and healing, Dr. Nadine Burke Harris writes that "Childhood adversity changes our biological systems, and lasts a lifetime" (Burke Harris 2018, p. xvi).

The relationship between adverse childhood experiences (ACEs) and long-term health consequences was first described in a groundbreaking paper by two interns in San Diego in 1998. They were attempting to understand the risk factors for dropping out of a weight loss program in a sample of mostly White, middle-class adults. Their research identified that those who had exposure to sexual and other forms of abuse, and growing up in households that could be classified as "dysfunctional" where children had parents or caregivers who used drugs, were involved in criminal activity, and domestic violence was witnessed, were likely to quit the weight loss program (Karatekin and Hill 2019). A subsequent Center for Disease

Control Study grant included researching up to 17,000 adults which led to a deeper understanding of adverse childhood experiences and the influence of early adversity on health (Burke Harris 2018, p. 36).

The ACE study proved that it's not only risk factors that trigger and worsen medical illnesses, but there is also an additive effect or dose response. In other words, repeated exposures to trauma can double or triple the risk for poor health outcomes. For example, in the clinic of Dr. Burke Harris (2018), she found that a child who had an ACE score of four or more was twice as likely to be overweight as a child with zero ACEs. Her patients with four or more ACEs were 32.6 times more likely to be diagnosed with a problem related to learning or behavior.

To understand this significant finding, we must go back to the brain's functions that we laid out in earlier chapters. To review our brain's stress response, remember that when we are faced with challenges, obstacles, or situations that make us feel on guard or confused, our lizard brain takes over. It pushes our body and brain to "do something" and that something could be to "fight, flight, or freeze." When triggered by thoughts or feelings, the amygdala or the body's fear center comes to attention after being nudged by hormones like cortisol. Every single hormone in our body can be triggered by stress after the amygdala sounds the alarm to a real or perceived threat. I don't know about you, but if my gut tells me to be afraid, I usually jump into action. If I were being chased by a lion through the brown lushness of an African Savannah, and were able to get away, then my revved-up stress system would have done well for me. The problem is that when kids are chronically exposed to stressful situations of abuse, trauma, and neglect, their stress hormones kick in and have a hard time getting back into balance. That creates a situation of chronic or toxic stress, which is where physical and mental problems can originate. The intensity, frequency, and duration of the stressful event and the presence and availability of a caring, supportive adult can all elevate the risk of toxic stress (Sege and Harper Browne 2017).

Toxic stress can impact the immune system, worsening every chronic medical condition. It can lead to high blood pressure, heart attacks, diabetes, stomach aches, and more colds. Most relevant to our purposes here, it can get in the way of learning and remembering. Think about it this way: If a child is chronically stressed, unsure and nervous, their focus and concentration is challenged by their hyper-alert brain sending competing thoughts like: "Are you okay?"; "you sure?"; and "I think it's time to exit." Think how well they'll be able to focus on the lesson. A kid with toxic stress will likely be hyper-vigilant about their safety, and with all their brain's precious resources devoted to self-protection, they might grapple with low self-esteem, insecurity about whom to trust, and just misery in general. Learning how to face fear is more effective in a safe environment like a courageous classroom. Chronic or toxic stress impacts memory. Learning is the consolidation of memories and the ability to recall them purposefully. Chronic stress can damage and alter the structures in the brain that are responsible for learning and memory.

The period of childhood into adolescence is one of physical but also cognitive, social, and emotional growth. Between the ages of 11 and 21 there are noticeable physical and sexual maturation stages, the emergence of more abstract and long-term thinking as well as a propensity for more risky behaviors (Soleimanpour 2017). Exposure to childhood ACEs during these times can impact how children and teenagers are able to navigate transitions and handle challenges. Traumatic experiences influence cognition and emotional development. Disruptions in positive supports are linked to potentially worse outcomes. Research on the biology of stress proves that excessive or prolonged exposure to stress hormones can disrupt early brain functioning, leading to impaired learning, behavior, and health from childhood to adulthood. Because the developing brain is very sensitive to toxic stress during periods of rapid brain growth in infancy, early childhood, and adolescence (Sege and Harper Browne 2017), it is very important to identify students who are exposed to trauma, recognize how they respond and provide preventive interventions.

The educational experience begins at home, outside the classroom. It is important to provide positive experiences for students in their homes. Parents and teachers should know that there are four key positive actions that contribute to a child's healthy psychological growth.

- The first is to be in nurturing, supportive relationships.
- The second is to provide safe, protective, equitable environments for children to live, develop, play, and learn.
- The third is to create opportunities for constructive social engagement and connectedness.
- The fourth is to actively search for schools where social and emotional learning is a part of the curriculum.

Situations at home that can lead to ACEs for students include physical abuse or neglect, sexual abuse, domestic violence, substance abuse or mental illness, parental separation or divorce, having a household member who is or has been criminal justice involved, and not being raised by both biological parents (Soleimanpour 2017). Almost one in five children in the United States will experience a traumatic event involving interpersonal violence by the time they reach adulthood (Mclaughlin and Lambert 2017). More than 50% of adults and 46% of children in the United States will have experienced at least one ACE in their early years (Ziv et al. 2018). A Center for Disease Control report found that an estimated 62% of adults across 23 states reported at least one ACE during childhood and almost 25% had three or more (CDC 2019a). Exposures that involve three to five or more exposure types can be more difficult to mitigate and be more common than we realize. Insecurity, unconnectedness, low self-esteem, poor relationships with peers, and acting out in school can be the result of neglect, because abuse affects social-emotional development (Ziv et al. 2018). School settings that provide safety, emotional support, and security are critically important as a safety net for traumatized students and their families. Schools also meet the basic needs for students who may have food insecurity or marginal food insecurity. In 2020, almost 31 million children in US schools received free daily meals. Due to the Covid-19 pandemic and school shutdown, one out of every four children experienced food hunger and their parents reported worsening mental health (Garrett 2020), both of which can contribute to trauma in children.

Children who live in poverty, belong to low-resource communities, and/or are members of marginalized minority groups may also face hardships outside abuse, neglect, or living in a dysfunctional household. Expanding the risk factors of the ACEs' scale could then include the impact of systemic racism, community risk factors and dysfunction, bullying/peer dysfunction, and environmental inequities. A researcher conducted a study on widening the early experiences of children who felt victimized and helpless after intentional trauma from ACEs related to emotional or physical threats to include victimization experiences outside the home and found that there is a cumulative impact associated with poorer mental health in young adults (Karatekin and Hill 2019).

Trauma and the Brain's Development

Trauma exposure in school is a serious problem for students. Brain development in infancy, childhood, and adolescence is impacted by the social and environmental conditions where children live, play, grow, and learn. The growth of the human brain from infancy through childhood is extraordinary, as it lays the foundation for future mental health and the capacity for cognitive control and problem solving. Peak brain growth is in infancy and early childhood, but the brain structure changes, refines, and alters from childhood to young adulthood in response to health exposures, genetics, and environmental conditions.

Famed neuroscientist Joseph LeDoux (2019, p. 9), writes, "We are our brains." Our brain's ability to allow us to think, feel, worry, reflect, plan for, and take action comes from the functionality of its evolution. Our brain evolved and has adapted to ensure our survival and to reproduce. It can also help us recover from our traumatic experiences and rewrite our own script when we recall them. As author Patrick Sweeney (2020) writes in his book, *Fear is Fuel*, you can erase the shortcuts or triggers that may intensify trauma when you use your feelings of fear as a source of courage, power, and success. Using language that is not "fluent in fear" like "I can't" or "Why does this always happen to me?" can be replaced with the language of courage, "I will figure this out" or "What do I need to learn from this?" Describing fear as an opportunity for courage is possible and our brain is wired for it.

There are several factors that impact brain functioning including age, neural circuits, sex, psychological traits, and brain disease. Neuroplasticity refers to the brain's ability to modify, change, and adapt both structure and function, in response to experience (Voss et al. 2017). When we look at the way our brain's development is susceptible to environmental influences and to learning or intense activity, we need to look to our white matter (Lebel and Deoni 2018). While gray matter is composed of neurons and parts of the brain involved in the control of muscles, and sensory perception, white matter contains a substance called myelin that wraps up axons, which come from neurons. Myelin helps with the transmission of information through interactions involving brain chemicals or neurotransmitters. Neurotransmitters can help by either amplifying or lowering the process of transmission through the use of receptors located throughout the brain and nervous system.

The fact that our thoughts, behavior, genes, and environment can influence the development of white matter has implications for trauma and learning because white matter makes up most of the brain. Myelinated nerves can carry impulses up to 100 times faster than unmyelinated fibers and the volume of white matter processing information, growing and shrinking with experience, shaping them as we develop. White matter is not just passing on data, it has a relationship with IQ (Newman 2017). Research suggests that exposures to chronic stress and trauma in children can contribute to developmental abnormalities in how a threat is emotionally regulated, leading to increased activity in the amygdala (fear) and impact the hippocampus (memory), contributing to the risk of lower thresholds for developing anxiety and depressive disorders in children (Herringa 2017; Sweeney 2020). This is another reason to monitor students for their exposure to past or current trauma and educate them in school settings that are safe and enhance their well-being.

Trauma Presenting in Children

My (Janet) professional experience has been that when a child presents with trauma that was either done to them or they witnessed in their home or living situation, there is a high probability that at least one of their adult caregivers has a past or current history of trauma. Traumatized children may grow up untrusting of the world, hypervigilant with constant anxiety, and have difficulty with emotional regulation and conflict resolution. When conflict erupts, they may go from 0 to 100, or completely shut down, unable to express their needs or inner feelings. As a result, their children may have parental anger or mood swings displaced onto them, which can make even young children feel responsible for their parent's or caregiver's moods. It's a very helpless place and far too many children find themselves there.

The majority of adults with a mental disorder are parents, in fact almost 68% of females and 76% of males have children (Zalewski 2017). As educators, you will interact with fellow teachers, parents, and staff who may receive some sort of mental health treatment. Getting mental health treatment is a healthy and good thing. It is important to never use shame or further stigmatize others who disclose their mental health status. Try to avoid linking a child's behavior to faulty parenting skills that you as an educator may associate with that parent. It's important to support them and to ask how you can help in a non-judgmental way.

Adult mental health is affected by their own early exposure to childhood adversity. The literature has several well-documented associations of ACEs and adult mental health, physical health, and behavioral outcomes. Common findings in adults who scored on ACEs include depression or a major depressive episode. Depression is a major risk factor for suicide and can create on average 28.9 years of quality-adjusted life expectancy, which is twice the burden of several chronic conditions like stroke, heart disease, diabetes mellitus, hypertension, and asthma (Merrick et al. 2017). Students who have high ACE scores can have lives associated with future violence and victimization, health risk factors, chronic health conditions, mental illness, decreased life potential, and premature death (Merrick et al. 2017). It's critical when we identify a child with a high ACEs score that we find ways to support the family to end the cycle of trauma.

Teachers are often in the best position to identify students who are exposed to trauma and provide preventive interventions – but without proper training, such efforts are unlikely to yield much benefit, and might exacerbate the burnout levels of these already overburdened professionals (Ouellette et al. 2018). In many schools, teachers provide mental health services without adequate training on how to manage disruptions, engage learners, and identify psychopathology in their students. Teachers face the challenges of working with limited resources, overcrowding, chronic disruptive student behavior, and high-pressure accountability policies (Ouellette et al. 2018), additionally, with Covid-19, responsibility for monitoring the students' health and their own. Teachers may also have their own childhood trauma, exposure to childhood adversity, or they may currently live in a home dealing with relationship dysfunction, physical abuse, or substance abuse.

Trauma as a Student and Educator

I (Jed) am exactly the student/educator Dr. Janet is talking about. I was a childhood victim of physical, emotional, and sexual abuse. It lasted on and off my entire childhood. In fact, it lasted well into adulthood, the physical and emotional part anyway. It began with my dad. He had a violent temper, and by the time I was two years old, he had beaten my mom more times than she could count and once he even threw me across the living room in a fit of rage. Thankfully, they divorced. But because of the South Carolina family court system in the 1980s, my dad got visitation rights. Can you fathom? He literally beat my mom so bad that he broke her tail-bone, and tossed toddler me across the room because he was angry, but the courts found him worthy of visitation! That's a whole other book. I digress.

His physical and emotional abuse was present in some form during every visit. Because he was so unstable, he rarely had an adequate place for me to visit, so I would go to his grandma's house, my great grandma . . . Maudie. Gosh I loved her so. Her house was mostly a safe haven as long as he didn't come. But, he was a pride-ful man and wanted nothing more than to prove to me that he was my daddy, and not that new man my mom had married. In many ways his "proving" to me became more of bullying me into loving him. I was absolutely terrified of him. His rage could come on at any moment, and it could happen over the smallest thing. I saw him raise his fist to my Maudie, to his own mother, to his sister, to his second wife, and to his second child. My entire childhood was filled with uncertainty as I waited for his next blow-up. One particular blow-up happened when I was around 10 years old. It haunts me to this day. It was Sunday, Father's Day to be exact, which often proved to be a super stressful day. As I look back on that holiday, I don't recall one good memory of it. My dad was either out of town, drunk, passed out, or in a full-on rage because I wasn't with him the whole day. That's what happened on this day.

I went to play golf with my stepdad early that morning. I was supposed to arrive at my Maudie's house to attend church with my dad by 11am. Unfortunately, the golf course was super busy, and I didn't make it over there until after church. It was about 12:15pm. I remember that because I thought, "I'm not too late for lunch so hopefully he won't be mad." Trauma does that to kids. It makes them think about things they shouldn't have to worry about. Because of his history of violent rages, I knew to be on guard for being tardy. I had no idea what was coming.

As we pulled up to Maudie's I saw my family sitting on the porch. Maudie was there. My dad. And my dad's parents. His second child hadn't been born at this time. I waved goodbye to my step dad and he drove off. The moment he was out of sight, my daddy charged down off the porch and met me in the yard. He was immediately yelling and cussing. Something about how he was my real dad and he deserved respect. I remember "honor thy father," a reference to Exodus 20:12. As an adult I learned Ephesians 6:4, "And, fathers, provoke not your children." If only I had known that then. Honestly, I am glad I didn't. What happened next may have been far worse.

I was apologizing profusely, looking to the porch for some help. Sadly, that help didn't come. His barrage of swearing and yelling continued until suddenly his anger boiled over and exited his fist as it met my face. I fell to the ground, my glasses flew across the yard, and I heard the words I have never forgotten. "Stay down there you fat four-eyed fag."

I didn't even know what a fag was then. It wasn't long after this a guy named Michael Hayes called me that same word in the hallway of Boiling Springs Elementary. Of course, I did grow up to be a Fabulously Awesome Guy, but I am sure Michael and my dad didn't mean to express such endearment to me.

Of course, my dad's outrage ruined the rest of the day. I ran down the street to where his parents actually lived and never went back for dinner. I called my mom to come get me. Needless to say my dad was furious. It didn't end pretty at all. Sadly, two weeks later, I had to go visit again. His torment of me continued well into adulthood until I finally learned that I didn't have to take it anymore.

The day after he hit me, I went to daycare. School was out because it was June, but I often wonder how I acted at Small World that day with Ms. June and Ms. Donna watching on. Did they know my dad hit me just the day before? Did they think I was a fat, four-eyed fag too? I am sure I pretended like all was well. I am so glad it wasn't a regular school day. No way Mrs. Curry would've been able to handle that either.

As I said previously, this emotional and physical abuse happened well into my adulthood. I wasn't always the recipient of fists, but I was a witness to my mother receiving more than her share. His name was Jeff. Mama married him my junior year of high school. He was quite the charmer. Everyone loved him so much. He was definitely what you would call the life of the party. But, behind closed doors, he was identical to my real dad. He could go from cool, calm, and collected to raging and reckless in just the blink of an eye. I remember one day when he hit my mom just moments before her parents arrived. We all had to play it cool lest we have more of his punishment once they left.

The finality of his anger in our family came in March 2003. I was in the midst of my student teaching. I lived with my best friend Matt, and we were both at our apartment when my sister called me in a screaming fit of panic and fear. "He's got her, brother. He just threw her down on the ground and punched her. Come quick!" Immediately fear and panic flooded my body. I yelled to Matt to grab a coat and come with me. He drove and I called 911. My night of lesson planning and preparing for my week with sixth graders at E.P. Todd Elementary had come to an abrupt halt. My mother and sister's safety was the ONLY priority.

The ride there was a complete blur of passing headlights and seemingly pointless questions from the 911 operator. "I have NO IDEA what he is wearing, lady, I am not there." I remember yelling at the emergency dispatch. I know she was only doing her job. But in the moment, it seemed so superfluous.

When we arrived at my mom's, a 20-minute drive from our apartment, there was no sign of my sister's car. She was pregnant at the time so I assumed she fled for safety. I could see Jeff running through the house turning off the lights to make it seem like they were peacefully tucked inside. Matt encouraged me to remain in the car until the police arrived. Which by the way, took WAY too long. How had we got there faster than they had? This man had a history of violence and I told the 911 operator he was very dangerous. Shouldn't that have sped them up?

It seemed like eternity before they arrived. I am sure it wasn't as long as I thought, but at that time it seemed like forever.

I got out of the car and identified myself as the 911 caller. Within moments they had Jeff in cuffs, locked in the back of a patrol car. It took hours however for me to get to my mom. The night time ticked away. It was almost 3am before I got to see her. She was a mess, both physically and emotionally. By 4am we were at the hospital. Sometime around 5:30am, I went to the courthouse to watch his arraignment. Of course, they let him right out. SC Criminal Domestic Violence laws are some of the laxest in the country.

Around 6:30am I made a call to my cooperating teacher at E.P. Todd Elementary to tell her I wouldn't be making it into school that day. Of course I had to explain why. Damn, was I embarrassed. Next, I had to call my college supervisor. The embarrassment continued. Somewhere around 8am we made it back to my mom's place. He was not there thankfully. He had been ordered to stay away. I still to this day cannot believe he actually left us alone. After we cleaned up her house and got her settled in, we all crashed. My lesson plans never got finished, but I still had to go teach the next day. I have no idea what we did. I was mentally, physically, and emotionally spent. I had nothing to give to those students. At that point, it didn't matter.

I saw him once after that day. Thankfully, that chapter of our family is closed forever. Or is it? Trauma has a lasting effect on people. It never really goes away. The memories of it remain. Somehow you learn to cope and survive with it as you grow and thrive in spite of it.

Bessel van der Kolk, noted psychiatrist and author of *The Body Keeps the Score* (2015, p. 247), writes, "Even traumatized patients who are making real contributions in teaching . . . expend a lot more energy on everyday tasks of living than do ordinary mortals." Traumatized teachers can be hyper-vigilant and primed at lower levels for stress, anxiety, and conflict. In a heightened state, they can be easily triggered by a student's facial expression, raised voice, or seeming defiance leading to a collision of sensitivities without awareness and understanding that is harder to calm down from. I have been in work situations where well-meaning professionals come into the office reeling from a stressful homelife and take their emotions out on colleagues and patients. It's unpleasant for everyone involved but by being willing to have a courageous classroom, both teachers and students can find tools to create calmness, effective communication, and be less stressed.

Let's Chat

Jed: Dr. Janet, As I retold my story I realized once again how many negative experiences from my childhood have affected my adulthood. How common is this occurrence?

Dr. Janet: The way we see, interact with, and view others and events in our life is shaped from birth by how attached and responsive our caretakers were to us, and we to them. Negative experiences in childhood shape many adults' views of how they see themselves and their relationships with others. It's very common. The level of attachment impacts how secure and safe we feel beginning at birth. As we grow older and are able to find meaning in how we are treated both emotionally and physically, words and actions can hurt and leave a lasting impact on our self-esteem and ability to take risks as we develop. Traumatic events that are meant to hurt and demean create semantic memories. Semantic memories are when we remember the action and emotion attached. Because they are never forgotten, they form the basis for unending trauma. Although they're not forgotten, they can be mediated or framed in a less harmful way that convey strength and growth.

Jed: How can teachers who have experienced traumatic childhood events similar to mine use our lived experiences to help cultivate courageous classrooms of safe space for our students?

Dr. Janet: We know that almost 70% of students have experienced at least one traumatic event in their life, so I would imagine that most teachers are similar. To be effective, teachers must acknowledge their trauma. I would suggest writing down every traumatic event that has happened. Rank them, then circle the top three that have left the most significant impact. From your top three, choose the top one. Dive into it, swim in it, feel it. Identify the impact of your trauma and how it makes you feel, then while breathing deeply (to access your subconscious), write down your thoughts. Work on reframing your emotion to the event with the growth and strength that you currently have. The goal is to reframe your past emotion with a courageous mindset. That means you have a perspective of what happened to you as being done for you, not to minimize pain and trauma but to put a stake in the ground for your growth. The goal is to be able to help students self-regulate and talk about their pain and trauma with a plan of moving from victim to hero because of their willingness to triumph over their circumstances. It comes with time and practice.

Jed: Two words in your response that jump out are "reframe" and "self-regulate." How can teachers use those techniques in their classrooms?

Dr. Janet: Cognitive reframing is a super easy technique to teach students. It relates to a general principle that we create and control our reality with our thoughts, words and actions. You can teach students to listen to what they say and listen for what others say as it relates to negative beliefs: "I'm not smart," "I always mess up," "Don't call on me." Ask them, "What's another way to look at what you said?" looking for a positive reframe.

Self-regulation can be taught to children as young as three and four. It involves being able to identify your thoughts and feelings in response to an event and choosing an outcome that either clarifies or confirms a positive or healthy outcome. It requires the use of the frontal lobe, which is important for executive functioning and less impulsivity and moves away from just reacting (fight, flight, freeze) to action. Children should be asked about how they're feeling daily and given the option to draw it out, choose a color that represents their emotions, or say it out loud. Ask them to share at least one way that they can feel better if they're having a bad day, giving them suggestions if needed. Teach and encourage them to take 10 deep breaths and smile when they want to elevate or change their mood.

Trauma's Effect on You

ACEs are linked to chronic health problems, mental illness, and substance abuse in adulthood. ACEs also influence education in a negative manner and job opportunities. If you score four or higher on your ACEs, you may be at greater risk for a number of chronic health conditions like heart disease and depression.

The good news is, ACEs can be prevented. Schools can assist in preventing ACEs by strengthening economic support to families by providing information and assistance related to financial security, helping with lunch programs, and instituting family friendly work policies. Schools can also promote the prevention of bullying (a topic that will be addressed in the next chapter) and intrapersonal and family violence with public education campaigns and by teaching conflict resolution. Early childhood education can provide preschool enrichment with family engagement and early teaching of social-emotional learning. After school programs in schools can provide mentoring, tutoring, and strengthen social networks. Schools are also places where trauma may be identified and students and their families can be directed to effective interventions and treatment (CDC 2019a).

We have included the ACEs Quiz here for you. Teachers, it is not recommended that you complete this with students. *This is provided here for your personal reflection and information.*

Take the ACE Questionnaire

This questionnaire will ask you questions about events that happened in your childhood.

While you were growing up, *during the first 18 years of your life:*

Did a parent or other adult in the household <u>often:</u>

Swear at you, insult you, put you down, or humiliate you?

Or

Act in a way that makes you afraid that you might be physically hurt?

☐ Yes   ☐ No

If Yes, enter 1_____

Did a parent or other adult in the household <u>often:</u>

Push, grab, slap, or throw something at you?

Or

Ever hit you so hard that you had marks or were injured?

☐ Yes   ☐ No

If Yes, enter 1_____

Did an adult or person at least five years older than you <u>ever:</u>

Touch or fondle you or have you touch their body in a sexual way?

Or

Attempt or actually have oral, anal, or vaginal intercourse with you?

☐ Yes   ☐ No

If Yes, enter 1_____

Did you <u>often</u> feel that:

No one in your family loved you or thought you were important or special?

Or

Your family didn't look out for each other, feel close to each other, or support each other?

☐ Yes   ☐ No

If Yes, enter 1_____

Did you <u>often</u> feel that:

You didn't have enough to eat, had to wear dirty clothes, and had no one to protect you?

Or

Your parents were too drunk or too high to take care of you or take you to the doctor if you needed it?

☐ Yes   ☐ No

If Yes, enter 1_____

Were your parents <u>ever</u> separated or divorced?

☐ Yes   ☐ No

If Yes, enter 1_____

Were any of your parents or other adult caregivers:

<u>Often</u> pushed, grabbed, slapped, or had something thrown at them?

Or

<u>Sometimes or often</u> kicked, bitten, hit with a fist, or hit with something hard?

Or

<u>Ever</u> repeatedly hit over at least a few minutes or threatened with a gun or knife?

☐ Yes   ☐ No

If Yes, enter 1_____

Did you live with anyone who was a problem drinker or alcoholic, or who used street drugs?

☐ Yes   ☐ No

If Yes, enter 1_____

Was a household member depressed or mentally ill, or did a household member attempt suicide?

☐ Yes   ☐ No

If Yes, enter 1_____

Did a household member go to prison?

☐ Yes   ☐ No

If Yes, enter 1_____

ACE SCORE (Total "YES" Answers): _____

The Story of Johnnie

Everyone in the building knew Johnnie. She had cussed out most of us, she had thrown desks and chairs, she spat, she kicked, and she screamed to the top of her lungs on a regular basis. Other students were afraid of her, and if I (Jed) am honest, I think some teachers were too. I witnessed her behavior many times because my classroom was on the same hallway as hers. Some days things got really intense for her and administrators had to be called in to help. Needless to say her behavior wasn't earning her many gold stars or sweet notes home.

Other than the "bad behaviors," I knew little about her, but I often wondered what was going on in her life that I wasn't aware of that led her to act out the way she did, but based on my own childhood behaviors, I knew that I acted out when I felt things at home were unsafe and unstable. What I needed most on those days was:

- routine
- safe space
- kind words
- to know that I was valued.

I confess, when I saw her name on my class list as she entered second grade, I experienced almost every emotion a teacher could feel. Admittedly, most of my feelings were self-absorbed at first. I was anxious about what she might destroy in my classroom. I was nervous that she would hurt me or other students when in the midst of one of her fits. I was worried that I wouldn't be able to handle the stress that was sure to come with her misbehaviors. I was terrified I would mishandle a situation and lose my career. I was confident that when my entire school year fell to pieces because I didn't have the skills to handle ALL children that my professional peers would mock me and I'd be humiliated.

As "meet the teacher" day arrived, I had settled my nerves, put my irrational fears aside, and dug deep into my teacher training to figure out a plan for Johnnie. My mantra, "love first, teach second," as you will read about later, was guiding every step of my planning and preparation for Johnnie's arrival. Sadly, she never showed up for the big meeting day. Her absence relieved me a bit, but it concerned me more than anything. Why wasn't she there? Who missed "meet the teacher" day?

As was protocol for the school, I called her house to check in. The number was disconnected. There were two other numbers on the contact information sheet, both disconnected. Wanting to start off the year on a positive note, and build a relationship with her family, I decided to visit her home since I couldn't get in touch with anyone. My thinking was that my visit would be viewed as a nice gesture and the beginning of building a connection with Johnnie's mom in hope of having a successful school year. When I arrived at the door, I could hear at least two kids crying, the TV blaring, and music playing even louder. I knocked several times until someone came to the door. When the door opened I saw a woman I had never seen before. Two babies, one on each hip, a cigarette dangling from her lips, and a dog barking at her feet. Assuming it was Johnnie's mom, I introduced myself as the new teacher for the year and she hesitantly invited me in. Hearing there was a visitor, four other kids emerged from a bedroom. One of them was Johnnie. She immediately said, "Oh Lord, It's Mr. Dearybury!" I chuckled then, and I still chuckle to this day because that response to my presence in her home was a classic Johnnie moment. Little did I know at the time the impact that she'd make on my life. After a brief and somewhat tense visit, some chatting about the upcoming school year, and watching the kids devour a bag of candy I brought with me, I left to return to school.

Driving back to school I began to process what I saw, smelled, and heard. Six kids total in the small apartment. Two babies. One of which was obviously a baby with special needs and the other was very young. Both in diapers. Two of the remaining six were also in diapers and not school age. That left Johnnie and her other sister, one year older than her. I later learned that Johnnie was the primary caretaker of one the youngest siblings when mom was at work. Unfortunately, this is a requirement for many students whose families may not be able to afford child care for preschool children.

The rooms I saw didn't have much. I saw a couch, TV, and a lamp in the living room. No table for the lamp, no stand for the TV. They both sat on the floor. I didn't take a tour of the place, but the bedroom I saw had a mattress on the floor and a lamp sitting beside it: no bed frame; no night stand. At the foot of the mattress was a pile of clothing. I never saw the radio that I heard when I knocked, but it continued to blare while I was there. I assume it was in the kitchen. I didn't see a table, but there was a Styrofoam cup on the counter being used as an ashtray. The place had a musty, smoky odor and the carpet had lots of stains. Mom was not very cordial and seemed annoyed that I was there. Her responses to all of my small talk were short, and I could sense almost immediately that she wanted me to leave. As the door closed, I heard mom cussing at the kids, asking them why I was coming to their house. She was very angry. Unfortunately, my visit got the oldest two, including Johnnie, quite a scolding.

Of course, I was grieved that I had got them in trouble. That certainly wasn't my intent. What is often missed by folks with good intentions is that we fail to consider the impact of our intent. What I assumed to be an innocent visit was very upsetting for the mom. I visited with one intent, but she saw it from her perspective. When I reflect on that moment, with the lens of knowledge that I have now, there is a whole list of reasons that my presence in their home could have caused tension. This is where better training would have helped me as an educator. I never once considered how my visit might play out, how it might make mom feel, how it might create tension and unease. I should have considered a few things first:

- Maybe mom had a bad school experience.
- Maybe mom had a bad experience with males.
- Maybe the bills were due, the house was a wreck, there was no lunch ready, there were six screaming kids, and now a teacher shows up . . .
- Maybe the presence of a strange white man from the school created intense anxiety.

What happened as a result of that visit has stuck with me for years now. I only considered my perspective, not theirs. I should have acknowledged all of the ways that my visit could create problems, but because I had never been taught to consider things like that it never crossed my mind. We teachers must be willing to see different perspectives and separate our own limited worldview to be more encompassing of ALL students.

Here where I teach in the South, a large majority of people are conservative, White, Evangelical Christians. The majority of your co-workers, neighbors, politicians, community workers, teachers, principals, school boards, etc., are thus conservative, White, Evangelical Christians. Their ideals are consistently accepted as "normal" in these parts, and any deviation from their principles and beliefs is abnormal. The most diversity you have in some parts of my state is Southern Baptists versus United Methodists. The biggest difference being a sprinkle or a dunk. (Google it.)

Large communities here are of the same general belief system and as a result it is often difficult here to see, hear, and feel from a different perspective. With the bulk of the masses being alike, you tend to fall in line and become like them in order to make it. It grieves me that I fell into that when considering the best move to help Johnnie. My lack of understanding for a family in her financial, social, and physical situation started our relationship on a rocky footing.

What I could have done differently is a question that I have asked many times.

- Should I have not gone to visit?
- Should I have taken a female teacher with me?
- Should I have asked her previous teachers more questions prior to visiting? Should I have not taken a gift?
- Should I have taken a bigger gift?
- Should I have scheduled the visit rather than arrive unannounced?
- Should I have just written a note and left it on the door?
- Should I have insisted on chatting outside the apartment rather than going inside?
- Was I being intrusive?
- Was I appearing to be nosey, meddling, or arrogant?
- Was my tone condescending?
- Was my body language communicating negativity?

These are just a few of the questions that have bombarded my thinking since that day.

Let's Chat

Jed: Dr. Janet, I know there are many teachers out there like me, who have good intentions but often make mistakes in helping students who come from homes where fear and trauma have had a great impact. How can we avoid those mistakes so as not to cause further harm?

Dr. Janet: The first step is the ability to assess and recognize if, in fact, there is trauma in their daily life. Statistics suggest a higher likelihood than not that there is. It's imperative that as educators, healthcare providers, or adults who cross paths with students that we are able to keep them safe. Asking about physical or sexual abuse does not create the problem but provides them the ability to answer. So ask, don't assume. Avoid re-traumatizing by treating conversations gently with respect. Listen without judgment, and use their words to clarify any questions. Let them know the reason for your visit or questions so that everyone is on the same page. Keep resources handy in the event that something reportable occurs or you need to make a referral. Reassure them that you are there to help.

Jed: You said step one is recognizing the trauma in their daily life. What should we look for?

Dr. Janet: As a reminder, trauma is not always physical, and emotional abuse is just as damaging to the psyche, but looking for things like bruises, scratches, etc. and gently inquiring is important. Physical hygiene changes, tiredness, or a change in mood may indicate some issues at home. Most kids will not tell you that they are feeling some kind of way in response to a stressor at home, but they may have behavioral or attitude differences in the classroom. The key point is to know their personality and individual behavioral patterns before there are outward changes, which may be noticed in the classroom. There may be little things that you pick on, and after asking a simple question, like "How are you?" or "You seem upset" may be clarifying for you and your student.

Jed: Upon visiting Johnnie and seeing her home, experiencing the anger of her mother, and realizing that her daily routine involved caring for her little sister while mom worked, it helped me better understand why Johnnie acted out at school. She carried a lot of pressure and anxiety, and presumably trauma, into the classroom. What strategies would you suggest for teachers who have students from similar backgrounds as Johnnie?

Dr. Janet: Disruptive behavior at school can come from many sources. Children often act out their emotional upsets, lack of trust for authority and/or pain, anxiety, or depression. When teachers can see behavioral outbursts or disruption as both a symptom and signal for help, then a path of understanding can begin. Being poor or ethnic does not confer dysfunction or psychopathology. However, we know that poverty, changes in family relationships and dynamics, situations like Johnnie's, where she had to take on adult-like duties and was not allowed to play, will alter one's individual temperament and functioning in the classroom, and needs to be addressed.

How to Help Students Who Might be Experiencing Adversity

1. Find out as much about their home situation (stability, stressors, potential abuse) as you can.
2. Teach them how to self-regulate by identifying their thoughts/ feelings and how to safely self-manage shifts in mood or thinking with their breath.
3. Look for patterns when the behaviors occur. For example, if behavior is worse in the morning, find a way to intervene and reinforce positive coping check-ins before beginning the day.
4. Teach them the power of the breath as a stress-buster and to relax.
5. Provide therapy resources at school.
6. Allow them to play, have fun, and be a kid as much as possible while in school.

Tips for the Courageous Classroom

Understand your ACE score and its possible effect on your teaching.

Learning Principle

Past or current trauma can impact teacher well-being and their relationship with their students and colleagues. Symptoms of unresolved trauma may include: substance use or addictive behaviors, an inability to handle conflict, anxiety, depression, and/or low self-esteem. Traumatic events can be additive with increased psychic pain if not dealt with. They can contribute to a feeling of anxiety, helplessness, or hopelessness. The first step to resolving trauma can be to examine your old wounds.

Take the ACE survey and be determined to deal with childhood or current trauma.

Learn to identify triggers that may cause an emotional response that challenges your relationship with colleagues and your students because of misread signals, low frustration tolerance, fear in the classroom, poor impulse control, and inattentiveness because of distraction. Don't be afraid to seek psychological help or counseling if your job performance or personal relationships are impacted.

Tips for Dealing with Your Trauma

Trauma is an acquired fear response; after exposure to an experience or experiences, the fear memory persists. With an experience of trauma, there are physical changes that happen in the brain that help the brain memorize elements of the traumatic experience to inform future behavior. This makes it hard to shake a traumatic experience as smells, tastes, what you see, and other fearful or traumatic experiences can quickly feel as if you are re-experiencing your event. Teachers and students need to be aware of the role of trauma and fear as a lived experience for them and the impact that it has on their functioning in the classroom. Outward signs of a trauma include withdrawing, easy startle reflex, aggressive or disruptive acts, anxiety, sadness, disengagement, and staying quiet or silent.

Trauma relief skills within the classroom are:

- Establish the immediacy of the trauma and stop it. If someone reports active physical, sexual, or emotional violence or abuse, shut it down by reporting it.
- Acknowledge the trauma and traumatic events in a safe space.
- Write about the experience for 20 minutes. Disclosing by writing it down or saying what happened out loud, can improve psychological well-being and help you understand the emotional impact of your experience.
- Acceptance not denial produces better health outcomes when facing adversity and paired with the commitment and motivation to face the trauma to help yourself.
- Understanding that you did not cause it, and are not to blame, can alleviate the burden of having to keep it a secret.
- After disclosing or talking, for twenty minutes, do a neutral positive activity like going for a walk, jump-roping or riding a

bike to avoid dwelling in negative feelings, knowing that you can return to the experience.

- If you have a hard time talking about it directly, discuss your event as if it happened to someone else, with a focus on what happened, what was felt, and how they could be helped to feel better.
- Traumatic experiences can create chronic stress and compromise physical health. Pay attention to sleeping patterns, try to eat nutritious foods, and do exercise as stress relief.

Chapter 4
Crossing the Threshold into Schools

Courage in Spite of Circumstances

The ultimate goal of teaching and learning in a courageous classroom is for students and teachers to view one's circumstances – however challenging – as a motivation to succeed. Don't get us wrong here. Many of the circumstances that our students are facing are horrific and should have never happened. Their stories are often heartbreaking, but countless students rise above their circumstance. Kit Summers is one such student and is living proof of what can happen when a teacher helps a child make that belief their North Star.

Now a professional, he describes his early life as one big struggle. Born into a spiritual, praying household in a leafy, stately but modest brick home in a suburb of Texas, Kit obtained his PhD at the age of 27. He never imagined that he would survive his upbringing, much less have a storied career.

Kit didn't meet his biological father (despite knowing "who he is and where he lives") until he was an adult, and is still ravaged with the thoughts of wondering what he, as a child, could have done to make his father not want to be a part of his life.

In his home he was subjected to violent, harsh beatings by the men that his mother would allow in. Remembering that time, Kit recalls being "angry and alert all of the time." Dearly loving his mother, at a young age, he remembers hearing loud crashes and her echoing screams as she was beaten by her boyfriends. At the tender age of seven, cowering in his bed but feeling like his heart would burst out his chest, he grabbed a plastic gun and ran out of his room to confront his mother's attacker. When he attempted to bravely stand up for his mother, he was picked up and hurled into the wall, and he remembers his then-tiny body hitting the wall, the wind knocked out of him, as he breathlessly faded to the floor. It was after that, at seven, he began plotting how to kill the man, who called himself his stepfather. He kept his thoughts, abuse, and feelings secret, until a teacher noticed that something just wasn't right. Being in school was where he felt in control, and you will read later how that paid off for him.

Courage at The Eagle Academy for Young Men

Although far too rare, schools do exist that are geared towards helping people like Kit. The Eagle Academy for Young Men in the Bronx was started in 2004 by 100 Black Men of America to meet the challenges of city life for Black and Brown young scholars, experiencing issues like gangs, drugs, difficult and violent home lives, with individual and academic expectations to achieve in spite of it all, much like the example of Kit Summers, who did not go there.

New York has the lowest graduation rate for Black men in the country (Lankes 2014). New York Black and Latinx males have the lowest graduation rates in the country, with males of color having a 37% graduation rate in four years (Schott Foundation 2004). The Schott Foundation for Public Education found that Black males have the lowest graduation rate at 59%, trailing Latinx males at 65% and White males at 80% (Schott Foundation 2004). Success in school can be determined by factors like poverty and parental educational levels; schools that have students who live in temporary housing, who receive free lunch or public assistance tend to have lower graduation rates (New York City Comptroller 2016). Very much aware of the dismal statistics around risk, education, and young Black men, David Banks, a lawyer and the founding principal of Eagle Academy for Young Men in the Bronx, was determined to take courageous action to make a difference for at-risk youth of color in the Bronx.

In 2004, he opened The Eagle Academy, a five-story red brick building with 115 students, all male, only expecting the best from these young men. Every day starts with a daily town hall.

He states that "student voices are always heard." Together, they begin with the powerful recitation of William Ernest Henley's poem, "Invictus." A brief glimpse into Henley's inspirational life and the circumstances out of which "Invictus" emerged, speaks volumes about the values The Eagle Academy seeks to instill in its students.

Henley wrote the poem in the summer of 1872, a few days shy of his 23rd birthday while he was recovering from an infection of his foot. When he was a teenager his leg was amputated secondary to tubercular arthritis and he was facing a second operation and the potential loss of his foot. As his condition worsened, so did his despair. Determined to improve without another amputation, he made his way to the wards of Dr. Joseph Lister, a British surgeon and founder of the antiseptic theory who combined research into bacteriology and wound infection. As Henley's foot healed, he turned inward and reflected upon suffering and his survival, writing a series of more than 18 "hospital" works. "Invictus" emerged out of those works and has inspired heroes like Dr. Martin Luther King, Nelson Mandela, and President Barack Obama.

Out of the night that covers me,

Black as the pit from pole to pole

I thank whatever gods may be

For my unconquerable soul.

David Banks knows well the relationship and storied history of ritual and ceremonies from the Diaspora and why it is important to bring a sense of home to those who have suffered loss and pain. He knows how daily trauma plays out every day as students cross the threshold of academic institutions bringing in their pain and states clearly that students "can't show up for class unless they're ready to unpack." Daily town halls at Eagle Academy provide time and structure for its students to share, unload, cry, grieve, give gratitude, and discuss their fears, worries, and successes.

It matters not how strait the gate,

How charged with punishments the scroll.

I am the master of my fate:

I am the captain of my soul.

It is possible to build community and foster cooperation by recognizing the importance of a safe, courageous, shared space as a container for trauma and traumatic stress. Nearly half of all children in the United States have been exposed to at least one traumatic event, and more than one in five have been exposed to several (Sparks 2015). In addition, children who live in neighborhoods with high poverty and who lack safe reliable transportation that forces them to walk or catch a bus in dangerous situations, may miss more school and, therefore, opportunities for support, mental health guidance, and resources. The question of schools, then, is not only how to provide a safety net within them but how to widen its reach to capture students who are missing and need to be found.

Even though Kit didn't have a place like Eagle Academy, he was fortunate. Early on, he recognized that being an excellent student could be his ladder to climb out of violent, demoralizing situations. He distinctly remembers in the fifth grade sitting stiffly with a fresh, deep bruise on his thigh not being able to focus, "there but not there" and not being able to stop hot, salty tears from rolling down his face. His teacher called him out into the hallway and gently asked if he was okay. He erupted with the truth of his trauma and fighting his fear about being sent away if exposed. His teacher listened, safely intervened with support for him and his mother, allowing Kit to stay focused on excelling at school. His teacher constantly checked in on him for the rest of his school year and beyond, constantly telling him that "he would be someone special." Because of his experience with courageous teachers, coupled with his determination to achieve by acknowledging and working through obstacles, he is an active mentor who teaches at university level.

Courage During Car-Line Duty

One morning while I (Jed) was on car-line duty as an elementary teacher, I witnessed one of these parent stressor moments. I could hear the mom yelling at the kid as they approached the curb. It was a heated fuss, the kid was crying, and the mama was using words not appropriate for a school. I reached down to open the door for this student like I did all of them, anxiously wanting to rescue him from the barrage of profanity being hurled at him by his mother. As he exited her car, she threw his toast at him. He didn't catch it because he never saw it coming. Neither did I. The mother sped off leaving her crying kid standing on the sidewalk as his toast lay in the grass just beyond. I talked with him just a bit to investigate what happened. They were running late because he had taken too long to find his shoes.

While I think we have all had those moments in the mornings trying to get out of the house, it grieves me to this day that she threw the toast at him. It was so demeaning. The look on his face when he saw his breakfast on the ground . . . painful. I checked on him several times that day. He wasn't my student, but I saw him at recess, lunch, and at afternoon car-line. He never did get better that day. He spent most of the day in a terrible mood that, as is often the case, led to behavior problems. I told his teacher about what happened that morning in hopes that she would show him a bit of grace. Sadly, that information didn't seem to matter to her. If only her heart was one bent towards a courageous classroom.

What could she have done with the info? Maybe allowed the student to have extra time to eat a snack to make up for the lost toast? Maybe she could have allowed him to have some extra special class privileges for the morning to build him up. Maybe she could have talked with the school counselor about it and got him some one-on-one time in the guidance office. Maybe she could have hugged him tightly and reminded him that he was loved and safe at school.

Multi-focal Approach

Part of casting a wider net means looking holistically at students by taking a multi-focal approach that includes nutrition, sleep habits, and transportation to and from school. Our brain never stops working for us and is the first organ in the body that responds to what we eat. What we put into our body greatly impacts our brain, feelings, and thoughts. To maximize the benefits of a healthy brain and body, students should eat protein: meat, fish, eggs, chicken, nuts and seeds, dried beans and lentils, dairy products and/or soy products. Protein assists the brain in sending messages through the body and can improve your mood with the creation of brain chemicals. Foods that are high in antioxidants like fruits, vegetables, berries, and juices (low or no sugar) can help delay or even prevent the brain from aging. Water is always necessary to keep the brain working to its maximum capacity and students should drink regularly.

To improve memory, foods that are high in monounsaturated fats like avocados, nuts, olive oil, canola oil, and peanut oil are suggested. Omega-3 can help the brain work harder and is good for mood. Foods high in Omega-3 are oily fish, flax seeds and flax oil, chicken, and beef. Eggs are good for cholesterol and Omega-3 oil work to promote the creation of cells in the brain.

Sleep is another important component of performance for students and educators. According to experts, the amount of sleep that a student gets during their school years ultimately influences the outcome of their academic performance (Chen 2019). Many students in middle school and high school do not get enough sleep. The National Sleep Foundation recommends that students should get at least seven to eight hours of sleep a night, with studies indicating that most students receive less than six hours. Sleep is important for brain development and critical when trying to learn new concepts. Not getting enough sleep can lead to health problems secondary to weakening the immune system and a lack of sleep can drop the number of white cells (necessary to fight infection in the body) in the blood. The National Institute of Neurological Disorders and Stroke reported that a lack of sleep can impact concentration, memory and physical performance, and reduce the ability to work out math calculations. "Some experts believe sleep gives neurons used while we are awake a chance to shut down and repair themselves. Without sleep, neurons may become so depleted in energy or so polluted with byproducts of normal cellular activities that they begin to malfunction" (NINDS cited in Chen 2019).

Having good sleep hygiene can start with a bedtime ritual. Parents and teachers should turn off bright lights when trying to sleep. Put computers, tablets, smartphones, or screens away from the bedside. Avoid doing work or stimulating activity in bed. Monitor caffeine and sugar intake throughout the day, avoiding both after midday. Practice thinking positive thoughts before going to sleep and focus on positive sleep habits.

Talk to your students about their walk or bus route to school. Listen for any concerns or questions that they may have. In the United States, almost 25 million students jump onto yellow school buses to get to school (Schneider 2016). For many students, being able to ride the bus, or get to school on their own can be exciting, seen as a way to be independent and an important facilitator of health and cognitive development. However, dangerous neighborhoods or interactions with people who are not always well intentioned can create anxiety or fear in students. It's important that teachers check in with students about their safety, and allow kids to vent and be ready to share any concerns. In Springfield, Massachusetts, after discovering that almost 90% of students were being driven to school through high crime areas, the community, parents, teachers, and police officers launched a Walking School Bus that fostered togetherness. It started in 2010 with six kids and now is used by nearly 200 (Schneider 2016).

Kids around the world go to school by hiking, rickshaws, ferries, cable cars, trekking, subways, boating, bikes, motorcycles and in Sichuan province, children climb a 2,625-foot-high ladder secured to a cliff just to make it into school. All prove the dedication of students, parents, and educators to learning.

Barriers to children walking to school have remained the same for decades. A report from the National Center for Safe Routes to school found that the most common reason that children don't walk to school is distance (61.5 %). Years ago, most schools were located as central points of a community. As schools needed to be remodeled or renovated, schools were built on the edge of communities to save costs and get more land. Longer school trips from home to school contribute to less physical activity for kids, higher use of motor vehicles or public transportation, and increased pollution. Other reasons that parents worry about children walking to school include: traffic-related danger (30.4%), weather (18.6%), crime (11.7%), opposing school policy (6.0%), and other reasons (not identified) (15%).

However you travel to school, be aware of the impact of stressors within your home as barriers to your effectiveness within the walls of the school and classroom. Use your travel time to school to reflect on how the day started and what you want to accomplish. Pay attention to personal issues and be aware of internal and external resources if you feel overwhelmed, alone, and need psychological assistance. Be mindful about diet, nutrition, exercise, and sleep and practice healthy habits that contribute to learning, physical health, brain health, and stress management.

The Story of Mary

It was about 9:30am. School had been going for more than two hours. Students entered my room starting at 7:20 so we got right into the fun of learning new things as they arrived. Mary opened the door and tried to sneak in because she was so tardy. Of course I (Jed) noticed her right away, because that's my job as her teacher.

I welcomed her out loud . . . "MARY!!! It is sooooo good to see you. I was worried you weren't coming and today is our special reading celebration!!!" I said it with so much excitement because the day only occurred every six weeks, and Mary needed to be a part of the big event because she had worked incredibly hard with her reading.

No sooner than I said the word celebration, Mary lost it. Not the good kind of losing it either. She was bawling. Big fat tears. They streamed down her face like a summer downpour. It was wintertime and she had just come in from the cold, so the tears quickly began to intertwine with a snotty nose. I am sorry to be so graphic here, but I am painting a picture for you as to the depth of her emotions. She was a mess.

I rushed over to the door where she had dropped her book bag to comfort her.

"Mary, sweetie, what's wrong? I am sorry if I hurt your feelings."

I had no idea how my welcome could've upset her. I was confused, but I had to apologize right away if I upset her.

"The PO-lice," she muttered

"The police?" I asked, even more confused.

"They took him." she cried. "They took him and my mama."

"Sweetie, tell me what happened."

"They took him?"

"We was leaving our apartment when the blue lights flashed behind us. They pulled him out of the car. Mama started screamin' then they took her out too."

I listened, in disbelief. This wasn't a moment that college prepared me for. This wasn't a moment that hours upon hours upon hours of mind numbingly boring professional development in the library after school had trained me for. At no time in my career had I ever been trained about a child of color being a victim of police brutality. Listening to her describe it, that's exactly what it was. She talked about how they threw her daddy to the ground. Then they did it to her mama. All right in front of her. She will never ever forget it and will likely never recover from the trauma. Regardless of what her parents did, she deserved better than that moment.

Realizing the emotional moment was going to get worse before it got better, we moved the conversation out into the hallway. I let her cry it out and tell me how scared she was. She told me that she was left alone in the backseat through the whole thing. Her mama screamin' for her, her daddy yelling at her mama, the police yelling at both of them. Handcuffs, threats of a taser, multiple cop cars, parents locked in the back.

Can you imagine how terrifying that must have been for her? As if all of that weren't bad enough, the cops loaded her up in the back of one of their cars and dropped her off at school. They didn't even bother to call a relative who could have helped comfort her through the traumatic event. They just dropped her off. She literally walked to my classroom holding the little red tardy slip.

I finally got her calmed down enough that she stopped crying, but the sniffles remained till she finally fell asleep on the couch in the back of my classroom. She slept for hours. I sent my students to recess with another teacher that day, so in case she woke up I would be with her. While she was asleep, I contacted the guidance counselor. Apparently after dropping her off at the door, the officer who brought her in talked with the office personnel about what had occurred on the way to school. The reason dad was pulled over . . . marijuana. Mom was arrested for supposedly interfering with the arrest. According to Mary though, she never left the car until the police pulled her out. They informed the school that an officer would pick her up from school and take her to the social services office. I knew her grandma personally and begged to call her instead of that horrible scenario the officer prescribed, but my hands were tied by bureaucracy. The guidance counselor had to explain to her who was coming to get her at the end of the day. The tears flowed again. It was such an emotional day for Mary. I hope I helped her as best I could.

It's important to send your child off to school or wherever they learn, from a place of forceful calm. By that, I mean they should not cross the threshold of their school rattled from being verbally abused, shaking from witnessing or being the victim of domestic violence, or fearful from the negative verbiage of bullies. Parents must be laser-focused on the awareness of their own stressors and remain mindful to not let that interrupt the self-esteem and well-being of their children. It doesn't mean that you have to sugarcoat real stressors that may be occurring in your home, but understand when and how you push out your own negativity to your children. When the last words that children hear from you are destructive, it will impact their mood, which in turn impacts their focus and schoolwork. Educators and parents should know that when students have a "why try" attitude, a multi-focal approach can be utilized to understand why they're feeling that way and inspire them to achieve in spite of their pain.

Let's Chat

Jed: When students cross the threshold from home to school they often bring so much with them. Reading the stories about car-line duty and Mary and her parents, teachers never know what to expect as students arrive. How can educators ready themselves for moments like these?

Dr. Janet: The establishment of rituals, whether it's a spoken debrief or check-in, is beneficial for students and teachers. The process can prime students to reflect on what they're feeling at that moment and be ready to share. Teachers can also observe the eye contact, body language, and responses of students as they arrive and be ready for an uplifting conversation or activity to get everyone on the same page to learn.

Jed: How can teachers help students be ready for school and learning in spite of the events that often precede their arrival to the classroom?

Dr. Janet: Teachers can help students by teaching them about their power over how they feel and think after a conflict or a challenge. They can teach them to check-in with themselves by simply asking "How am I doing?" and invite them to notice their sensations within their body and use their senses. They can use an exercise like "I see, I smell, I taste, I touch, I notice . . ." and reflect on how they are feeling. A positive word or thought (mantra) has the power to enhance their feelings of happiness. A terrific classroom exercise is to teach children how to create a mantra that makes them tap into their superpower. When you look at your own mantra for only 30 seconds a day daily, it will become a habit and change your outlook.

Jed: Can you explain a bit more about how having a daily mantra can help students and teachers to move further away from the effects of their trauma that may inhibit them from being successful, whether it be at school or home?

Dr. Janet: Trauma impacts the brain by increasing levels of stress and anxiety and having a brain that is hyper-alert to what could happen next. Uncertainty derails the ability to focus and can alter one's mood. Trauma can also be triggered by sounds, smells, words, and sites. A mantra can help calm students down and help the brain relax and focus on new thoughts and hopefully behaviors. The brain has the capacity for neuroplasticity or growth in different places in the brain. When the brain re-fires it re-wires, so a mantra assists the brain in rewiring in a positive manner. It takes practice but can be done.

Dr. Janet's mantra: "Where am I?" I use this question as an emotional check-in with my mood, thoughts, and feelings. My touchstone word is "more," (reminding me I always have more to give).

Jed's mantra: "Make a mark." This mantra helps me remind myself that I matter and I have the ability to make a mark on the world with my life.

Tips for the Courageous Classroom

Recognize and relay to parents about the effects that trauma on the way to school may have on learning.

Learning Principle

Poverty, violence, sexual abuse, food insecurity, and home instability can impact the ability of school children and teenagers to learn. The stress of trying to meet their own emotional needs and recognize the needs of others may be severely compromised because their growing brains are also stressed. The flow of stress hormones like cortisol and epinephrine can trigger fear, which can be a distraction for memory function and learning. When the world, your household, and traveling to the classroom appear as threats, it's very difficult to learn and thrive.

The educational experience begins at home and continues when children return. Learning occurs best when everyone feels safe in their environment.

Tips for Parents Working at Home with Their Children (from Alan J. Watson 1994)
- **Pause:** Create the time and space to be there with them. Breathe, listen and be non-judgmental.
- **Prompt:** Give appropriate prompts while allowing your child to try to figure out and understand their work.
- **Praise:** Use praise selectively and effectively by stating specific aspects of what they're working on and are doing well.

Chapter 5
Fear Inside School

School Shootings

Concerns about school shootings are well-documented concerns for students, educators, and parents. In 2017, 4.1 million students participated in lockdown drills and many reported excessive worries afterwards with frequent bedwetting, writing goodbye letters to their parents, and giving away their possessions in case they didn't make it home (Pinkser 2019). One can only imagine their suffering and confusion. The statistics about actual school shooting victims tell a different story.

If we start from the basic premise that one child or educator who dies from shooting violence is too many, an examination of the facts is imperative. It is estimated that 3 million US children are exposed to shootings every year (EveryTown Research and Policy n.d.). As the Covid-19 pandemic led to school closures, March 2020 was the first March in almost two decades without a school shooting in the United States (Lewis 2020). Since the Columbine High School shooting in April 1999, there have been 68 school shootings and although school shootings appear to be common, they are still very rare when compared to daily gun violence (Melgar 2019). For example, gun violence in the United States is an extremely serious public health issue. The US firearm homicide rate is 20 times higher than the combined rate of 22 developed countries, and more than 150,000 students attending 170 schools have experienced campus shootings (DeSaulnier n.d.). What we know about school shootings is that in 93% of cases, the shooter has planned the attack in advance and in four out of five shootings, at least one other person had knowledge of the pending attack and did not report it (Sandy Hook Promise n.d.). The Government Accountability Office (GAO; 2020) has found that most shootings at K–12 schools more commonly arise from grievances or disputes between students or staff or between gangs (31%). Accidental shootings (16%) also occur and are followed in incidence by school-targeted attacks (14%).

Factors like the relationship between the shooter and the school and characteristics of the school economically and racially are important. It has been found that schools that are urban, poorer, and have high minority populations are more likely to have shootings characterized as coming from a dispute or grievance. Suburban, rural, wealthier, and low minority schools had more suicide and targeted shooting and are more likely to have higher fatality rates (GAO 2020). To date, there is not one standard definition of "school shooting" nor is there one single database that organizes related statistics that tracks the number of shootings, people killed, demographics of the shooter and victims, types of firearms and ammunition, and the motivation of the shooter. The creation of programs to prevent shootings on school grounds would be greatly enhanced if that information was located in one place. When a shooting occurs in a school, it leads to increased vulnerability, fear, and anxiety for students and educators. Anxiety can occur even if educators and students are not directly involved, or in the region or vicinity of the shooting.

The Monday after the Sandy Hook shooting, I (Jed) was standing in my classroom making gingerbread houses with my second graders when a flood of emotions came. I was devastated at the loss of students and teachers at the hand of a man who was described by a national news outlet as someone obsessed with mass murder and a scorn for humanity (Ortiz 2014). I was overwhelmed with fear that it could have very easily been my school. My classroom was the closest to the office and if an intruder ever came in, my students and I were first on the list. I was grieving so deeply as I helped my students coat their houses in icing and gum drop roofs that I began to cry as we worked. I couldn't explain to my kids why I was crying. I didn't want them to worry or be afraid. I remember telling them that they were happy tears because I was so proud of how hard they were working. That wasn't a total lie. I was happy. Happy that they were safe, and that I was safe. But then, grief set in all the more. Why hadn't a gunman charged into our school? Why had we been lucky enough to be in a classroom that wasn't victimized? You see, just like Dr. Janet said, anxiety can occur even if educators and students are not directly involved, or in the region or vicinity of the shooting.

School communities should be built around a commitment to day-to-day classroom safety. A positive classroom creates a virtuous cycle whereby students and teachers experience less emotional dysregulation, which fosters a less stressful environment, increasing their self-efficacy to monitor their moods and ask for help. Educators can teach children how to manage aggressive feelings and have zero tolerance for aggressive behavior. At the same time, we must identify, treat, and support mental health conditions like depression, anxiety, and substance abuse in a manner that lifts students up and doesn't stigmatize their mental condition. School communities must also provide the same support for those who often have to manage student mental health issues while managing their own stressors. If we focus on peer wellness and activities that mitigate loneliness and isolation, we can promote a classroom community of togetherness and work on social problems together – instead of pointing fingers.

One step is to create classrooms with a resilience or growth mindset, instead of fixed. Noted psychologist Dr. Carol Dweck writes extensively about the importance of applying psychological processes and solutions to social problems. When a student or educator responds to a challenge or obstacle with a "fixed mindset," it's a recipe for a negative outcome. The stifling "why try?" approach to education and life creates a false narrative: the feeling that character, intelligence, and creativity cannot be changed and therefore limit one's ability to strive, grow and achieve. The alternative is to have a "growth mindset," a frame of mind in which we seek out challenges and relish the opportunity to learn from failure. Our intelligence, personality, and capacity for intellectual growth is not fixed but in fact impacted by what we choose to see as possibilities and the work that we put in to achieve our goals. With a growth mindset, the basic belief in the power of your own possibility opens the door for love, friendship, intelligence, creativity, and yes, even courage. Dr. Dweck (2007, p. 7) writes:

> Why waste time proving over and over how great you are, when you could be getting better? Why hide deficiencies instead of overcoming them? Why look for friends or partners who will just shore up your self-esteem instead of ones who will challenge you to grow? And why seek out the tried and true, instead of experiences that will stretch you? The passion for stretching yourself and sticking to it, even (or especially) when it's not going well, is the hallmark of the growth mindset. This is the mindset that allows people to thrive during some of the most challenging times in their lives.

It is possible to build a community of students, educators, and parents with a single unifying purpose of each contributing to courageous classrooms. When groups of people from varying backgrounds and motivations can agree on a common purpose, their individual approach or method takes a backseat to the unified goal. Simply stated, there are many ways to accomplish a shared goal and all methods should be welcome. We know that diverse ways of thinking, different ethnic backgrounds, and unique styles of communication can enhance productivity when all feel like their contributions are accepted, wanted, and respected. In other words, a community committed to diversity, trust, and respect are important building blocks of a courageous classroom.

To make this happen, we need allyship: people standing side-by-side, in solidarity to move towards a goal. Differences in ethnic background, gender, socioeconomic status, and sexual orientation should not hinder but help allyship when all involved exercise tolerance. This means creating a safe space for difficult conversations through a willingness to listen and understand with the goal of improving communication and action.

During the fight for Civil Rights in the early 1960s, a time marked by racial unrest and tension over unfair laws and policies of exclusion, Black and White people came together as allies to protest injustice together. The results were impactful and resulted in the passage of the Civil Rights Acts of 1963. The racial reckoning and unrest that will define 2020 in the United States has given rise to a story of multicultural, multigenerational protests, similarly looking for equity and equality related to policing, healthcare, and the economy. The power of people recognizing a shared voice in the quest for a new humanity gives rise to lessons that students, educators, and parents can use in the determination for safe, courageous classrooms.

As educators work with students, they must think about how to amplify positive youth development and assist them in finding their voice. When youth realize their own power, identify their needs, and see the needs of others, it can lead to a shared community of courageous advocates working together as in the Civil Rights Era.

Many researchers have focused on the role of amplifying individual strengths and establishing positive purposes as necessary to improving mental health and creating a buffer for mental illness. Dr. Martin Seligman (n.d.), a psychologist known as the "father" of the Positive Psychology movement, views human strengths as contributing to well-being and sees the need to teach cognitive problem-solving skills including learned optimism. Learned optimism can help students by teaching them not to see the disappointment of a bad grade or the humiliation of being disciplined as permanent but rather temporary and a challenge that can be overcome. By adopting the habit of seeing obstacles as *specific* ("this time I got a bad grade") versus *pervasive* ("this always happens") students can learn to tackle them, step-by-step, instead of viewing them as insurmountable. Learned optimism can also lead one to delegate responsibility, instead of feeling like "it's always up to me," which can create negative pressure. Delegating builds community; it means that a loss or defeat is not wholly the individual's fault, allowing others to share the responsibility. Taking steps to change one's mindset takes time and practice, but the payoff is clear: it can ease anxiety, alleviate depression, and improve overall well-being, for students and teachers alike.

Getting ready for the first day of school always excited me. Tossing and turning in my wooden twin bed, I (Janet) would sneak quick glances at my short red skirt and crisp, white, cotton blouse hanging on the closet door, relieved that it was still there. My favorite black patent shoes and white tights were paired together like the ebony and ivory keys worn smooth from hitting the same notes. I was good. Shyly walking into the classroom holding my proud mother's hand, my butterflies always calmed down once our feet landed on the gray cement steps, and we navigated to a classroom full of wonder and the promise of a new year. I look back on those years fondly, but when I think about what the first day of school is like for many children in America, now, I get a little sad. As Jed recounts here, the first day of school isn't always so great.

The first day of school doesn't always happen in August/September. Sometimes it happens in the middle of November or late February. Traumatic experiences can cause families to flee from one place to another under the cover of darkness as a protective cloak. Sometimes it's not just a fearful moment that causes a new start, but often an unexpected death can relocate students from school to school. That's what happened to a former student of mine, Lucy.

Lucy was the sweetest first grader when I had her. I was so sad to see her go to a new teacher as she entered second grade. She had such a great personality and was super smart. She lived with her great grandparents across the street from the school. Her young life had been filled with traumatic events. Mom had abandoned her. Dad was in jail. Grandparents were still working full time, thus she ended up in the home of the great grandparents. As much as they loved Lucy to pieces, it was hard for them to give her the life that she needed. They were very poor and lived mostly off government assistance. They provided for Lucy the very best they could, but she carried around emotional scars, from the incarceration of one parent and the abandonment of another, that needed attention. The school guidance office could only do so much.

One afternoon Lucy arrived home to find both great grandparents dead. They had died while Lucy was at school, both of an apparent heart attack. Can you fathom the fear that ran through Lucy in that moment? How does one ever recover from that type of childhood trauma? I don't know the exact details of the story after she discovered them, but I do know that the next day Lucy wasn't at our school. In fact, she never came back. She seemingly disappeared, never to exist within our walls again. She had been there daily from kindergarten to second grade. She came to every summer event we hosted and was at anything that ever fell on a Saturday. Our school was her life. A few days later we received word that another school about 30 minutes away had requested her records.

As Dr. Janet spoke of being sad about the first days of school, I couldn't help but think about Lucy's first day at her new school in the middle of October. Her entire life had been snatched away from here in a blink of an eye. Suddenly the safety of her friends, her teachers, her school, and her great grandparents was gone. In a way, it was like all of us at the school died too. I imagine that there was nothing exciting about her first day like there was for the young Dr. Janet in her black patent leather shoes. Rightly, as she said, the first days of school can be sad.

Luckily for me (Janet), there was never a time when I sat in a classroom during my early childhood or teenage years and felt afraid. Fire drills were the extent of any preparation for our demise, and they were silly affairs where kids would goof-off, jumping out of order to get attention. I only was petrified within the walls of my school one time – and what caused me to recoil in fear was my mother. My mother was a high school teacher and she had a rule about wearing your coat in school once you were there and settled. I think that I had been warned once. Well, I was in seventh grade and wearing a corduroy skirt, tights, turtleneck, and a leather red motorcycle jacket with tufts of white fur. I loved that jacket. I was meandering to the restroom when I saw my mother out of the corner of my eye. Before I could get my jacket off, my mother superhumanly leapt to me from the end of the hallway, yanked off my jacket and yelled at me so loudly that a teacher appeared from another classroom. Realizing that everything was all right, she left. I was on my own with my livid mother. To this day, I don't wear my jacket indoors for any event without wondering what my mother would think.

Fear is important. Had I not associated wearing my jacket in class with fear, it would not be seared into my memory. Reflecting back however, my deeper emotion was disappointment because I know that my mother always wanted me to present myself as ready academically with complete attention and presence for my teacher, just ready to learn. As deep as my association between the feeling of disappointment and the jacket, the lesson was never really about outwear.

For many children, fear in school is a reality of their lives. The fears of children tend to be a reflection of their perception of the environment that surrounds them, as well as their emotional well-being (Jones and Borgers 1986). In today's culture of 24/7 news and a daily diet of the 100 ways you could be harmed, it's easy to imagine the angst that our children entertain on their way into school and while they're there. From school shootings, to being kidnapped, earthquakes and tornado drills, zoo animals escaping and trampling down the hallway, (okay maybe a skunk), peanut allergies, parental custody battles, and now sneezes behind a mask – all can trigger vulnerability, and a sense of lingering dread. To be fair, worrying about and working through fears is a natural part of a child's development but anxiety and fears that exist in school are real and have to be dealt with, so that children can have the best possible learning experience. One of the most all-pervasive sources of anxiety and fear within a school environment is bullying, which can destroy a child's self-esteem for a very long time.

School Bullying

As of the writing of this section of the book, I (Jed) am 42 years and 9 months old. Not quite 43, but some days I still feel very much like the insecure teenager that roamed the hallways of Boiling Springs Junior High. Writing this book about students' fears and trauma has brought to mind so many of the things I faced as a child. The junior high building I attended is still there, albeit empty and promising to be replaced by a Target one day. I pass it often. Every time I do, the anxiety and fear that I experienced as a student in that building floods my mind and body. It has been almost 30 years since that time, but the reaction I have internally when I see the building is often visceral. My stomach turns, my hands shake, and sometimes, I have to close my eyes just to avoid a breakdown. That's not a really great move if I am the one driving. Thankfully, it is a quick moment that doesn't last very long, but the results of the trauma I experienced there have definitely stuck around.

The bully's name was Brad. He didn't like me one bit. He was older than me. I, in the seventh grade, and he in the ninth. His sister, Becky, was in my grade, and she had told him that I liked boys, not girls. How did she know, I wondered? I hadn't even decided for sure at that point. I was still figuring it all out. Sure, I liked Justin and Christopher a lot more than I did Angie and Jessica, but why was that any of her concern? Maybe she saw Justin rub my leg under the desk in Mrs. Hawkins's science class out in the portable. Maybe she heard that Christopher kissed me in the bathroom after band practice. I really couldn't figure out how she knew anything about me. I didn't even really know her at all. But, she didn't like me, thus her brother didn't. Every single day the boy tormented me. I *hated* school because of it. I don't think I remember one bit of curriculum from that time period of school because I was constantly on guard, looking out for the threat of Brad.

One day in particular, I heard through the grapevine that he was looking for me so he could beat me up. Of course, the little band nerd me was terrified. I was looking over my shoulder all day.

The only time he and I ever really crossed paths was at lunch and after school. Unfortunately, both of those times were when teachers weren't readily available to protect students from bullies. They were busy doing their duties as they called them.

I saw him walk into the cafeteria and immediately my insides turned outside. I was scared to death so I left my lunch tray on the table and made my way to the bathroom. I was going to hideout in the stall until lunch was over. I turned around to look behind me as I left, and Brad was walking right towards me. In my best fight-or-flight mode, I chose flight and ran to the bathroom. He was right behind me, but luckily I was locked inside the stall before he could get to me. I lost count of the number of times he banged on the door and yelled faggot. Surely a teacher on duty heard him. Surely they saw me fleeing for my life as I ran into the bathroom. Surely one of my friends had gone for help. No, nope, no one.

After what seemed like an eternity of him trying to tear the door down, he wised up and started to crawl under the stall door to come in after me. I wasn't a straight-A student by any means, but I knew to get out of that stall as fast as I could. I hurriedly crawled out the other side of the stall, leaving him locked inside. It took him just long enough to stand up and unlock it that I was able to escape the bathroom and run for help. Literally right outside the door, I ran into one of the principals, Steve Johnson. I was so thankful to see him. I knew he would help me. That was his job after all, right? So you would think, but I have never forgotten the words he uttered to me at that moment. He said, "Well son, if there is a bully after you, I suggest keeping a baseball bat in your locker to protect yourself."

I hope your mouth just dropped. I hope that you are as outraged as I am that I even typed those words. Think back to our introduction of this book where we discussed the goals. Was Mr. Johnson promoting engagement? Was he developing a positive adaptation to adversity? YIKES! He was the worst! He had no empathy for me, and didn't make even one attempt to walk into the bathroom located no more than 10 feet from where he stood planted in the breezeway overseeing lunchtime hall traffic to speak words of disdain to Brad.

Even as I typed this whole story, I cannot believe that it actually happened. But sadly, I am sure that even in 2021, there are Steve Johnsons out there, refusing to be courageous and stand up to bullies that torment students.

I didn't tell my mom and step dad about this incident until well after high school. I was embarrassed, humiliated, afraid, ashamed, and petrified. What if my daddy found out? He would probably hit me because I didn't defend myself? See how the trauma of having an abusive father affected the trauma brought by the bully? It was a lose-lose situation. A vicious cycle of trauma begetting trauma begetting trauma. Maybe that baseball bat in my locker was the best idea after all. No, of course it wasn't. Violence isn't the answer. I continued my seventh-grade year living in fear. Thankfully, he never beat me up . . . physically. But mentally and emotionally, he kicked my ass. I am still recovering.

School Safety

Can you fathom how unsafe Jed felt at his school? What a terrifying experience to read about, much less experience as a junior high student. Sadly, there are stories like his happening around the world. Students come to school hoping for a safe space to learn and thrive, yet they may be left under the charge of educators or administration who do not fully understand the consequences of fear and trauma. Unwittingly, they magnify it by verbal abuse or not shutting down bullying.

Bullying is one of most pervasive sources of fear and anxiety in school, but children face a range of fears that vary with their stage of development. The average fears of children from the age of 5 to 11 years old involve things like the dark, monsters, being alone, animals – all things that you wouldn't commonly associate in a classroom setting. After 11, the fear of being hurt by someone, getting bad grades, being in trouble, or being punished are more common. With the teen years come fears related to a failure in school, relationships with other people, war, being alone, family concerns, pregnancy, and issues with various diseases (Robinson et al. 1991). Children who have experienced more personal trauma or disasters may have an increased risk of developing more problems related to fears. Those problems could include a depressed mood, anxiety, or constant worries or rumination. Children who live in stressful conditions or have changing unstable situations may also be at a greater risk for having fears at school.

Being a bully and being a victim of a bully both impact childhood self-esteem, school engagement, positive youth development, and challenge resilience. Studies show that being a bully negatively impacts academic competence, predicts lower self-reported grades over time, and can be more detrimental for girls than boys (Lerner and Steinberg 2009). Bullying can happen on school grounds, in the classroom, and online or by text. One out of every five students reports being bullied and almost half of them will notify an adult (National Bullying Prevention Center 2020). This means that almost half of all parents will not know that their child is being bullied. More than two-thirds of students who are bullied worry that it will happen again, which can impact their emotional health and ability to focus within the classroom. Bullying can present as being called names, made fun of, physically assaulted, shoved, tripped, spat on, and/or being excluded from events on purpose. Girls are a little more likely to be bullied than boys (24% to 17%), but the difference may result because girls are more likely to report it. The Center for Disease Control (2019b) reports that students who experience bullying are at increased risk for depression, anxiety, sleep difficulties, academic trouble, and dropping out of school. Students who are targets of bullying and bully other students may be at bigger risk for behavior and mental health problems. Students who experience bullying are twice as likely to have headaches and stomach aches and negative effects on how they feel about themselves and their relationships with friends and family, school work, and their physical health (National Bullying Prevention Center 2020). Bullying can be related to ethnicity or bias and LGBTQ identity leading to a higher dropout rate and lead to fears in students.

Research has shown that when a child has a persistent fear, almost 83% will have that same fear one year later (Morocco and Camilleri 1983). In fact, many childhood fears can extend through the teen years into adulthood. Different studies reveal varying opinions on whether gender impacts fear. However, what is clear is that cultural and social influences related to current political and national events can impact the fears of children and their personal safety.

Parents may underestimate how many fears their child may have (Jones and Borgers 1986). (Remember, fear can be defined as a mental or physical reaction to a danger or threat.) The intensity of a student's fears, especially at younger ages, may affect their self-esteem, increase feelings of insecurity and inferiority, and damage their overall mental health. As Jed mentioned, he is almost 43 years old and is still recovering from the trauma of his junior high school bully. He started therapy several years ago to process the childhood, as well as adulthood, trauma he experienced because of an abusive father and his sexuality.

The idea that schools should be a place where students can work to alleviate their fears is not new. A research study conducted in 1951 (Noble and Torsten Lund 1951) used a large metropolitan high school in order to analyze what students listed as causes of fear and anxiety. In it, 127 students were asked to list two things: The first was "incidents or experiences, either in school or out of school, which caused them to feel fearful, nervous, excitable or tense," and the second, was "an example of a culture pattern which you think causes friction, unhappiness, fear or hospitality in an individual or in a social group." Issues like school tests, school grades, teachers, and giving a speech topped the list with being late at the bottom. Even in 1951, the authors concluded that in addition to teaching academics, schools should be aware of what can be done to lessen tension and fear in students and provide a greater feeling of security.

Feeling afraid or not safe in school has serious implications for students and teachers related to learning, socialization, emotional well-being, and their health status. Just ask Jed how much he learned during his seventh-grade year. Many fears are shaped in early childhood and can be influenced by peer attitudes, parental response, teacher/counseling support, and actual or perceived risk. A student's fear of something specific, like a terrorist attack, may serve as a symbol of other fears or general anxiety, unease, or be in response to societal changes at large. For example, there is a scientific phenomenon known as "the fear of crime paradox." In 1973, "widespread public anxiety about crime and victimization" was prevalent, but there was a big discrepancy between a high reported level of fear and a low level of risk. If the overall level of fear was too high compared to the risk, there could be a build-up of irrational fear in people who shouldn't have felt threatened" (Cops 2010, p. 387).

There are many factors that impact how fear can be interpreted by students. In the home, students witness their parents' or caregivers' reactions to fear, watch and listen to their peers and educators, and more broadly see how different topics that could instill fear are covered in the media. What a student fears may reflect a direct correlation to a particular item or be symbolic and used as an expression to represent general feelings of societal tension or unrest caused by social changes, like the Covid-19 pandemic and racial unrest.

School Anti-Bullying Programs

Back in the early 1990s when I (Jed) was trapped in the bathroom by a gay-hating bully, when principal Johnson was telling me to keep a protective baseball bat in my locker, there was no such thing as an anti-bullying program. Fast forward to the present and there are 13 million hits when searching "school anti-bullying programs" on Google. Diffusing bullies and the trauma they create is essential to a courageous classroom. But we would be remiss if we didn't take a pause here to discuss the effectiveness of many of the programs and the methods by which they are implemented in schools across the country.

While I have not visited every school in the United States, I have been to many of them in more than half of the country. I am friends with educators in all 50 states, and I have heard from almost all of them about their schools' anti-bullying program. Almost all of them say the same. The plan was adopted over the summer by district office personnel who no longer have direct contact with students. The initiative was then introduced to school faculties at the back-to-school meeting in the fall via a well-crafted slideshow after lunch. A new "anti-bullying" district-level position was created (or added onto an already full staff member plate) to monitor teachers' implementation of the new program. No training provided whatsoever, but 14 accountability rubrics were developed to hold teachers accountable for the new plan that cost the district thousands of dollars.

Why did they do this? Not because they valued the mental, emotional, and physical safety of their students, but because their insurance companies said they would be liable if they didn't. Is this true for all districts? Of course not. Many districts are much better at implementing these programs than others. Not discounting the work of any evidenced-based anti-bullying curriculums, but even the most effective are only as good as those who consistently do the work of building strong cultures and climates of empathy in their classrooms, schools, and districts. No matter the plan used, if the people responsible for its delivery have the mindset of principal Steve Johnson, it will not work.

Bullying at school whether it's student to student, student to teacher, teacher to student, or teacher to teacher is unacceptable. According to the American Psychological Association, almost half of all students will report being bullied at least once, and 5–15% report constant harassment and bullying (Dikel 2014). Bullying is not a normal part of child development and should not be accepted. Many times, students and responsible adults will have an attitude that the bullied child or teen must have done something. Bullied students will also too often adopt this erroneous explanation of what's happening to them. Bullying is and should be considered a public health problem (Rivara and Le Mensestrel 2016). Historically, bullying happened on school grounds or within spaces where children interact; cyberbullying on digital platforms has expanded the opportunity for bullying to occur. The Centers for Disease Control and Prevention (CDC 2019b) defines bullying as:

> Bullying is any unwanted aggressive behavior(s) by another youth or group of youths who are not siblings or current dating partners that involves an observed or perceived power imbalance and is repeated multiple times or is highly likely to be repeated. Bullying may inflict harm or distress on the targeted youth including physical, psychological, social or educational harm.

Students who are bullied within classrooms and have a learning experience within a school climate that doesn't stop bullying are more likely to drop out of school or avoid school, have lower academic achievement, including in math and reading, have lower self-esteem and higher levels of anxiety, depression, and loneliness, and are more likely to attempt suicide during childhood and later in life (APA 2017). It's a wonder Jed made it through school after the trauma he experienced being harassed in the bathroom by a bully, then only to be told to bring a baseball bat by the very person there to protect him. Children who are bullies show higher levels of impulsive activity and aggression, have higher rates of alcohol and drug abuse, and engage in more delinquent and criminal behavior. Schools with positive climates have students with better attendance and study habits, are more motivated and succeed academically, engage in cooperative learning and achieve higher grades, test scores, and subject mastery (APA 2017).

Children may be targeted for bullying because of their race/ethnicity, sexual orientation, physical or mental disabilities, gender identity, weight, or religion. Students with disabilities can often be the subject of bullying, physical abuse, or social rejection. LGBTQ+ youth report very high rates of bullying at almost 80%, coming from students, staff, and teachers (APA 2017).

Teachers should be familiar and be reminded about reportable offenses like sexual or physical abuse or hate violence. They should be encouraged by administrators to report incidents and rewarded for their effectiveness. A safety plan with resources for students who may have psychological needs, housing, and food insecurity, and may need assistance with hygiene structure or assistance is necessary.

Bullying in the Classroom/Supporting Students: Tips for Teachers and Parents

Teachers
- Create classrooms that are a positive safe environment with zero tolerance for bullying and specifically bullying that targets children or teens based on ethnicity, sexual orientation, or secondary to a disability.
- Provide support for students who are bullied and change the behavior of bullies with discipline that teaches rather than is just punishment.
- Intervene to stop the bullying behavior and not force children to fix the problem themselves. Actions you can take are (a) to listen to the student and believe them, (b) check on them after they reveal their bullying, and (c) direct the student to psychological resources if needed.
- Learn to call out bullying behavior and teach bystander strategies including rewarding students who report bullying, positively support students who have been bullied, and together discuss rules to stop bullying outside and within the classroom.
- Have a list of mental health resources for students and their families.
- Discuss situations in a classroom setting so that all of the students are on the same page and have a plan about what to do if they witness bullying, are the victims of bullies, are bullies, or feel unsafe.

Parents
- Teach your children to use their voice and tell if they are being bullied or feel unsafe.

- Teach peers who they can safely report concerns about a student who is threatening to hurt themselves or others with or without a plan or firearm. Speaking up is not snitching, it's safety.
- Know how to get mental health resources for your child.
- Play "what if" with your child to role-play how to speak up and what to say if they're in a dangerous situation.
- Listen to, and avoid minimizing, your child's fears or reports of bullying.

Schools and LGBTQ+ Bullying

"Mr. Dearybury, what's a faggot?" I (Jed) will never forget it when David walked up to me at recess and asked that question.

In the few seconds after he did, my mind instantly leapt back to 1989, in Mrs. C's fourth grade at Boiling Springs Elementary School. A classmate named Michael introduced me to that word. He yelled it at me in the hallway. I didn't even know what it was. I doubt he really did either, but I could tell by the way others laughed at me that it wasn't good. Mrs. C didn't punish him for it. She only said, "We don't say that word at school." Soooooo it's okay to say that word at home? At ball practice? At church? Just not at school so you don't have to deal with it, Mrs. C? Yeahhhh okkkkay. Needless to say Mrs. C didn't make it on the top five favorite teachers list. Not even in the top 20. I digress.

"David, where did you hear that word?" I asked him.

"My brother calls me that all the time. My diddy* too. It kinda makes me sad when they say it because they are mad at me when they do, but I don't really know what it is."

"It's not a very nice word, David. I am so sorry that they call you that. They shouldn't do it," I said. (I made a mental note to run this by the guidance counselor and ask about reporting it. This is 100% mental abuse.)

"They call you one too," David continued.

When he said this it cut so deep that I almost couldn't breathe. The fear, the anger, the rage, the intimidation, the embarrassment, the confusion, the worry, the . . . ALL THE THINGS!!! Why was I being forced into this conversation because of some redneck daddy and brother who were ignorant and hateful! Yes, that's the exact thought I had.

At the time David was in my classroom, I was still very much in the closet. Being an openly gay male teacher in Spartanburg, SC, was NOT allowed. Well, no one in my district said that directly, but trust me, it was very much implied. We are, after all, located on the tip top of the diamond stud on the golden cross shaped buckle of the Bible Belt South. It is terrifying to be gay here most days. As a public educator, I did everything possible to keep who I was from everyone. I went as far as being a faithful member of a church that regularly condemned people like me. Just this morning as I was typing this section, I had a conversation with a friend about how embarrassed I was at the lies I told about myself. She reminded me that it wasn't lying; it was survival.

"Well David, sometimes people call me bad names like that, and I try to ignore them, but I sometimes feel sad like you too. Like I said, that's not a very nice word. I have actually been called that word before too."

"What does it even mean?" he asked.

"Well, it's a bad word that people often call boys, but I gave it a new meaning so it wouldn't hurt me anymore. The first three letters are F, A, G. I told myself that it means Fabulously Awesome Guy!"

"Well you are awesome so that makes sense," David said with a big ole grin on his face.

"And you are too, David. Don't ever let anyone tell you any different."

He walked back out on the playground and never mentioned it again. I was told by school administrators that it wasn't a reportable offense. I called Department of Social Services anyway. Nothing came of it because the Department of Social Services at the time was likely run by folks who didn't like gay people. That is my assumption of course, but when you live around here long enough, you realize how "things" work.

David was an amazing kid. I absolutely loved having him in my class. He was absolutely obsessed with Hannah Montana and Reba McEntire. Almost every morning before school began, he would put on a performance in the front office. Sometimes he wore his Miley Cyrus wig and brought a microphone. Whenever it rained outside and indoor recess was the only option, I'd play Reba McEntire on the sound system, and he'd perform for the class. You haven't lived until you've seen a second grader throw down with "Fancy" on a rainy Friday morning!

I wonder about him almost every day. I believe he is now in tenth grade. I hope that he is in a safe place with the support he needs. I also wonder what might have happened to him back then. What if he hadn't had me as a teacher at that moment? What if he was in the class of a religious zealot who didn't like gay people and thought that the word faggot was okay to use against a student who didn't fit the stereotypical molds of their view of masculinity? What if he was in a class of someone who lacked empathy and brushed it off flippantly? What if it was in the class of a person who had just disowned their own LGBTQ+ child?

Teachers must be trained how to handle situations like this. They will happen to every educator who enters the field. It is not a matter of if, but when. It is terrifying to think of the negative impact an untrained educator who lacks empathy for ALL of their students could have on a child. Sadly, there are thousands of teachers out there who lack understanding and compassion on a variety of sensitive topics like this, and are often negatively vocal about their opinions regarding the LGBTQ+ community in a very public way.

One such educator voiced her concerns on November 22, 2018.

That day probably doesn't mean much to you at first glance. Let me remind you. It was Thanksgiving, and the country was watching the 92nd annual Macy's Thanksgiving Day Parade. It was the coldest on record according to commentators, but that didn't stop the fun! The traditional balloons floated down Fifth Avenue, the bands played their familiar tunes, and superstars poorly lip-synced from their flowery floats. Parade hosts made corny jokes and Broadway musicals filled our homes as their stars performed in Herald Square. Two actresses from the musical, "The Prom," Caitlin Kinnunen and Isabelle McCalla, even kissed at the end of their performance. It was the first ever lesbian kiss of the parade's history, and it was broadcast live for all to see. What should have been seen as a beautiful moment of love between two adults quickly shattered the interwebs with bigotry and outrage.

As you can imagine, there were some pretty bigoted and hateful comments that filled social media. One of them, from a teacher I knew personally. Someone I went to high school with actually. She was just so outraged because her seven-year-old son had witnessed such an atrocious thing. "How am I gonna explain this to him?" she exclaimed on Facebook. "Do better Macy's!!!!" she continued.

I will tell you how she should've explained it: "Aww. Two grown ups love each other, son." Period. The end. Move along.

But instead she took her disgust and angst to the public space of her social media page, and many of her teacher and principal friends started chiming in with likes, hearts, and comments of support. It was maddening for me as a gay man. I immediately thought about David, and what if she had been his teacher. I begin to think about kids I may have in the future . . . What if someone like her were their teacher? It was a real possibility because the school this bigoted teacher taught in was employed at the school that my future kids would attend. I immediately took a pic of her post and explained my concerns to her principal and superintendent. The responses I received were canned politeness at best. Neither of them seemed to have much empathy for me because their straightness and lack of training, which could lead them to be the courageous educators folks like me need, kept them from compassion. "I can't make her take it down," said the principal. "She's entitled to her opinion," said the superintendent.

While yes, she was indeed allowed to have her opinion, this same district had punished other educators for far less offensive material on social media. The difference here was that they likely agreed with her opinion. I didn't back down, and didn't give up. I wanted to be heard. I wanted the post down. Students like David were likely in her class. They needed protecting. They needed to have educators that understood the negative impacts of such hateful words. I had worked with this school many times prior to this event. I have not been back since. The words of the teacher and the reaction of the administrators severely damaged the relationship. Imagine how an LGBTQ family in that building would have felt reading those words, experiencing the lack of concern and empathy.

Two weeks later, the post was finally taken down. She got nothing more than a slap on the hand. Sadly, the district continues to this day to support her and bigotry-minded educators like her.

The need for courageous educators is greater now than ever. According to GLAAD (Gay and Lesbian Alliance Against Defamation 2013) 61.6% of LGBTQ+ students who reported bullying said the school staff did nothing about the incidents. With that in mind, it is not surprising that 55.5% of LGBTQ students feel unsafe at school (GLSEN® 2013). Courage is not only facing down fear or adverse situations. Courage can also be summoned as truth. The truth to deal with your own issues, the truth to question your own approach to self-care, the truth to mindfully self-regulate in order to maximize your health and well-being. Building a safe, courageous classroom requires teachers to be fully aware of the barriers to both children and themselves having the psychological freedom to express themselves and not worry about challenges to their safety.

Let's Chat

Jed: Dr. Janet, there is a lot to unpack in this chapter. Fear in school is real and the evidence shows that it is harmful to students and their learning. What can teachers do within their classrooms to help alleviate those fears?

Dr. Janet: Fear is a response to an event or experience that involves the brain and sensory input. Teachers should understand

and teach students the power of mindful self-regulation to identify and recognize the source(s) of their fear. Within their classrooms, teachers can minimize conditions in the classroom that may trigger fear, not allow bullying, be role models by using language and actions that are respectful and calming, and have small spaces or nooks where students can go, reflect, and find a courageous response to their fear.

Jed: The conversation I had with David on the playground was an attempt to divert any pain/fear/concern he had about being called a homophobic slur. He was a second grader and didn't actually know what it was, so I reframed it. Teachers often utilize strategies like that to lessen the words others may use to bully. I often wonder if I should have told him what it was, but I chose not to, in the moment. Was this helpful or harmful?

Dr. Janet: Clearly David felt comfortable enough with you and trusted you to ask a question, which is important. How your response landed with David is indicative that he felt it helpful. This being said, it's okay to ask, "Was that helpful? Do you have more questions for me? What did you think and feel when you heard it?" Helping students understand the context, and meaning of words is an important strategy for their own clarity but can also teach them the power of what words they choose to hold onto, and let go of words that hurt them.

Jed: If you were in charge of a school or district, what policies would you implement from a psychological standpoint, to create a school full of courageous classrooms?

Dr. Janet: I would have mandatory courses for students and teachers about anti-bullying (www.stompoutbullying.org), how to have a courageous (growth) mindset (www.mindsetworks.com), and mindful self-regulation (www.self-compassion.org). A courageous classroom will come from spaces that value difference, have open communication, and appropriately handle conflicts or challenges with approaches that teach and inform not belittle or bully. The more schools and districts focus on valuing ALL students, the more courageous their classrooms will become.

Tips for the Courageous Classroom

Acknowledge the characteristics of bullying when you see them and act to change behaviors with a courageous mindset.

Bullying, aggressive, unwanted, repetitive behavior can impact mental health, leading to depression, anxiety, and issues with self-esteem. Whether it is verbal, social, or physical, it is characterized by an imbalance of power (physical strength and the use of verbal, embarrassing information). Although more common in childhood, bullying can occur at any age. Act to prevent bullying by understanding and having a clear understanding of bullying and being able to distinguish bullying from teasing.

Fear experiences drive brain changes at a neuro-cellular level. These changes can be reversed with a thought, command, and witnessed examples of how to be. A courageous mindset can be taught and be used for safety, motivation, and to foster achievement. When students learn that they can "grow their brains" with stronger neural connections to stretch to learn hard things, reframe challenges, and overcome obstacles, they engage more and have increased motivation.

A Courageous Mindset

- Learn, reflect, and know your triggers of fear and anxiety.
- Identify where your body feels fear and anxious responses.
- Label at least one fear and where you feel it in your body.
- Replace your fears with curiosity and mastery, by seeing them as overcome-able.
- Act with courage, don't react to fear.
- Exercise your body to keep your mind healthy and ready.
- Exercise your mind as your survival system, make it stronger, clear your negative thoughts by replacing them with purpose.
- Inhale and innovate. Be creative.
- Build buddies of courage by identifying social supports.
- Be mindful by staying in the moment and being ready.

Chapter 6
The Brain and Learning

The Impact on the Brain

Genes and experiences impact a young brain. Recall the stories you have read thus far. While student genetics definitely play a huge role in who they become, there is no doubt that their traumatic experiences are impacting their growth and development. Our brain shapes itself based on its environment: at home, at school, and in the surrounding culture. When we learn something new, neurons – the cells that gather the information – become better and better at their task of receiving and sending messages. In fact, as their signaling becomes more efficient, it takes less energy to work. They become wired for that task.

Another type of brain cells that becomes more active as we learn are glial cells. Glial cells wrap around the axon, like a warm, fuzzy blanket and in doing so form a myelin sheath. Made up of protein and fatty substances, myelin protects axons by insulating them. Myelin also speeds electrical signals in the brain. When we are learning new tasks and skills, researchers have found that the amount of myelin cocooning axons increases. Having a thicker myelin sheath can improve tasks like reading, creating memories, playing a musical instrument and, decision-making (Pearce 2014). When trying to learn, sleep is very important because as we sleep, memories and new information from the past day is stored. During sleep, cells that help us learn fire in reverse and the next day are wired more tightly to each other. Sleep is critical in the retention of new knowledge. The fact that we need this nightly integration is why our brain responds best when we learn new information a little bit of a time, instead of trying to cram it all in.

As an educator, how many of you knew all that? Maybe you have heard bits and pieces of it. You may recall learning about sleep being critical in the learning process during a human growth and development class. Maybe some of the vocabulary seems vaguely familiar from the psychology class you took years ago. But did you know, getting a good night's sleep contributes to having a thicker myelin sheath and can improve tasks like reading, creating memories, playing a musical instrument, and decision-making? I (Jed) confess to you as an award-winning educator of almost two decades, I didn't know that, and I was awarded the title of county reading teacher of the year in 2010. One would think that this knowledge of the brain would be more on the forefront of our work as teachers. Next to brain surgeons and psychologists, we educators should be experts in this area. Sadly, we're not, and the ripple effect of this missing piece in our degree programs is damning. As of the writing of this book, I am the instructor for four courses in education training programs and I am eagerly adding more brain research into all aspects of my teaching. If we are going to teach, we must have a better understanding of the brain. Thanks for the "aha" moment here, Dr. Janet!

Research shows that an "aha" moment doesn't just happen. The epiphany is the result of a steady gathering of information. Accumulating new information can unlock memories associated with the task, leading to the formation of new and stronger connections inside your brain. Progressively, comprehension grows until you have a "eureka" moment.

The Science of Learning (Deans for Impact 2015) was developed by Dan Willingham, a cognitive scientist at the University of Virginia, and Paul Bruno, a former middle-school teacher, in collaboration with other educators. Together, they established core principles about learning for students. They found that students learn new ideas by relating them to ideas they already know. Prior knowledge from a well-sequenced curriculum is critical to master new ideas. To learn, students have to build on information from working memory (where it is consciously processed) to long-term memory where it can be stored and later regained. They noted that it's important for teachers to make sure that what they say complements their visual presentations, to avoid dividing students' attention and impairing their learning ability.

Teachers can help students focus their attention on the meaning of what they are teaching by having students explain information. When students have to explain by answering questions about how something happened or why it happened, they are forced to meaningfully organize what they are learning and build on new concepts. For example, it's suggested to review content over time to help students remember content over a long period. This can be done by interweaving concepts and having students practice new facts that are related to each other, instead of solving one problem and moving onto a new one.

The Brain Needs Time

I (Jed) can hear all of you teachers as you read this: "But we don't have time. We must keep moving." This is a true statement. We don't have a lot of time. Especially those in heavily tested grades that have both state and national assessments required by an antiquated system. With the pressure placed upon us to meet benchmarks and increase scores, there is no doubt that other than our students, time is our most precious commodity. That said, we must find more time. The students who pass through our classrooms for 180 days at a time are counting on us to do so.

As you have read, their brains need more time. What many states are asking us to do with their mandated standards just doesn't align with the evolutionary development of the human brain. Moreover, many of the goals expected of students do not take into consideration the effect that trauma may have had on their development. The bias that often pervades the whole process of deciding standards further adds to the unrealistic expectations that these requirements place on our students as well.

What do we do then? We find more time, and we find it by slowing down by using our breath. No, that doesn't add more minutes to the day, but it does provide more opportunities for deeper learning and understanding that many of our most vulnerable students need. One of the most valuable lessons I learned early on in my career was that I would NEVER effectively teach every standard required of me. There was just no possible way to do it. If you are a teacher who puts a check by each standard as you cover it, that's great. But, I can almost guarantee that "covering" it doesn't mean that all of your students learned it. The definition of teach according to the dictionary means "to show or explain how to do something." If a student cannot show or explain how to do what you covered, then you didn't teach them anything because the same dictionary tells us to "learn" means that one gains or acquires knowledge or skill by being taught. Teachers teach. Non-teachers cover. The best teaching I have ever done is when I took my time, worked through the lesson, considered all of the needs of all of the students, and solved the problem (standard) at hand.

It's easier to problem-solve when students commit basic facts to memory. For example, math facts and letter-sound pairings can ease reading comprehension and math calculations when committed to memory. Students are also better able to solve problems when they are given clear and specific feedback that focuses on the task, not the student, and is explanatory, focused on improvement rather than evaluating their performance. Effective feedback is often essential to acquire new knowledge and skills (Deans for Impact 2015).

For students to transfer their learning of new situations in and out of the classroom, teachers can encourage students to identify and label the steps necessary to remedy a problem. They can be taught to apply their problem-solving skills using the context of a problem and the underlying structure of a problem. For example, if there is an issue about bullying, they can be encouraged to look at it from all angles in an attempt to understand it and mitigate it.

By using praise, teachers can increase student motivation and their feeling of being in control. Teachers who encourage students to have a growth mindset, believing that their intelligence and ability can be augmented through hard work, can motivate their students. Student beliefs about their intellect and smarts are important correlates of their behavior. Student motivation that is self-determined (related to values or interest) leads to better outcomes than motivation based on a consequence of punishment or a reward. Teachers control factors related to punishment or reward by realizing when their students are already motivated to perform a task, how they link reward and punishment, whether praise is offered and the timeliness of praise or a reward. Teachers can encourage students who self-monitor their own thinking about what they understand and how they learn to ask more questions to facilitate their learning. It is critical that teachers reassure students that they are accepted and belong in their academic environments. Students are more motivated and successful in academic environments when they feel included and capable of meeting academic standards.

When teachers challenge their own myths about who can learn and how students think and learn, they can improve student learning and functioning. Learning is not fixed; all students do not think or behave at the same age and growth stages. Teachers must be able to think in individualized ways about the needs and academic functioning of their students recognizing the impact that health behaviors, environment, beliefs, culture, and trauma can impact learning and behavior in the classroom.

The Brain and Sleep

Sleep issues can be a huge problem for students and are associated with greater student-teacher conflict (Holdaway and Becker 2018). For children and teenagers to have healthy development, they must sleep. Many children report sleep issues secondary to inconsistent bedtimes, nightmares, insomnia, and daytime sleepiness. Children who have ongoing sleep problems may have academic difficulties and impaired socioemotional functioning. Research has found that a child's sleep patterns and functioning were significantly associated with maternal sleep problems and specifically maternal fatigue, parenting stress, and overload (Holdaway and Becker 2018). The significance of these findings may be a yo-yo effect between the child and parent sleep disruptions resulting in child mood difficulties and perhaps marital or relationship conflict. Daytime sleepiness in the classroom directly impacts the attention, perseverance, and participation/initiative in school. Teachers should remind their students about the importance of sleep for learning, emotional regulation, and their physical health.

Younger students who display higher deficits in their processing of attention and memory and their ability to regulate their mood and behavior, secondary to poor sleep patterns, can worsen as they get older. The student-teacher relationship can be made more difficult because of the nature of students who require more discipline and are less likely to function doing independent work or interacting appropriately with their peers. Teachers should screen for sleep problems in students who may be struggling with learning and behavior.

Teachers may also have impaired sleep patterns leading to physical and emotional risks for their health. Remember Jed's story about his student teaching experience. How do you think he slept that week after being up with his mom in the hospital all night? Being a teacher can be (IS) stressful and besides dealing with challenging workloads, many teachers are also faced with demands including caregiving, taking care of elderly parents, managing collegial conflicts, and a lack of administrative support. Work stress can lead to decreased sleep. Research evidence directly points to difficult and adverse job characteristics challenging healthy sleep patterns in educators. One study by Kottwitz et al. (2018) showed that 38% of teachers who had diminished sleep quality reported experiences of failure at work, social exclusion, and emotional ups and downs. Being able to recover with more sleep while away from work on vacation was positively associated with improved health and well-being. Managing stress with healthy coping practices was key.

A lack of consistent sleep can challenge emotional well-being for teachers. Sleep deprivation is a stressor and skipping one night of sleep can lead to an increased vulnerability to the perception of risk and cause a rise in anxiety and fear (Tabibnia and Radecki 2018). Emotional dissonance, or the feeling that something's just not right, can force many teachers to hold their emotions in check when dealing with students, their parents, and colleagues. That can be a difficult task as teachers diligently work to reach their educational goals and maintain a positive equilibrium in the classroom. Having to suppress most negative emotions often allows them to persist, while feeling like they have to monitor everything that they say, which promotes a feeling of lack of authenticity (Kottwitz et al. 2018). Emotional dissonance can be related to teacher burnout and has been found to be the highest in call centers, hotels and bank employees, and kindergarten teachers. Teachers should be taught how to deal with negative emotions at work using mindfulness, and re-appraising situations that facilitate changing their own emotions and allow for positive self-expression. Administrators must monitor the health and well-being of their teachers and promote interventions like yoga and mindfulness practices to increase stress management, well-being, and socioemotional competence for educators.

The Brain and Adversity

Students who have had adversity early in their lives show changes in their brain and behavioral development. The brain adapts to stress and can promote survival in the short term but can influence long-term changes in the young brain that may be maladaptive (Duffy, Mclaughlin, and Green 2018). The network pathways in the brain that are influenced by early-life adversity are threat-detection processes, reward-related processes, and cognitive control. Easily activated threat-detection processes can contribute to children having more emotional reactivity and more easily feel threatened in safe environments. Children who have been in deprived situations or experienced neglect may not readily respond to a reward, and more intense rewards may be needed for them to feel a pleasure response. Increased reward-seeking can lead to an increased risk of substance abuse or rewarding stimuli (high sugar, fat foods).

While not all children who experience adversity exhibit negative outcomes, research suggests that impairments in executive functioning can lead to a shift from goal-directed, flexible responses to inflexible ones. Children may have difficulty with the emotional regulation of their responses and delay immediate gratification. All of these can have psychological and behavioral consequences in the classroom.

The Brain and the Long-Term Effects of Trauma

Reading Dr. Janet's words here, I (Jed) take pause to recollect more about my own life growing up. I was never a behavior problem in class. In fact, I would say I was a model student in that regard. I was the kid who got to run errands to the office, the one who got to show new students around the building, the one who was picked to organize group work, and most importantly the one who was trusted enough to go outside the building to clean the chalk erasers by banging them on the side of the building. I may have just dated myself there, but that's who I was. I lived for cleaning those erasers. Even more so after the school got one of those fancy machines that cleaned them. It was *life*!

While my behavior wasn't a problem, the psychological effects on my student life were deep and long lasting. I could write for days about this really. I cannot tell you how many times I went to school on a Monday morning after a traumatic weekend with my dad. It was almost a given that I would spend my day in the guidance counselor's office as I started my school week. I don't remember much of what she said to me during those times, but I do remember crying to her a lot. The crying would always start in the classroom and like clockwork the teacher would send me down to "get some help."

All of them except Mrs. Miller, my second-grade teacher. She was the least empathetic teacher I have ever known. She didn't care if I cried all day, I was expected to sit in my seat, face the front, and listen to her every word. Thankfully, she is no longer an educator. Last I heard, she opened a shoe shop not long after she tortured me and the rest of our class that year.

I often wonder what I missed in the classroom on all of those Mondays hanging out with Mrs. Townsend and her puppets. Was that when they learned spelling tricks that helped them with words like *receive*, *neighbor*, and *separate*? (Yep, I spell-checked at least two of those.) Was Monday when they learned the nifty finger trick that helps you remember your nines on the multiplication tables? Maybe that's when they dissected a frog because I never once got to do it. I bet Monday was the day they all learned how to be gifted. Talk about a psychological effect on learning.

My abusive father always called me names like dumbass, stupid, and fool when he was drunk and angry at me. (He was really angry at my mom, but taking it out on me.) Naturally, I took those names with me right into school. As I mentioned, I wasn't a behavior problem, but my grades . . . ehhh not so much. It really started with the D on my report card in third grade and went downhill from there. That same year was the first time I remembered being tested for the "gifted and talented" program. All students were tested per new state mandates that year. In hindsight, I really believe it was a state-sanctioned resegregation attempt, but I don't have the evidence to back that up so I must digress.

As it was required for my teacher to assess me along with the other students, I took the test. I didn't pass it. I don't remember much about the test, but I do remember what happened when the results came back. It was then I learned that those who did "pass" were the smart kids. As a reward for their intelligence, they got to leave our classroom for one full day every week so they could go to learn in a special place. The classroom that they went to was AMAZING! They had polyhedrons hanging from the ceiling, models of the solar system, skeletal system, and the Earth all around. The best part was the "gifted" teacher collected all of these specimens of animals in glass jars full of some kind of juice that preserved them so that the smart kids could ooh and ahh at them every day as they arrived. As if that weren't enough, these newly crowned honor students got to go on adventures outside school to the most incredible places. Once I realized all of the perks of passing that test I failed, I was devastated . . . and dumb. Or so I thought.

The next year, I took that test again. I failed it . . . again. And the next year I tried once more, and failed again. "You're just not gifted," they said. Well, maybe not just like that, but that's what I heard. So sadly, my time to try to get into the fun class had ended, and I wasn't smart, just like my dad said.

It was those gifted test failures that led me to a life of basic tech classes in high school. Occasionally I made it into a college prep course, but never into Honors, and no way was I ever in an advancement placement (AP) course. My lack of intellectually challenging courses in high school of course led to a terrible SAT score. Only a 900. How did I ever get into college? No idea. Intelligent was never an adjective used to describe me. Until one day. . . .

A friend of mine named Cindy Riddle invited grown-up, educator-me to be a part of a special arts day at a school she worked with. I was excited to go because artsy people are MY people. I have always been able to be myself in the fine arts world. It is very different from the world of academia. As I arrived at the school that day, I found my way to the gymnasium where we were meeting, placed my bag at the table I wanted to spend the day at, and found Cindy. She is one of those people that I instantly became friends with. I never felt like she judged me for being gay, and she didn't care that I wasn't "gifted" in elementary school. She loved my work as a teacher and as a fellow creative in the arts world. She and I had met while serving on the board for a statewide arts organization so she was pretty familiar with my work. Thus, the invitation to be a part of her event.

When I found her, she was chatting with the daughter of a former legislator in our state. I knew who the lady was because of her relationship to her well-known mother, but of course I played it cool so as to not be too eager to meet her. As Cindy introduced me to her, she said, "This is Jed Dearybury, he is one of the most intelligent people I know."

WHAT?
Did she *just say?*
Surely she didn't call *me* . . . ?
Maybe I mis*heard her.*

That was my brain talking to itself as she continued to introduce me and my work to this semi-celebrity. I cannot tell you much else about the meeting because emotions filled my whole mind. As far as I could remember, no one had ever told me I was smart, intelligent, educated . . . *ever*! Since the D on my report card, through Cs in tech classes, and all of the insults my dad hurled at me, I had always thought of myself as a mediocre brain at best. It was in that exact moment with Cindy Riddle that I realized the long-lasting effect the psychological trauma of my dad's words and that damn gifted test had taken on my entire life as a student. Wonder how much different my life would have been had I passed that test and my dad called me smart.

Let's Chat

Jed: This section is titled "long-term effects." I am confident there are many teachers like me who are coping with the effects of fear and trauma from their own childhoods. How can we use our experiences to help our students who are facing similar issues in their own childhood?

Dr. Janet: Your question highlights why we wrote this book. There's a saying that "hurt people hurt people." We want teachers and students to manage their fears in a healthy way. Living with memories of trauma and/or constantly trying to manage fear has an impact on your ability to focus, pay attention, emotionally regulate, and sleep. In the classroom, that could present as irritable, disengaged, fearful of conflict, or being a poor role model for students. One way is to acknowledge your pain from trauma and identify your fears. Reflect on situations that occur and identify if your own feelings impacted the outcome. Teach your students about trauma and fear so that they can identify their own feelings and learn to emotionally regulate. That means recognizing how you feel and doing something positive about it. Also, talk about when it's time to meet with a mental health specialist to go deeper and learn more about yourself.

Jed: We educators know that the power of the words we speak into the lives of students has a lasting effect. What does neuroscience say about that?

Dr. Janet: Words matter. We create our reality with our words, thoughts, and actions. Positive thoughts can change our brain when repeated over and over, creating new neural networks. Teachers can also be supportive of teaching students to conquer their fears when they clearly challenge a fear with their words. Reframing a negative thought or comment by asking themselves, "What's another way to look at this?" Reframing leads to a growth mindset where you're focused on potential, not a fixed attribute that someone says to you or you think about yourself. Research shows that when a student acknowledges being anxious about a test and writes down their concerns, says them out loud, or tells a peer, they are able to dampen the part of their brain that reinforces negative thinking.

Jed: You told me once to write down five positive things about myself each day in order to combat any negative thoughts that tried to creep in. Would this be a good strategy for teachers to do with students? Any other strategies like this?

Dr. Janet: The ability to turn negative thoughts into positive ones is a skill and practice. Our brain naturally holds onto negative comments that may originate from our childhood or present day. There are always two ways to look at issues. For every negative thought, it takes five positive thoughts to combat it, so writing them down is a very good exercise. Another one is the power of intention. Say what you want to happen, avoiding negative things like "I never" or "This won't happen but . . ." instead say "I will," "I can," "When this happens I will . . ." Another fun habit to cultivate is to encourage the class to take "smile breaks" every 15 minutes. Smiling makes you feel better and just anticipating it can lift your spirits.

The Brain of a Coping Teacher

Teachers who may be coping with their own experiences of trauma are in unique positions to utilize their own experiences and assist their students. A teacher who has had trauma also may experience their own reactivity and be sensitive to classroom situations that may be perceived as threatening. Experts recommend that teachers with trauma make a commitment to their own healing. Acknowledge when you may be having a bad day to your students and don't be afraid to ask for help. Having a support network of peers inside the school building is vital to teacher well-being. Please don't go it alone. The work is hard and there is no shame in needing help. To quote President Joe Biden, "Some days you need a hand. Some days you lend one."

The same self-calming techniques and trauma-informed practices that work for students also work for teachers. It is recommended that teachers look for ways to practice mindfulness, self-awareness, and how to emotionally regulate on a regular basis (Donahoe 2018).

Exposure to violence and trauma (childhood sexual and physical abuse) has been linked to changes in intelligence scores and impact cognitive functioning (Platt et al. 2018). To be clear, it is proposed that the effect of exposure to trauma alters brain adaptation and response and the effect of lower socioeconomic status may occur because of decreased cognitive stimulation and living in environments where there is high stress. There also may be less verbal and positive sensory stimulation. The absence of expected neural inputs has been shown to influence neural development, including the development of the frontoparietal system, which is involved in executive functioning and impulse control. Working memory, cognitive control, and language processing are all dependent upon high-quality environments, childcare, and academic environments (Platt et al. 2018). Trauma-sensitive classrooms, whether in under-resourced or well-resourced communities, are necessary for our children's growth and educator satisfaction.

In the United States there is an increasing need for trauma-sensitive schools, as nearly half of all US children have been exposed to at least one traumatic event, and many have been exposed to several (Sparks 2019). Finding a way for teachers to help students who have been traumatized can be a heavy lift and more than 1 in 5 teachers describe it as "one of their most challenging tasks." More than three-quarters of school psychologists report having had "little or no training in trauma-informed practices" (Sparks 2019).

Schools first began the process of working with and integrating trauma awareness into education almost 15 years ago. Educators would focus on learning a student's trauma story to explain a student's behavior, which would often result in a student/teacher trap of being caught in the narrative but not being equipped to support and understand the effect on the student learning and behavior (Hall and Souers 2015). Students are more than their story.

The National Child Traumatic Stress Network (n.d.) reports that the essential elements for a Trauma-Informed Schools System are:

- Identify and assess traumatic stress.
- Address and treat traumatic stress.
- Teach trauma education and awareness.
- Have partnerships with students and their families.
- Create a trauma-informed learning environment (social/emotional skills and wellness).
- Be culturally responsive.
- Integrate emergency management and crisis response.
- Understand and address staff self-care and secondary traumatic stress.
- Evaluate and revise school discipline policies and practices.
- Collaborate across systems and establish community partnerships.

The Brain and Classroom Needs

After spending almost 20 years in various classroom settings, I (Jed) have learned a multitude from experienced educators across the country. A great friend and colleague, Kara Foster-Lee, program coordinator at USC Upstate's Child Protection Training Center in Spartanburg, SC, is often a go-to for trauma-informed best practices. She and I talked on the phone for a moment as I wrote this list of tips for educators seeking to have a more trauma-sensitive classroom.

Safe Space: First and foremost, students need a space that is conducive to learning. Many of you will read that as a nod to a cute or well-organized classroom, but what we mean here is not only the physical space, but the emotional space as well. Students learn best in environments where they do not have fear. Avoid loud noises such as doors slamming, banging the desk, or shouting. No teacher should ever be yelling and slamming doors, but sadly, I have heard them. There was a teacher across the hallway from my classroom for years that yelled. She was absolutely terrifying. I often felt sorry for the students in her room, especially the ones who came from homes full of yelling and fussing. Sometimes those things may happen accidentally, but being aware that the noises in your learning space may trigger harmful memories for students will help to minimize alerting sounds. Also, harsh lighting and interactive white boards with too much flash and bang can remind children of traumatic events. There is no way we can know all of these things about our students, but awareness of the role emotional and physical space plays in the learning of a student dealing with trauma is a key step in helping them heal.

Structure/Routine: Fear of the unknown and unexpected can be paralyzing for some students. As someone who deals with my own anxiety daily, routine and structure during the day greatly reduces my own stress. Students who come from homes with lots of upheaval often look forward to the daily movements and practices of school. Lunch is at the same time every day, almost guaranteed, and that makes students feel safe. The predictability provides stability that many students with trauma don't have in their out-of-school life. If there is ever a change in schedule coming, it's often a good idea to alert students that there will be a deviation from the routine.

Clear Expectations: The emphasis here is on the word "clear." Students must know exactly what you expect from them, when you expect, why you expect it, and how you expect it. Vague directives, whether in regards to behavior or academics, often leave students feeling confused and worried about the task at hand. This can lead to a spiral of anxiety as not meeting expectations at home could lead to abuse. Remember the story of my dad hitting me in my Maudie's yard? I didn't meet his expectations and still to this day I hope to know exactly what is expected of me in every situation I am in. Not because I want to please someone, but because I fear the brain battle that will take place if I don't.

Voice and Choice: This idea is one that can be difficult. Allowing students to have voice and choice in the classroom means that teachers have to relinquish some of their control. College education programs don't fully prepare new teachers for this as they often instruct them to over-plan for their day of learning, but allowing students to lead the way in various aspects of classroom life is actually very helpful in helping students of trauma to heal. For example, does it really matter if Johnny is the last person in line versus the third person like you want him to be? Maybe Johnny likes the back because he can see all of the other students and no one will catch him off guard. The abuse he has faced has likely created this as a self-preservation technique. Does it really matter if Susie wants to stay in her seat while you read a story to the class on the carpet? She may feel insecure about her body being close to other people who may touch it. She too has learned how to self-preserve.

Ongoing Assessment: I am hard pressed to make definitive statements about the effects of uniformed teaching because we all react differently to the way we are treated, but judging the entirety of a student's abilities based on something as arbitrary as a letter grade is, in and of itself, a traumatic event. You read about the long-lasting effects that the D on my report card had on me. That D was literally based on the results of two tests testing a whole nine-week learning period. Students who have experienced trauma often come to school with more grief than we educators will ever know. Our assessment of their abilities cannot and should not ever be relegated to one or two pieces of graded work. It is never how you start, but how you finish that matters most to me. In my college courses, I always allow my students to redo their assignments if they feel my assessment doesn't reflect their actual learning. Ongoing assessment of students who have experienced trauma is imperative so that they are afforded the opportunity to showcase their true abilities.

If you would like to learn more about creating a trauma-sensitive learning space, visit www.learningforjustice.org.

The Brain's Health

Learn to face your fears and identity trauma memories by labeling them and knowing how trauma and fear feels for you in your body. Facing a fear in a safe environment can change associations in your brain and dampen the stress response, providing you with calm and relief. Active coping with feelings of anxiety also helps rewire your brain and makes it easier for you to relax the next time a triggering memory presents itself. When you actively, consciously ignore a fear, the medial prefrontal cortex suppresses the amygdala-based fear response and those are skills that you can utilize and teach students.

With a brain that is healthy and functioning optimally, control is possible.

A healthy brain is fueled by:

Exercise: Exercise improves your mood, lowers the stress response, and improves your cognitive functioning. Exercise releases Brain-Derived Neurotrophic Factor (BDNF) when your body is challenged, which promotes neuroplasticity, connectivity in the brain, learning, stress regulations, and social bonding. For example, four weeks of regular exercise on the treadmill reduces impairment from the stress response. In other words, you bounce back from stressful situations faster (Tabibnia and Radecki 2018).

Mindful eating: Eating nutritious foods that are antioxidant rich (dark chocolate, blueberries, strawberries, kale, artichokes, beets, pecans, raspberries, red cabbage, and beans) helps your cells stay healthy. It is also important to avoid foods that are high in fats and sugar, which is usually what we crave during stressful times, as our body snaps into survival mode and tries to pack on as many pounds as possible, in case our access to resources becomes scarce – an evolutionary throwback. There is evidence that fasting and limiting food intake when stressed or having trauma memories can facilitate the brain to unlearn early traumatic memories through serotonin- and amygdala-related neural plasticity related to the vagus nerve.

Have an attitude of gratitude: Being thankful can increase physical and psychological well-being. Two weeks of keeping a daily gratitude journal has been found to increase life satisfaction and decrease anxiety. Gratitude has lasting effects on the brain region that is important for regulating emotion and social reward.

Connect with others: Finding support and a support network increases feelings of belonging, companionship, self-esteem, and self-efficacy. Being in a good mood can be contagious and should be spread. Connection to others lowers cortisol, which can lessen the stress response and decreases activation of the HPA.

Check in with yourself, noticing your thoughts and feelings, and remember that you are your greatest resource when you use your brain.

Resilience

The term "resilience," was introduced by French psychiatrist Boris Cyrulnik as the capacity to carry on in environments that ought to lead to breakdown. Informed by his experience in Nazi-occupied France, Cyrulnik understood resilience as the capacity to acknowledge trauma without later being affected by it, or to find a way to reconstruct one's sense of self in the aftermath. In a broader sense, a resilient person is able to continue their life after a traumatic experience, thanks to their capacity for reorganizing their sense of the world. In other words, resilient people are able to survive trauma and return to their everyday life, no worse for the wear.

Another psychological resource that has been associated with positive aspects of work, is that of finding meaning in what you do. Meaning may potentially help explain the variation in educator outcomes examining well-being. The construct of finding meaning is rooted in the seminal work of Victor Frankl. He is known as the "father of Existentialism." His theory is based on the framework of how we find meaning in life and our ability to find meaning through suffering. It is based on four basic principles. They are (1) humans have the capacity to make choices in how they see or respond to a difficult situation like caregiving, which in many ways is like being a teacher; (2) an individual's personal and philosophical values shape their response to caregiving; (3) persons have the responsibility for doing what is right and good or doing what the situation demands; and (4) humans have the capacity to find provisional and ultimate meaning. Provisional meaning is the management of day-to-day events that provide an educator with a sense of purpose. Ultimate meaning is the educator's sense of the spiritual or philosophical power that is available to them that provides greater purpose for their particular situation (Farran et al. 1997).

Resilience can shape expectation and transform a negative experience or failure into one of growth and positive learning. Instead of reacting with defensiveness, avoidance, or silence because of the threat to one's self-esteem or self-integrity, one can flourish. To flourish is to blossom and self-regulate emotions while using cognitive reframing for a new perspective. When one finds a new meaning for an adverse situation, new possibilities for growth can be found and problem solving can begin.

Tips for the Courageous Classroom

Guide students with a trauma-sensitive lens.

Learning Principle

Students who have experienced trauma can feel unsafe within their own selves and be easily triggered by a lack of structure and boundaries. Classrooms that are guided by structure, clear expectations, tolerance, and consistent warmth can alleviate tension and help provide comfort and ease of learning.

Teachers

- Provide a clear agenda of expectations and rules for academic and behavioral outcomes.
- Promote student self-efficacy by providing choices related to decision-making and rewarding good behavior.
- Good teaching tools for socioemotional learning include meditation when a student is upset, breathing exercises to maintain calm, and mindfulness to recognize and resolve feelings.
- Create a ritual for safety in the classroom that students can do when they arrive.
- Teach students how and when to verbalize their feelings, monitor them, and ease their suffering.

Chapter 7

When Teachers Are Targeted

Aggression Against Teachers

While the threat of school shootings is real and understandably the first thing that comes to mind when you think about school violence. Less prominent in our thoughts is the problem of violence against teachers more generally.

Violence against teachers is a serious problem. In 2015, a US Department of Education report indicated that from 2011 to 2012, almost 20% of public-school teachers reported being verbally abused, 10% stated that they had been physically threatened and 5% were physically attacked (APA 2016). The costs of teacher victimization include both hidden and obvious factors. There are issues of lost wages, absent days from work (927,000 days per year), time lost away from instructing and teaching students, the increased need for substitute teachers or training new teachers to replace those out or injured, medical and psychological care and intervention secondary to verbal threats, bullying and actual physical abuse, student disciplinary proceedings, student absences because of expulsion or incarceration, and worker's compensation claims and premiums

(APA 2016). In order to focus on prevention, the determinant factors of violence against teachers need to be explored.

Teachers are the barometer for the emotional temperature in a classroom. How students react, respond, behave, and participate is largely guided by the ability of a teacher to be a warm, positive force or know when to dial it down. When teachers are stressed or operate from fear, not only do they convey their inner feelings to their classroom, they compromise their ability to connect and direct. Karen Agne (1996, p. 131) states, "Teachers functioning in states of fear are less tolerant, less patient, and less involved with their students." Stressed or fearful teachers can be perceived as uncaring, demonstrated by being more authoritarian, and offer fewer rewards to students who deserve it. In other words, their fear controls their ability to interact in a flow of positivity with their students. Because fearful teachers are unable to be "guardians of their spaces," (Brown 2019) they do not allow students to breathe, be curious, and explore.

Working in a threatening school environment means teachers must worry about their basic safety. This drain on their mental bandwidth can diminish their opportunities for professional development and their capacity to understand what students need. A fearful brain frequently makes one want to hide or freeze, which inhibits creating a safe, containing space of learning and growth for students – the goal of a courageous classroom. A containing space is one where, author Robert French (1997, p. 2) writes, the role of the teacher is to "contain anxiety for the sake of teaching," so that learning can be experienced as an "expansion of potential" not just as the mastery of a subject measured by meeting the objectives of a lesson plan. "All learning occurs in relationship."

Teachers have long been asked to balance the relationship between managing an educational curriculum with the psychological well-being of themselves and their students. In fact, developmental psychology – the study of how and why human beings change over the course of their lives – has its roots in teaching and education. William James, a US philosopher and psychologist, introduced psychology to education as a teacher handbook in the early 1900s (Bland 1979). Teachers were seen as responsible for a child's personal growth, and their classrooms were meant to be trusting environments that gave students an opportunity to choose their own ways to learn and teachers a chance to become "living feeling resources" for their students. Humanist Clark Moustakas wrote of the crucial relationship between the teacher and student in his book, *The Alive and Growing Teacher* (1959), that "Being a genuine person means that the teacher will meet each situation as a human challenge, with all the accompanying contingencies, uncertainties and risks" (cited in Bland 1979, p. 283).

A Story of Lawrence

Times have definitely changed since 1933. I (Jed) was never physically harmed by a parent, but I have been hit, kicked, punched, or spat upon by 11 students over the course of my elementary classroom tenure. I taught first–third grade for 13 years before moving to higher education. That means only two years without a student who inflicted violence on me. I am sure you are reading this and thinking, "Well those are little kids." Little they may be, but a punch, hit, or kick to the throat or groin is painful, not to mention psychologically damaging. The ones who spit on me hurt the most. Those are things you don't forget as a teacher. To this day I can mentally see the face of every single student who harmed me.

One student in particular that I remember is Lawrence. He was possibly the most violent one I ever had. It was my second year of teaching when I met him. He was in kindergarten at the time. He was a really sweet kid on his good days. Big brown eyes, toothless smile, and quite the jokester. He could make anyone laugh. On his bad days though, watch out. He could completely demolish a kitchen center play area and used every swear word known to mankind and he was only five years old. The day I met him was when he had barricaded himself in his K5 classroom and a fellow teacher asked me for help. I was way too inexperienced to be handling a kid like him, but I tried my best to coax him down off the emotional ledge he was on as he hid behind a rolling easel.

My words didn't work quite like I had hoped. I did get him out from behind the easel, only for him to dart out of the classroom and down the hall to a supply closet where he hunkered down in all of his stubbornness until his mother came to get him. I remember walking out of the closet so grateful that he wasn't my student.

Fast forward to the beginning of the next school year, and guess whose name was on my class roster . . . Lawrence. I was terrified when I saw it. I knew I didn't have the skills to help this kid. This was before the interwebs and thousands of articles were available at my fingertips. I didn't have time to get another degree. I went to my principal and got as much encouragement and support as a thirsty man gets water from the desert. She was the worst. She'd never taught any grade below seventh and had no idea about first graders.

It took about three days before I was reacquainted with the Lawrence I met the previous year in kindergarten. He wanted to keep drawing when it was time to move on to something new. He threw his crayons at me, spat at me, and kicked his chair into my shin. It was the first of many violent episodes that happened with him throughout that year. Each incident got gradually more intense. Instead of kicking the chair he threw it. Instead of spitting at me, he walked to my face and spat on me. He knocked over desks, punched me in the groin, and would tear through the room like a twister. It often ended with him banging his head against the wall and screaming uncontrollably. I lost count of the times I had to evacuate the room because of his behavior. The ever-so-helpful principal rarely came to help. It was usually the guidance counselor and me while the rest of the students waited in another classroom. Not only did he disrupt the learning for my learners, but it usually caused enough chaos that the two other first-grade classes had to stop what they were doing to accommodate the influx of my fleeing students.

I made several attempts to provide him with the counseling and therapy he needed beyond what the guidance office and I could provide, but I was always stopped by his mother. She didn't believe he needed any help that she couldn't give him with corporal punishment. She herself was a very intimidating person who yelled and cussed a lot. It was not uncommon for her to make a scene in the main office resulting in a call to the police. I never was able to get him help. The next school year they moved away and I never saw him again. I often wonder if he is safe, if he got help, if he ever figured out what trauma caused his hurt to come out the way it did.

Aggression and Teacher Safety?

There's no question that for many teachers, individual students come with their own traumas and experiences, causing them to view the world through an ambivalent lens that causes it at once to appear safe and dangerous. Whether we realize it or not, these students look to the reaction of their teachers as they learn about themselves. Teachers monitor the immaturity of a growing brain, compete with raging student hormones, respond to bullying – all are situations that require the teacher to have the gaze of a friend, the wisdom of a counselor, the skills of a nurse, the pedagogy of an instructor, the patience of pseudo-parent, and the courage of a safe-keeper, an exhaustive list that takes its toll on teachers daily.

The National Center on Safe Supportive Learning Environments (n.d.) describes "School safety as schools and school-related activities where students are safe from violence, bullying, harassment and substance abuse." Without disputing the validity and importance of this definition, it begs the question: what about teacher safety? With violence and violent incidents occurring in school halls and classrooms, how safe do teachers feel?

Many teachers feel like the requirement to self-report data about school violence leads to under-reporting, and a survey of School Resource Officers found that 89% of school police thought that crimes at school were under-reported (Bucher and Manning 2005).

Defined as any act that negatively impacts the internal school climate, violence "is the most extreme manifestation of a range of behaviors that run contrary to schools' expectations and purposes" (Bucher and Manning 2005). You think? Ideally, schools provide freedom from violence, fear, and intimidation for students and teachers, yet far too many teachers suffer from a silent crisis of violence. Teachers have to counsel bullies, break up fights, monitor verbal escalations, and have appropriate interactions with students, parents, and caregivers, while maintaining their own emotional and physical well-being.

Research suggests that teachers are increasingly exposed to violence from students, and/or their parents, and it's one of the most serious contributors to work/stress for teachers (De Cordova et al. 2019). Factors like misbehavior and aggression can not only lead to physical injury but also harm teacher well-being, preventing them from developing positive relationships in the classroom. Although it is apparent the violence directed towards teachers is prevalent and increasing in some schools, violence against teachers is also under-researched and under-reported and thus inconsistently documented (Espelage et al. 2013), which is a problem. To adequately analyze teacher-directed violence for the purpose of education, and also to develop support structures and prevention strategies, it is imperative to know the extent of the impact on teachers. Teacher violence and victimization can negatively affect the relationships between students and teachers, which in turn impacts student learning and classroom morale, to say nothing of the damage to overall teacher morale, recruitment, and retention.

The costs of nationwide teacher violence and victimization by students, parents, and other teachers is estimated to exceed $2 billion dollars a year (APA 2016).Teachers report that most incidents are with students (94%), parents, (37%), and colleagues (21%) (Espelage et al. 2013). Therefore, it is important to note that the economic costs do not include those to the individual perpetrators of violence against teachers who may incur costs secondary to incarceration: lost wages, dropping out of school, medical care, and utilizing social services over their lifespan.

You may have glossed over one of the most jarring statistics there, but let's bring it back to your attention; 21% of teachers reported an incident of violence or victimization by a fellow professional in the school. That is alarmingly high considering that schools are supposed to be filled with those who model for our children how to be good citizens. I (Jed) was accosted by a co-worker once while in the middle of teaching first graders. I upset a fellow co-worker regarding bubbles (yes, bubbles. Like the soapy water in a plastic canister with a little wand) and he stormed into my room and threatened physical harm as I read students a book about the life cycle of a pumpkin. His face was red, his body shaking, and his anger flowing out of him like a freshly erupted volcano spewing lava. I could feel his breath on my cheeks and ears as he leaned in to tell me how he was going to "punch my face in." It startled the students and terrified me. The shock of it was so bad that I left the classroom unattended to immediately report him to the principal. Needless to say, the rest of my day was shot. I wish that I could tell you he's no longer in education. Sadly, he is.

The economic and psychological costs to everyone involved in violence against teachers, including educators, students, parents, and other teachers/administrators can be best viewed from a public health lens and scrutinized with the necessity of prevention, awareness, mitigation, and timely treatment interventions for those drawn into this multi-systemic web.

Aggression Defined

Understanding aggression and how to identify potentially violent students, parents and fellow teachers can lead to the development of effective interventions. Aggression should be thought of as an intentional behavior that is socially influenced with the goal of causing harm to another person who is motivated to avoid that harm. Aggression is deliberately used to change the behavior of others (Allen and Anderson 2017). You can also see aggression; it is observable. If a student states that they are thinking about harming someone, it can be a sign of potential violence but is not aggression. Aggression must be intended to harm someone. A student who accidentally bumps into a teacher or another student is not aggressive as there was no intentionality. The victim of aggression must be motivated to avoid the potential harm caused. As it turned out with Jed's co-worker, it wasn't his first incident with aggressive behavior towards another. There was a history of anger management issues that had gone unchecked in the building, thus creating a climate where his behavior was allowed.

Violence is aggression that causes serious harm and was intended to do just that. Actual physical harm does not have to occur for an act to be considered violent. For example, a student who brings a knife, gun, or other weapon to school with the intent to harm, terrorize, or hurt others should be considered violent. Again, referring back to Jed's story, while the co-worker never hurt him physically, the act of terrorizing him in front of his students had a lasting effect. Their relationship never recovered even though the two had to work together for the rest of the school year, when the aggressive co-worker transferred to a different school.

All acts of violence are forms of aggression, but not all acts of aggression are considered violent. The various forms of aggression are *physical*, which would include physical action and/or the damage of property. *Verbal* aggression includes name calling, spreading rumors, and verbal bullying. *Relational* aggression is when words are said, texted, written, or distributed with the intent to harm by demeaning the victim's social relationships with others. *Passive-aggression* is another form of aggression demonstrated by allowing emotional harm to happen to someone by ignoring and excluding them in what should be a pleasant social interaction. All forms of aggression can be hurtful both psychologically and physically, which is why aggression and bullying should be taken seriously.

Schools are social spaces bringing together people and their personalities, their ability to manage impulses or not, and a desire to make other students and teachers feel their unresolved pain. When a teacher or student with full awareness, planfully, thoughtfully, and proactively displays aggression towards another, it's known as "cold aggression." Many school shooters would fall under that category. Their actions are premeditated, incrementally planned, and unemotional. Their intent may be more motivated than a goal to simply harm others. Other goals may include attention, revenge, or robbery. Reactive or "hot aggression" usually occurs in response to a feeling of anger or disrespect. It is hostile, angry, full of emotion, retaliatory, and direct. Indirect aggression is when a student or teacher targets a substitute victim because their intended target is unavailable. Individuals often come to work after an argument with their spouse, or children thinking, "I'm going to mess up the next person who crosses me," in an effort to take their frustrations out on the person who was the source of their argument. Indirect aggression is a dangerous form of aggression and should be taken very seriously as its consequences can often be just as harmful.

In the brain, aggression is related to an outside stimulus that triggers negative emotions or feelings thus triggering feelings of flight or flight. These feelings can occur automatically through memories, physiologic reactions (like butterflies or sweaty palms), and are processed unconsciously as the need for an expectation (reward or pleasure) or a behavior. Individual motivation and self-awareness are key factors during this process. Students with enough motivation and insight can identify their feelings and think about why they feel that way. They can consciously choose to remain calm, plan an outcome or remedy that doesn't involve reactivity through violence or aggression, use their words, and avoid conflict. Avoiding conflict, expressing oneself, and not inflicting harm is the ultimate, doable goal.

Research demonstrates that an increase in aggressive behavior comes from a student's direct experience and observational learning (Allen and Anderson 2016). For example, when students see other children rewarded for negative behavior or being actively aggressive, they are more likely to be aggressive themselves. Social learning can mitigate that behavior because when students are motivated and taught to think about witnessed aggressive behavior, they can change their beliefs and expectations about that behavior, which may lead to a perceived reward.

Aggression and Social Learning

Social learning can be rehearsed and practiced. The process consists of linking sequences of related events to memory with positive, enabling conditions that students want and can list as goals, actions, and plans that link to potential outcomes. This can be accomplished by classrooms practicing "if-then" scenarios and learning individual script items that link together so strongly that they morph from learning sentences to knowledge structures. Knowledge structures can be thought of as "to know something as organized in a certain way" with the ability to recognize knowledge and use it for one's self by focusing and repeating it. Student expectations and behaviors in social situations can be changed with script rehearsals and practicing positive engagement to avoid conflict. This happens because more rehearsals create more links and connections in the brain to other concepts and memory. More links increase the strength of brain connections for students between concepts of identifying potential aggressive or hurtful situations and using their words and feelings to script out a different outcome.

For example, teach students beginning in preschool how to identify their feelings (in their body, known as arousal), their thoughts (cognition), and their effect (overall emotional state). Have cards with colors that correspond to all of their effects by using colors like red – mad, blue – sad, yellow – happy, white – neutral, orange – emergency (please check-in with me) that they can display first thing in the morning and throughout the day. The lesson here is that how we feel, our emotional state can influence our thoughts and feelings about ourselves and our interactions with others. Teachers should role-model the process.

Before verbal or physical conflicts take place, teach "what-if" scenarios for students to brainstorm around in the classroom to take a deeper dive into the role of thoughts and feelings in confrontations and how to problem-solve by talking to avoid hurting others.

Here's an example.

Tammy was late to school because she couldn't find the right socks. Her mother yelled at her saying, "You're always making me late for work. I told you to find your socks last night. You are so dumb!" (Ask the class open-ended questions, like "Has that ever happened to you? How would you feel? Where in your body would you feel it? Show me a card that describes your feelings and thoughts.) Continue telling the story: When Tammy got to school, she was mad, and pushed John because he was in her way. He pushed her back and the teacher made them both sit down. (Ask the class to think about why they pushed each other. What could Tammy have done or said if she was mad? What could John have done instead of pushing Tammy? How can we fix our feelings when we are mad, sad, or upset? If you see someone push someone else or say something mean, how can and should you react?)

Allowing students to link their experiences with words and actions that make classrooms feel safe and courageous builds knowledge and self-efficacy. Instead of removing disruptive children or teenagers, students and teachers can calmly examine the behavior from an empathic viewpoint to understand, address, and mitigate future behavior. Doing that promotes social learning and teaches self-regulation, which is crucial for successful learning and anti-aggressive performance. We can teach students to listen and be aware, unite around a collective classroom culture of safety and calmness, and act with knowledge instead of being reactive.

Aggression Disclaimer

Neither of us are saying that you should continue to keep disruptive, or potentially harmful students in your classrooms. But often, the removal is the end result the student may be hoping for. Almost all of us have had a student who didn't like us very much. They'd do anything to get out of our classrooms. Their disruptive behaviors may be just that. Remember the story of Johnnie from Chapter 3? She butted heads with her first-grade teacher every single day. They couldn't stand each other. Unfortunately, once Johnnie learned that she would get removed from the class if she acted out, she used the behavior as an escape mechanism. The teacher, a three decades veteran, sadly played right into her disruptions by not remaining calm and defusing the situations as they arose. Her immediate response was to have the disruption removed rather than focusing on what could be causing the reactionary, and sometimes violent behaviors.

Instead of seeing our students, their parents, or colleagues as the sum of their aggression or violent output, it's critical to understand the factors that contribute to it and the internal psychological systems that we can utilize to manage or avoid aggression. Our personality factors in as it determines how we view ourselves and others in situations where we live, work, learn, and play. We inherit some aspects of our personality so it's largely shaped by biological factors like temperament and our environment. When a potential threat or input from outside us triggers the sense of "fight, flight, or freeze," our brain sizes up the threat into two categories, person or situation. Our brain and body become acutely aware of what we are thinking (cognition), where we feel it (arousal), and the overall state of our emotions (affect), which is the route leading to potential outcomes. If we take the time to appraise the situation, think about desired outcomes, available resources, and possible options, it becomes easier to avoid impulsive action (violence or continued patterns of aggression or violence) and choose a thoughtful action (walk away, resolve with words, agree to disagree). The key is to break patterns of repeated aggression by altering knowledge patterns and practicing thoughtful actions and behaviors (see Table 7.1).

There are certain markers that may indicate a person has a high potential for aggression or violent acts, including if they:

- have unstable high self-esteem;
- are narcissistic;
- have issues with their self-image;
- have difficulties with setting long-term goals;
- have low self-efficacy for resolving violence and non-violent behavior;
- have normalized beliefs about aggression;
- feel like retaliation is normal;
- have negative aggression scripts running constantly;
- dehumanize others;
- culturally stereotype others;
- morally justify violence;
- push responsibility onto other people;

- interpret ambiguous behavior as hostile;
- think that aggression is common and acceptable. (Allen and Anderson 2017)

Circumstances that can lead to violence include: a break-up with a partner, arrests of family members including parents or siblings, parental divorce or separation, the death of a family member or close friend, clashes with other students or teachers, economic pressures, being the victim of racism or homophobia, being bullied over a medical condition, irregular sleep patterns, changes in housing stability, food insecurity, involvement or pressure to be involved in gang activity, substance abuse, victimization from sexual, physical, or emotional neglect or abuse, stress from academic pressure or frustration, being socially isolated, and having untreated mental issues.

Safe, courageous classrooms allow teachers to provide instructional learning more effectively and promote healthier learning environments for students. In order to create safe, courageous classrooms and minimize – or eliminate – disruptive, violent outbursts, we recommend the following best practices in behavior management:

- Daily recitations of classroom guidelines and expectations that should be clear and understandable.
- Consistent consequences of actions not complying with expectations, modeling, teaching, and rewarding positive behavior.
- Demonstrate caring for each individual student verbalizing their strengths as individual learners and highlight their resilience.
- See students as capable of learning knowledge and as socioemotional learners.
- Be flexible with a student's ability to make a meaningful choice.
- Have resources for student psychological emergencies.
- Do not ignore red flags.
- Teach, model, and welcome problem solving, empathy, conflict resolution, impulse control, and anger management. (APA 2016)

Creating courageous classrooms and teaching anti-aggression/violence strategies may feel daunting and frankly exhausting, but creating a framework to combat school violence against teachers will benefit overall school safety.

Aggression Management

Many teachers think classroom management means discipline and rules to keep an orderly class, or managing aggressive behaviors however severe or docile they may be. After conducting a recent survey that included some of the nation's most effective educators, the results show that it is much more than controlling students and their behaviors. Table 7.1 will help you to debunk the classroom management myth and have a better understanding of what it really means to manage your class.

A number of factors come together to contribute to teacher well-being, including their own resilience and psychological function. However, a key component that is often overlooked is the relationship between teachers: teachers can be allies for each other by paying attention to events outside their own classrooms. We should commit to continuing to support more experienced teachers, the way we do with newcomers, especially when they experience obstacles (De Cordova et al. 2019). Allyship is taking other's challenges as your own, working in solidarity not for reward but because it's the right thing to do. Teaching is stressful work but collegial support and allyship can promote psychological fortitude.

Aggression and Responding to Potentially Violent Students

- Observe non-verbal behaviors, pacing, throwing things, and rapid changes in movement.
- Calmly verbalize your observation i.e., "You seem upset, How can I help?"
- Maintain a soothing tone, even when the student's voice escalates.
- Respect student space but move closer to engage and potentially redirect the student.

Table 7.1 Classroom Management

Is...	Is Not...
relational	disconnected
• Connect with students. Build relationships. Establish trust. Love first.	• Students are not robots. Try as you will to make them be, you will quickly learn you are wrong.
based on expectations	a list of rules
• Set expectations high and students will strive to meet them.	• A list of don'ts is not the best way to build a collaborative learning space.
sharing procedures and routines	discipline
• Everything from sharpening pencils to lining up, from restroom usage to turning in work.	• Correcting students all day will leave you tired, but well-modeled procedures will keep this from happening.
purposeful	meaningless
• As a professional educator, you have the knowledge and ability to create routines that will support your instruction.	• Focus on procedures that will help students achieve, not create more uninspired work for you.
intentional	spontaneous
• Start strong the first day, and continue every day after!	• You cannot decide the sixth week of school to have a well-managed classroom. Adjustments are always possible of course, but start day one with some kind of plan.
modeled	assumed
• If there is a certain routine you want in your class, show students what that looks like.	• If students aren't doing what you want them to, don't overlook it. Reteach it!
encouraging positivity	reinforcing negative
• Spend your day thanking, praising, and acknowledging students who meet expectations.	• Constant fussing or hovering over students who aren't performing may reinforce the negative.
rewarding	punitive
• Celebrate classroom successes often and teach students how to be better citizens.	• Walking at recess, silent lunch, extra homework, etc.
teacher and student collaboration	always teacher-directed
• Student buy-in to the classroom is vital. Partnership in the planning is key.	• Two heads (or 24) are better than one.

(Continued)

Is. . .	Is Not. . .
reflective of your philosophy of education	reflective of your co-worker's philosophy of education
• Think about who you are, what you stand for, and the goals you have for students. Let that guide your day-to-day classroom plan	• Don't be pressured into making your classroom exactly like your co-workers'.

- Have a safety plan to alert administrators and maintain safety for all of the students.
- If a student insists on leaving the classroom, let them go but alert administrators and/or security personnel.
- Avoid letting other students de-escalate situations in your classroom by taking control.
- Never engage students with put-downs or sarcasm. Check yourself and be a role model with appropriate behavior.

A Story of Tatum

Tatum was not a full-time student of mine (Jed). She left her regular second-grade classroom to meet with me and 11 other students to improve their reading skills. Tatum was very behind in reading compared to many others in her class, but as I often say, reading is like walking. We all eventually learn to walk, but it takes some of us a bit longer than others. My little sister took longer than others and had to wear braces on her legs, but now as an adult she walks just fine. I knew Tatum had the ability to read because she knew basic sight words and read kindergarten-level books comfortably. She just needed my class as a sort of "brace on her leg" so to speak. Prior to the first day of my reading class, I met with each teacher to gather data about the students I would be teaching. Tatum had quite the history of violent outbursts and often would run from the classroom. She had been tested for learning disabilities and evaluated by the school psychologist but just missed the threshold that would have qualified her for special services. My class was the only option other than regular education to help her get on grade level with her reading. Prior to having Tatum, I had my fair share of violent students who liked to run. Remember the story of Lawrence? There was another one too that I didn't write about, Lexi . . . boy could she run. And I cannot forget about Frankie. So, as you can see, I wasn't new to the actions of aggressive students. But the stories of Tatum were almost unbelievable.

I picked her and the others up for our first day of class and we made our way out into the "rec center," a shared public facility with the community that was adjacent to the main campus building. I was the only teacher with a class in that space other than the PE teacher in the gym. At the time there was no communication line with the office so cell phones were vital to communicating any urgent needs. My cell didn't work down there due to the spotty service in that area. It never once occurred to me prior to the events that unfolded that day with Tatum that I might need to call someone for assistance. I was a veteran teacher. I could handle it, I thought.

Soon after I got all the kids seated for the day's first lesson, Tatum threw her book across the room and loudly said, "I don't wanna do this shit." The eyes of all the students widened as big as a full moon. They didn't look at Tatum though, they looked at me, as if to question, what are you gonna do about that? I picked up her book and asked her to speak with me privately off to the side. She immediately began screaming no, no, no as loudly as possible. She kicked over her desk and threw her chair at me. At this point, my teacher training kicked in and I evacuated the room so the others would not be injured. In the brief moment that it took for me to escort the students out into the foyer of the rec center, my classroom was demolished. My desk had been turned over, bookshelves emptied, and a blind had been pulled down. When I walked back into the room I could feel my heart rate quicken and fear flooded my body. I reached for my phone . . . no signal. Knowing that help wasn't available, I immediately recalled the CPI (Crisis Prevention Institute) training that I had taken while Lawrence was my student. As I tried talking to Tatum, she became irate. Screaming at the top of her lungs as if I was her worst nightmare. Running as if she had seen the devil, she ran to a walk-in supply closet and barricaded herself inside. At that moment I yelled to one of the other students to go to the main building for help. Simultaneously, I could hear a wave of destruction crashing inside the closet. No doubt a tsunami of rage was destroying everything in there. Not long after she slammed the door as a divider between herself and me, she began to scream "let me out." The doors weren't locked and there was nothing prohibiting her from coming out, so I calmly told her that the door was open for her whenever she was ready. In a flash, she flung it open and bolted for the door. She ran out of the classroom and out of the rec center. I quickly ran behind her because there was a small road just beyond that was often used by senior adults as they came to exercise classes in the same building. I was terrified she would be struck by a car so my sprinting feet took over. I caught her just as she was about to enter the roadway and we both fell to the ground. It was raining and we were both soaked and covered in mud. As we landed, she seemed to find release from whatever prompted her outrage and she began to cry. My fear and anger towards her suddenly transformed into compassion. As she cried, I cried. Finally, help arrived. I got cleaned up as best I could. The principal took Tatum and I somehow went back to teaching reading.

Because of the incident that day, she ended up being placed in an emotionally disabled classroom by the district. What kind of trauma could cause a student to act this way? No one will ever really know.

Let's Chat

Jed: I will never forget that day. I have so many thoughts, questions, and emotions as I reread the story. No part of college prepared me for this kind of student interaction. What else could I have done to help diffuse this situation?

Dr. Janet: I feel your pain and anguish and hers too. In any situation like this, the safety of both you and your student is important. Unpredictable violent screaming or throwing things causes fear in teachers and other students. Removing other students can help and getting other adults to help calm the situation can show support for all. It's also important not to yell back at students and ask in a slow, steady voice, "What do you need?" or "Please help me understand what you're feeling." Letting students use their voice to "get it out" may be helpful. It's a very stressful situation, and once the immediate crisis is resolved, it needs to be discussed and evaluated while looking at what worked and what didn't, so that all can be prepared for the next time.

Jed: I had little-to-no information about this student prior to her being in my class. What questions should teachers be asking counselors and school administrators once they notice these kinds of behaviors from students?

Dr. Janet: When a student is disruptive or has emotional or conduct problems without a plan to help them tolerate being in class and participate with other students on a consistent basis, more than a diagnosis is needed. They need a plan involving parents or caregivers, teachers, guidance counselor, and school administrators. In addition to getting an assessment, it is important to understand her home life and potential stressors, including housing and food insecurity. It helps to have a clear understanding of her history with other teachers and identify any strategies that optimized her behavior with a focus on highlighting them and maximizing her strengths. It takes work and a lot of effort, but the payoff for all involved can last a lifetime.

Jed: Behavior Intervention Plans (BIP) are common in schools. What kind of behavior interventions would you suggest to teachers who may have students like this in their classrooms right now?

Dr. Janet: The first intervention is for teachers to treat themselves with self-compassion. Self-compassion is being mindful, showing loving-kindness to yourself and understanding that you're not alone in your suffering. Secondly, reassess your goals for students like this in small steps. If you have a student who goes to the principal's office daily, and one week they only go four times and the next week, three, that's progress. Involve the student in labeling their behavior, contributing to consequences, and building to a reward. For example, give them stars for good behavior with a goal of 30 stars equaling a reward that you all agree upon. Set up incentives for good, positive behavior.

Tips for the Courageous Classroom

Empower students to make thoughtful, courageous decisions to defuse their aggression.

Learning Principle

CALM is an acronym for controlling anger and learning to self-manage.

C: Count to 10. Teach students to recognize that they're feeling upset. Have them state what and where they feel it in their body and what their thoughts are. They can say out loud one word that describes their emotion. All of this can happen as they are deeply inhaling/exhaling 10 times.
A: Ask themselves why they are angry. What happened?
L: Listen to the other side (if another person was involved), to understand how they are feeling. If only one person is involved, think about what to say to yourself to calm down (use positive self-talk) saying things like, "It's okay, I will figure this out," "I will be alright," "I don't want to hurt anyone, I just want to understand."
M: Make a funny, goofy face. Smile. Try to find the humor in the situation. Humor is a terrific anger buster.

Students have the capacity to mindfully self-regulate by using their breath, if they have a desire to stay in control and the confidence to manage their situation. Reward them with positive words of encouragement when they try, and discuss what worked and what didn't, so that they can continue to improve.

Tips for Teachers Who Have Fear in the Classroom
- Acknowledge your fear.
- Establish practices that make you feel safer by identifying exits, knowing who you can call for assistance, and establishing safety protocols for you and your students in the face of a threat.
- Discuss your concerns with a colleague and administrators.
- Recognize red flags in students or colleagues and have a safety plan.
- Pay attention to your own self-care.

Chapter 8
When a Child Is/Might Be in Danger

Relationships Are Paramount

When students need mental health services, schools are one of the most frequent links. Teachers are the eyes and ears for children who may be in distress from physical or sexual trauma, emotional abuse or neglect, and witnessing interpersonal violence within their household. They also may be witness to bullying (when it occurs in the classroom) or its fallout (when it occurs on social media). Teacher self-efficacy, and their ability to identify, assist, and refer students who may be in danger is critical in lowering job stress for teachers and increasing their job satisfaction.

Teacher training is not enough to increase teacher satisfaction: teachers must feel connected and safe and see possibilities for organizational change (Ouellette et al. 2018). Factors that contribute to teacher satisfaction are student academic success in the classroom, supportive principals with positive leadership styles, and a positive school climate (Ouellette et al. 2018). The relationships that teachers build with students is paramount to the effectiveness of mental and public health initiatives within schools (Garcia-Moya, Brooks, and Spencer 2018). Teacher connectedness serves as a protector for in-school health disparities and lessens student involvement in risky activities. School commitment involves student connectedness to staff, and student relationships to their peers influence their learning and behavioral choices within school walls. Positive relationships with teachers are a key way in which the school environment affects the health and well-being of young students (Garcia-Moya et al. 2018). School connectedness originates from the relationship between the school's structural and organizational systems and the dynamics between supportive interrelationships in the schools. School size has been researched the most and findings suggest that smaller schools promote more teacher-student connectedness (Garcia-Moya et al. 2018). Gender plays a role in student connectedness with girls reporting higher levels of support, perhaps because more teachers are female. Teaching goals and self-efficacy also vary in male and female teachers (Garcia-Moya et al. 2018). Studies show that teachers will make differential instructional decisions based on their own gender, and teaching experience. Other significant factors include the socioeconomic level of the school, and the self-efficacy of the students (Rubie-Davies, Flint, and McDonald 2011).

Beliefs are powerful predictors that influence thoughts and ultimately actions. Individual teacher judgments about a few students can impact a whole class secondary to a teacher's attitude and can compromise classroom morale and safety. In other words, teachers and classrooms benefit from a resilience or growth mindset. A growth mindset for teachers can contribute to a more positive relationship with teachers and students who may exhibit disruptive behavior or have mental health issues. Teachers with a growth mindset don't view unmotivated or disruptive students as threats but as a challenge and opportunity for them to improve their skills, increase their understanding, and become a better teacher. Psychologist Carol Dweck (2014/2015, p.14) noted that some teachers with a growth mindset tell their students, "Every time you make a mistake, become confused, or struggle, you have made me a better teacher."

When instructing students, teacher beliefs and expectations can influence the learning experience, teacher expectations for students, and students' opportunities to learn (Rubie-Davies et al. 2011). From a teacher perspective, teacher expectations relate to *where* the teacher believes the students in his/her class will arrive, teacher efficacy relates to *what* the teacher believes that they can do to get the class there, and teacher goal orientation relates to *how* the teacher believes lessons should be structured to reach their goals (Rubie-Davies et al. 2011). If teachers believe that student outcome is predetermined or determined by factors beyond their control (like socioeconomic status and gender) they may have little motivation to be curious and find ways to reach their students (Auwarter and Aruguete 2008). Poor adult expectations (including both parent and teacher) for lower socioeconomic students are associated with disrupting the performance of low-income children. Many studies examine parents and teacher expectations separately, but they should be considered together. When both parents and teachers feel uncomfortable with their interactions, their joint discomfort can lead to miscommunication and difficulty with their relationship, potentially negatively affecting the child's academic success (Minke et al. 2014).

Relationships with Student's Parents

Parental involvement is associated with higher academic achievement, improved social skills and decreased behavioral problems (Minke et al. 2014). It includes all parental behaviors that support their child's learning, those that are visible to teachers (attending parent-teacher conferences, volunteering at school) and not visible (supportive learning at home). It is not surprising that both teachers and parents have varying descriptions of what parental involvement means. Teachers may emphasize parental behaviors that they can see and parents may reference their support from within home, or within the school. Parents usually see themselves as more productive than teachers do. Teachers initiate contact when there are problems and parents may initiate contact as well. All of the above can lead to serious misunderstandings. From a behavioral improvement standpoint, the quality of the parent-teacher relationship is an important factor for children with behavioral problems (Minke et al. 2014).

Courageous educators build relationships with parents/guardians by . . .

- Making positive calls home.
- Mailing letters of praise.
- Attending extracurricular activities and making small talk.
- Treating parents/guardians as partners in education.
- Showing dignity and respect during conferences.
- Using language that parents/guardians understand.
- Being as personable as possible while maintaining professionalism.

Relationships with Students

The relationship between a student and their teacher is an incredibly important variable for student success. Students who may have a mental health disorder are at risk for not completing school if their poor mental health goes unnoticed and unchecked while in school. Remember, high school (and college) graduation rates are a key predictor in health and income potential. Courageous educators build relationships with students by . . .

- Getting to know their personal likes and dislikes.
- Attending extracurricular events when possible.
- Identifying their strengths and praising them often.
- Allowing them voice and choice in the learning space.
- Trusting them.
- Listening to them.
- Respecting them.
- Acknowledging their humanity.

There are many risk factors for the development of a mental health disorder including:

- genetics (family history);
- environmental influences (poverty, overcrowding at home);
- exposure to violence (neighborhood);
- trauma (sexual or physical, or witnessing trauma);
- neglect (emotional);
- substance abuse;
- social (incarcerations of parent/s, food insecurity, housing instability);
- new medical conditions (diabetes or thyroid disorder);
- bullying; and
- economics (lack of health insurance).

The role of teachers is not to diagnose, but to be aware of how their students are living and to be responsive when the student's academic and physical well-being is being threatened or challenged. That requires a basic understanding of how life stressors, thoughts, words, and emotions can trigger behavioral changes, outbursts, or withdrawal, an inability to focus, crying or laughing or worse: psychosis with suicidal or homicidal thoughts.

Relationships and Mental Health

Most students are not suicidal but many may have behavioral infractions that belie underlying mental health issues. In the past, students who were disruptive were automatically seen as a bother and removed from classrooms without impunity. When teachers are under pressure to restore order to potentially chaotic classrooms, they might focus on discipline without understanding the root causes of behavior. They often miss an opportunity to teach their peers about conflict resolution or discussing the potential impact of a behavioral intervention on a class. In today's classrooms, there is probably not one teacher who has not had to navigate a student with mental health problems. Documents from the Surgeon General of the United States report that one in five children, adolescents and, adults will have a diagnosable mental health disorder, and 1 in 20 have severe emotional disabilities (Dikel 2014, p. 31). Almost 11% of teens will have a depressive disorder by the time they are 18. Depression is more common in girls than boys, and the Center for Disease Control (CDC) reports that the prevalence of mental health disorders in children and teenagers is increasing (Dikel 2014, p. 31). Researchers from the National Institute of Mental Health states that most mental illnesses present before the age of 14, and that's a guarantee that our schools and classrooms are seeing these students and teachers are teaching them.

Teachers should be aware of the signs and symptoms of a student who has a mental health disorder. Be prepared to intervene when a student: has changes in their mood (how they feel) or affect (how they appear to you); has trouble focusing; reports high anxiety, repetitive behaviors or thoughts; appears disoriented; has psychotic processes; expresses a desire to hurt themselves or someone else; and are more aggressive or withdrawn. Awareness can lessen stigma and create a healthy dialogue between the student, their parent or guardian, and their teacher. Teachers should familiarize themselves with school interventions (counselors or mental health clinics that offer services for students), talk to the student's parents to learn their concerns and/or review the previous history of the child and current treatment with mental health professionals. Express that a child's medical and mental health is confidential unless there is an expression of self-harm to a child or another person. Asking, "How can I help?" is a good first step, but requires a strategy on how you can assist parents and their children with their mental health needs. If this book inspires you to do one thing, we hope that you take a moment to reflect on your knowledge of school intervention protocols and begin to look and listen with fresh eyes and ears for those students who are hurting deeply and need a courageous voice to help them.

Any student, parent, or teacher who is violent (with or without a visible weapon) and/or threatens to hurt themselves or someone else should be treated as a psychiatric emergency. Administrators at the school should be immediately notified and a safety plan implemented. Students in a classroom who are exposed to violent situations and witness traumatic occurrences on school grounds should be debriefed and supported. Teachers who are victims and/or witness trauma should also utilize existing structures to gain support for themselves.

A Story of Frankie

What happens when it seems life is the bully, not a person, and there is no way to stop it? That's what I (Jed) often feel about the circumstances of Frankie's life. He wasn't my student. He was in the class across the hall. I knew him very well though. He spent lots of time visiting me because he couldn't stay put too long without having a meltdown. The change in scenery did him well, and I was happy to help a fellow teacher out. The more he came to my room, the more I learned about his story. His parents were super young and his grandma was raising him. He was legally blind and had to wear very strong corrective lenses to help him see. His family had no insurance and his dental hygiene had gone unchecked his entire life. Most of his teeth were rotting or had already fallen out. It was assumed that drugs had been used in-utero affecting his mental cognition and his speech was incoherent most of the time. The clothes he wore were often too small and his belly poked out just below the frayed edges of his shirt. We often called the department of social services regarding neglect, but they always said as long as he was fed and had no visible marks of abuse that there was nothing they could do. My heart broke for him daily. See what I mean about life bullying him? He couldn't catch a break.

One particular day during Frankie's year his breaking point arrived with a fury. Recess was ending and the teachers were calling for students to line up when I noticed Frankie sitting on the top of the monkey bars. His teacher was below trying to coax him down. He refused. Loudly. He was screaming "no" so loudly that I am sure they heard him inside the building. Apparently, he wanted to stay outside to play. He was laughing as he yelled, almost a devilish sounding laugh that chilled you to the bone.

I told his teacher to take my class inside with hers and I would coax him down. I climbed up the equipment with full intentions of just hanging out with him until he decided to go down. He and I had a fairly good relationship, and I felt confident he wouldn't mind me joining him. I was wrong. Really wrong. As I ascended, he jumped from the top and ran as fast as he could away from the building. Thankfully, the entire area was fenced in so he couldn't leave the school grounds, but that didn't stop him from running. Back and forth he went, sometimes in straight lines, sometimes in a zig zag, sometimes in circles. All I could do was keep an eye on him to make sure he didn't climb the fence. He wasn't in danger, and I feared that if I had intervened he may have hurt me or himself. It was about 1:30pm when he started. He didn't give up until about 2:15pm as busses started to dismiss. Just as quickly as he started running, he just stopped, walked over to me with a big grin, and we headed inside. I escorted him to his classroom thinking the worst was over. I was wrong again. It was only the beginning.

As his teacher walked her students to the bus loading area, Frankie screamed his way down the hall exclaiming that he didn't want to go home. It was Friday of a three-day weekend and most kids were ecstatic for the extra day off. Not him. As the class line passed by the main office, he jumped out and hid himself under the secretary's desk, and there he stayed until about 3:30pm.

His grandma came to pick him up. He hadn't moved in an hour and a half. When she walked into the school building she looked exhausted. The tiredness showed on her face with every worried line that marched across it. "Where is he?" she asked. The interim principal showed her where he was and she began to coax him out. Within just a few minutes it became apparent that he wasn't coming. I was in the classroom nearby working a bit late and could hear the commotion. I walked over to the office to see if I could help and they asked if I could carry him to the car. As I made my way under the desk to get him, he sprayed me in the face with a bottle of cleaner that was stored underneath. It burned my eyes, but I was determined to remove him so he wouldn't hurt himself or anyone else. All along the way to the car, he hit me, kicked me, and spat all over my back. When we got to his grandma's car it took every ounce of my strength to get him inside as he screamed and yelled. The interim principal asked me if I would ride home with them to keep him inside the vehicle. As I look back on that moment, I cannot believe that I was asked to do it because of liability issues, but in the car I went, holding Frankie for dear life, afraid for his safety, worried what the evening held for him.

After a short drive, we arrived at their home. It was a mobile home with no underpinning that sat very high off the ground. It appeared to be very dilapidated and the yard was in shambles. His screaming had continued the entire ride and got louder when the car stopped. I had never seen a kid so adamantly reject the idea of leaving school for home. Once I got him to the door, I fully understood why. Inside, the foul odor was so strong. It smelled of trash, smoke, feces, and cat urine. It took everything in me not to vomit. In the middle of the living room floor was a hole about two feet wide. Cats were jumping in and out of it when we walked in. I was carrying Frankie over my shoulders, continuing to be beaten like I was on the walk out of the building. I sat him down on a couch covered in animal fur, cigarette burns, and countless holes and I fled. His grandma said nothing but slammed the door behind me as I ran. I could hear him screaming as I opened the door to the interim principal's car who had followed behind so I could have a ride back to school. When I sat in her car, I fell apart. No wonder he didn't want to go home. With the bully that life had been to him, I would have kicked and screamed to avoid it too.

Let's Chat

Jed: Dr. Janet, this student's home was traumatic. It wasn't safe. It wasn't healthy. I reported it to the right people as the school required of me, but his situation never improved. From a psychological standpoint, what should a teacher do to help the mental health of a student who has this type of home life?

Dr. Janet: As teachers, you are the eyes and ears for students when it comes to potential trauma and dangerous home situations. Reporting it to guidance counselors and getting Child Protective Services (who do great prevention work) are two resources. As frustrating as it might be, teachers still need to repeatedly attempt to engage parents and caregivers. Being a positive force by listening, supporting, and helping children problem-solve can help you and them.

Jed: Looking back, I wonder if I caused more harm than good by removing him from underneath the desk and carrying him to the car. I was instructed to do this by my superior. At the time we feared for his safety as he hid. What strategies do you suggest for situations like this?

Dr. Janet: Having a plan for handling these kinds of situations before they get out of control is optimal for school management, instead of in the middle of the situation. There are certain aspects of curtailing behavior that are painful, but must happen. It's better that you did it, than the legal system. After something traumatic happens like a forceful removal or disciplinary action, what is the follow-up? Who checks on the student and finds out how they're feeling and processing? There should be a plan for that as well, to inform the process to make it better and handle hurt feelings.

Jed: When teachers are faced with events like the one with Frankie, it is traumatic. What should be the steps educators take for their own mental health in the days following an episode like this one?

Dr. Janet: Teachers and administrators have to recognize the toll that being on the frontline and a teacher-healer can take on you mentally, physically, and spiritually. You can find ways to "empty your cup" at the end of every school day, and sometimes during the school day, by checking in frequently with yourself asking, "How am I doing?" Find time for at least five minutes of meditation, stretching at your desk, exercising in 5- to 10-minute intervals and eating mindfully. Learn to manage your stress levels and bring yourself back into balance with positive words of self-encouragement. Get extra psychological support if you need it and lean on your colleagues to share stories of success and survival. Try not to go it alone.

Tips for the Courageous Classroom

Open your mind to evidence-based strategies to address mental health problems in students and yourself.

Learning Principle

Mental health issues impact almost half of all US residents and fewer than half will ever get treatment. We must dispel the stigma associated with seeking mental health treatment so that we can better manage ourselves and families.

Check-up from the neck up

- Pay attention to your mood. If you have sadness or a depressed mood that lasts longer than two weeks and impacts your work, love, and/or play, talk to your healthcare professional. Depression is treatable. Get help.
- Get a physical. There are medical conditions that can impact mood, sleep, fatigue and thoughts. Medications and illegal substances also play a role. Talk to your healthcare provider, openly and honestly about stressors and coping.
- Utilize mental health professionals. Refer students to the guidance office for assessments and therapeutic assistance.
- Don't forget the importance of regular exercise, mindful eating, and utilizing positive coping skills daily.
- Keep a gratitude journal. Research shows saying or giving thanks and counting blessings helps with sleep, lowers stress, and improves relationships with others. A study in 2018 found that gratitude journals lowered materialism and improved generosity for adolescents (Singh 2018).

Chapter 9
Building Courageous Classrooms

A Courageous First Day of School

Who doesn't remember their first day of school? I (Janet) know that I do. I remember carefully figuring out what outfit I would wear and nervously wondering if I would see one familiar friendly face in my classroom. A night of tossing and turning with anticipation left me excitedly tired as I made my way into my classroom. The death grip on my mother's hand would be loosened only as I saw the wide-tooth grin of a smiling teacher. Gently dropping my mom's hand as my panic gave way to curiosity, I carefully looked for construction paper bearing my name at a desk. Sitting down slowly, careful not to place my hands into gum wadded up under desks, waiting to snare unsuspecting fingers like a juicy-fruit-smelling Venus flytrap, I felt satisfied that I was there and ready.

On November 14, 1960, a year before I was born, a six-year-old, bright, Black, and courageous pigtailed girl had a very different journey into her classroom. Her name was Ruby Bridges and she made her way through name calling, death threats, and the hateful and vile rhetoric of adults as she calmly walked into the all-white William Frantz public school in New Orleans, Louisiana. Federal marshals were sent to New Orleans to keep her safe. Her first day of school was spent in the principal's office because almost every single parent at her school was protesting her presence. There were schools in the South that closed their public schools rather than have them integrated. Five years after Ruby Bridges fearlessly integrated her school, 75% of schools in the South remained segregated (Serrato 2017).

A courageous teacher named Barbara Henry stepped up to teach Ruby Bridges when no other teacher would. In fact, Ruby was Mrs. Henry's only student for the whole school year, and they sat side by side, working on her lessons (Serrato 2017). Speaking of her time with Mrs. Henry for an NPR interview (Simon 2020), she stated

> But I remember her graciously saying, you know, come in and take a seat – and there I was sitting in an empty classroom with her for the whole year, you know she showed me her heart. Very early on, and I realized that she cared about me, she made school fun, and ultimately I felt safe in that classroom.

A Courageous Man

Ruby Bridges had to display extreme courage in order to receive a classroom education. Frederick Douglass, born enslaved around 1845, had to seek out opportunities for learning in some of the least likely places. At the time he was born, it was against the law for slaves to read or write. Surviving hardships, beatings, and indignities that no human should bear, Douglass bravely and courageously escaped to Massachusetts, a free state. In his memoir, *Narrative of the Life of Frederick Douglass*, he describes the mental darkness he endured by not being able to learn. His mistress had started to teach him the alphabet when he was a child, until her husband found out and forbade her to continue. Determined to continue, he made friends with "little White boys" and turned them into his teachers. He would always carry a book with him and at 12, read a book about escaping slavery and the power of emancipation. He came to understand that to be free, he would have to write his own pass. He then taught himself how to write after years of secretly practicing whenever he could. Frederick Douglass wrote five autobiographies to inspire equality and human rights. He was a brilliant public speaker, leader in the abolitionist movement, and advocate for women's rights. Without any formal education, he taught other enslaved Blacks to read using the Bible while risking his life using his personal motivation in the service of others' education and freedom.

Today's world has created a new series of challenges for students seeking to get an education. The disruption of learning secondary to COVID-19 has closed some public schools, created hybrid learning schedules and remote learning, and revealed too many public-school hazards with poor ventilation and no access to hot water. Like both Ruby Bridges and Frederick Douglass, there is a new generation of students whose stories have been both inspiring and heartbreaking: students desperately doing schoolwork on their phones because they lack computers, struggling through the digital divide. A widely circulated photograph in August 2020 showed two young girls sitting outside of a Taco Bell using the fast-food chain's free Wi-Fi to complete their homework. The girls lived in a California school district where over 2,500 families were waiting for the delivery of hotspots so that their children could do their work. A Common Sense Media report found that 25% of K–12 students did not have adequate internet access at home and almost 20% did not have the proper equipment for remote learning, according to CNN (Chandra et al. 2020).

The impact of cultural norms and values, oppressive policies, and pandemics have made unlikely heroes out of everyday students, their parents, and educators determined to continue their passion of growing, educating, and developing young scholars. There are no easy answers in such times, but when teachers and students adopt a growth mindset, it becomes possible to expose our weaknesses while developing our strengths. When students are taught that their abilities are not fixed but that they can grow their brains and make their neural connections stronger when they stretch, practice, and try to learn new things, they show more motivation to learn, which becomes all the more valuable in times of great uncertainty.

A Courageous Definition and Neurobiology

We need courage in our relationship with ourselves because that allows us to engage, and communicate with empathy, trust, and honesty. Inner courage is important because life can be dangerous. The environments where we live, love, and work can be dangerous. Those threats – real or perceived – can pose a danger to people that we love. When we feel fearful, we create barriers to our own potential. When we have a sense of purpose, confront challenges, establish commitment, and do what's under our control, we grow. Courage is not about being fearless or performing a brave feat in reaction to someone in distress; courage is developing into all that you were meant to be.

The purest form of courage is perseverance (Rachman 2010). As educators, being able to teach through situations when there is a real or perceived threat exemplifies courage. Students who persevere through difficult home lives, strained relationships, or bullying with peers, horrific trauma histories, home instability and/ or food insecurity display courage when they show up at school motivated by the desire to just be present, to learn in a safe environment, and simply be better through education. Courage requires a confidence of skills that can be both taught and enhanced. Research has identified that the ability to recover quickly from a fear reaction, positively adapt to repeated stress or danger, have high morale, and display a courageous attitude all contribute to a courageous skillset. The good news is that all of the above can be mastered with practice.

A Courageous Story

I (Jed) have written this part of the book four times now. I keep deleting it and starting over because I cannot seem to find the words. Anyone who has ever written anything of deep personal significance knows the feeling. If you are reading this, it means I finally got through it and was happy with it, or I just gave up. In all honesty it is probably the latter. How does one write about one's own deeply personal trauma and feel happy with it? It fits here. It needs to be shared. People need to read it. Especially educators. They need to know that there are gay students, trans students, bi students, gender non-conforming students, non-binary students, pansexual students, asexual students, lesbian students in their classrooms who are petrified that someone will find out about who they really are, and school is a terrifying place for them. They also need to know that their LGBTQ+ co-workers have the same fear. That was me. Every single day. From my first teaching gig in 2001 to December 26, 2012, when I finally came out. I lived in constant fear that my students, their parents, my principal, my co-workers, my district officials, my school board would find out that I was a gay man teaching among them and fire me.

My story is a complicated one. It is rope tightly braided with strands of physical, sexual, and emotional abuse, religious indoctrination, conversion therapy, combined with being raised in the middle of the infamous Bible Belt. Raised by those who were deeply convicted Evangelical Christians, despite their legacy of divorce, alcoholism, drugs, pornography, and racism, I was taught that homosexuality was the most abominable of sins. Only worse was suicide, which was considered to be blasphemy in its highest form. More than once I heard a sermon about Sodom and Gomorrah and how their god destroyed them for their sexual perversions. My uncle regularly talked about his hate for "fags" as he called them and almost every day of my formative years I was taught to "be a man" so I wouldn't turn out gay. Gays were evil, bad, and bound for hell. You can imagine how terrified I became the first time Christopher put his hand on my leg and I liked it. What should have been a momentous moment of my teenage years, the first time I kissed a guy, sent me into deep depression that I went through completely alone because not one soul other than Jake could know about it. As much as I enjoyed the secret playful moments of exploration with Christopher and Jake, all I could think was . . . Damnit . . . I'm gay and going to hell for all of eternity. The very thing my family, friends, and society condemned, I was.

Fast forward from the moments of that first kiss to 2001 when my teaching career began. The in-between time was filled with twists and turns sharper and more sudden than a ride on Space Mountain. Long story short, I was definitely gay, but only the random guys that I met in AOL chatrooms knew. My Evangelical Christian conversion therapist knew too. And his constant advice to me was to never admit that I was gay because then the devil had me. So, afraid of eternal damnation, I followed his advice and told everyone I was straight, all the while meeting guys online and living a secret life.

Secret lives will drive you crazy. I don't recommend them. Especially if you are a teacher starting your career at a private Christian school. They have spies everywhere and find out things. I am convinced that they had someone monitoring local online gay chatrooms to make sure all of their people are avoiding "abominations." Regardless of how they found out, they did, and it ended my time at their school. There is a lot more to the story that maybe I will share in another book one day, but the emotional and psychological damage that their termination of me did to my psyche was enough to drive my gayness further back into the closet.

A few years later I landed another teaching gig. Just like every district in South Carolina, it was a conservative district. All-White school boards, mostly men, most of them active in prominent churches in the area. I was surprised I got the job honestly given my exit from the previous school. I vowed the day I signed my contact that I would never ever let them know I was a gay man. The trauma from the firing was still very real. It had squashed my very identity so far back in the closet that I had convinced myself I wasn't gay after all. I couldn't bear the thought of reliving the humiliation and degradation that I faced the last time, so straight I would be.

Are you reading this? Are you fully understanding that trauma and abuse had literally caused me to deny my very existence? I was 23 years old in 2001, 25 in 2003 as I began the profession again. I was fully capable of finding my words and expressing my fears, but because of the scars and hurt, the pain and grief, the worry and paralyzing fear, I couldn't exist as my authentic self for concern of being shunned, fired, disowned, and condemned to hell. Talk about someone being able to "teach through situations when there is a real or perceived threat exemplifies courage" as Dr Janet mentioned above . . . I was terrified. Every single day as I walked into school from 2003 to 2015, I was afraid. But, I taught right through it the best I could.

You may notice that the end of my period of fear, 2015, is well after my coming out date mentioned earlier. That's because it took about two years before I had the courage to come out to everyone. Once I did, I was still afraid of losing my job. So rather than live in constant fear, I took control of my own path and left my second-grade classroom forever. The years since then have been filled with ups and downs connected to my sexuality. I got in trouble at one job for advocating for my equality online. I lost another job because someone complained about my "gay agenda." I am confident that other opportunities in the great Palmetto State have avoided me altogether because of who I love. The post-traumatic stress of living my life in this place even led to me telling a potential employer not to hire me if they didn't want an outspoken gay man who fought for LGBTQ+ equality. I will never forget when Dr. Laura Reynolds, dean of the School of Education at USC Upstate, looked at me and said, "Jed, that's why we want you!" Talk about a moment of healing. I will never forget her words. The empowerment she gave me to further accept my true self will live with me forever. Every lesson and class I have taught since then has been delivered with more confidence than ever because of her. I am not sure she knows this so I hope someone shares this book with her. The irony isn't lost on me that it was an educator who helped me find the courage I needed.

Let's Chat

Jed: Dr. Janet, as you can tell from the story above, I carried a lot of my own fear into my classroom. I know there are many teachers like me who are facing life dilemmas that their co-workers are not aware of. How can teachers in a courageous classroom take care of themselves while they are simultaneously taking care of students?

Dr. Janet: We bring our experiences, pain, and suffering as well as purpose into our work spaces. Fear is the body's response to real or imagined stressors and thoughts and can present itself emotionally, psychologically, and physically in relationship to other colleagues and students. The first step to handling fear or trauma is to identify it by writing it down. Spend 20 minutes writing a trauma or fear timeline, by listing what happened and then adding your emotional response to it. Try to breathe deeply while you are writing. Figure out at least one strength or positive coping skill. Build on ways that you can utilize self-care while managing your own stress. Just like the message is to put on your oxygen mask first before helping others on an airplane, teachers have to prioritize their own self-care before helping their students using courageous principles.

Jed: What advice would you give to teachers who feel that they do not work in a district that supports the ideals of a courageous classroom for all students, but cannot afford to relocate or resign from their position?

Dr. Janet: Working tirelessly to support your own values and purpose and not having it reflected through administrative policies and practices can lead to burnout or, as you mentioned in your question, the desire to leave or quit. Burnout is characterized by insomnia, changes in mood, irritability, and compromised physical health. Teachers should focus daily on why they chose to work in the school they're in and look for little wins to help them stay focused and have less burnout. Find like-minded colleagues for social support. Balance emotional stress with mindful eating, regular exercise, sleep, and a positive attitude. Try to reframe negative thoughts with positive ones and take control over your own classroom.

Jed: What effect can a teacher's own fears and trauma have on students if they don't seek help?

Dr. Janet: If a teacher doesn't seek help for their own fears and trauma, then their ability to relate and socially connect in a healthy and helpful way can be compromised. Fear also is a trigger for stress and stress impacts learning and memory and can create feelings of irritability, anxiety, and depression. Fear can lead to a feeling of avoidance (flight), hiding (freeze), and fight (aggression), all can lead to a dysfunctional relationship with students who need teacher empathy, respect, and trust.

A Courageous Choice

Developing courage happens at the individual and the community level. Our students need to learn to develop positive self-talk, but they also need positive feedback from their parents and teachers to motivate them externally.

Both fear and courage can be modelled which is not to say that you shouldn't be in touch with your fear. The real message is to pay attention to your thoughts, feelings, and emotions, tap into your capacity for perseverance and courageous behavior – and teach your students how to do the same. "Life is chaotic and threatening, such that the person lives at best, if they react courageously" (Woodward 2010, p. 110). Our classrooms provide a tremendous opportunity for students and educators to react courageously. That reaction is rooted in authenticity: being committed to actions that display an ability to react to fear and still achieve a meaningful and important moral goal. Authenticity is a courageous choice because meaningful goals provide steps for our journey in life. While the path may not always be clear, and barriers arise, our ability to face an obstacle with courage is always there within us. Choosing courage can lead to a sense of completeness, enhance spirituality or faith, deepen our creativity and connection with ourselves, and push us closer to our potential. Courage comes when we embrace the awareness of our conscious threats and release our own authentic strengths of words, thoughts, and behaviors to be motivated and overcome an obstacle. Courage is the most important choice that we can make by saying "Yes" to who we are and what we want.

The educational setting is a wondrous place for educators to model and teach students about the different types of courage: social, moral, physical, and what's the most applicable to this book, psychological. Psychological courage demands that you act in the face of risk or threats to your mental well-being for the good of yourself and/or others. Standing up for yourself or others who may be being bullied or abused, requires courage.

A courageous mindset begins with the conscious goal of wanting to develop courage as a personality trait or classroom attribute. It requires choosing a positive state, when faced with a verbal, emotional, or physical threat. It means relying on self-efficacy, resilience, courage-building tools, and a sense of hope when faced with risk or fear. It stems from values like selflessness, feeling a sense of duty, integrity, and honor, that combine with beliefs of independence and tolerance for others in life. Personality factors like being open to new experiences, conscientious, and dependable play a role in individual emotional stability, which helps with tapping into your courage. A willingness to self-reflect, discuss, and give or receive feedback allows us to practice "to not always be right, but not to be wrong," which is a foundational quality for a courageous classroom.

To address issues like racism, bullying, discrimination based on one's sexual identification or immigration status requires courageous attitudes and actions from all involved. Those situations create an atmosphere of uncertainty, threat, and stress. Classrooms and students that are intentional about their value of tolerance for all and are equipped with the tools of being courageous will create change. Although we might not see our students as agents of change, they are more invested than we might think: "Children are more interested in matters of right and wrong, virtue and vice, then we sometimes acknowledge them as parents or teachers" (Goud 2005). Situations occur in schools and classrooms, where a small action of courage could have a major, lasting impact. Students as young as nine frequently report performing courageous actions (Muris 2009) that many teachers and parents may not be aware of, because they didn't ask.

As we tackle the long history of racial injustice in the United States including the myth of White supremacy, a courageous mindset is a necessary tool. Frederick Douglass, Ruby Bridges, and countless students after them embody such a mindset. But such a change cannot be the work of individuals. It will take all of our effort to lift the rhetoric and violence of bigotry, and create a new humanity, based on anti-racism with a platform of equality and equity for any population that feels marginalized or oppressed.

We need to create courageous classrooms whose inherent values are authenticity and courage. But it is not only necessary for us to do so, it is possible.

Tips for the Courageous Classroom

Utilize student strengths to help them overcome their fears and societal challenges.

Learning Principle

Encourage students to have a growth mindset and teach them that when they learn new things, their brain grows too. Challenge their inner thoughts about their abilities and academic potential by turning goals into small achievable steps and reminding them of their innate potential and progress daily.

Tips:
- Stay open about your possibilities and potential when faced with a challenge.
- Reflect frequently.
- Write down your strategies for solving challenges and achieving goals.
- Be patient with yourself. Keep trying.
- Don't go it alone.

Practice Praise for the Process (suggested by Carol Dweck 2014/2015):

- Encourage challenge-seeking, doable tasks.
- Acknowledge hard work by having them recognize the achievements of themselves and others.
- Teach good strategies in clear frameworks. For example, "Let's do two math problems then smile and breathe deeply 10 times."
- Increase their focus by teaching them how to identify and eliminate their distractions.
- Remind them of the benefit of effort and persistence for their own development. Allow the students to talk about people they see in their own lives who work hard and discuss their feelings and actions.

Chapter 10

Creating a Landscape of Calm in the Classroom

Acknowledge Diversity

In our critical development period, our experiences with our earliest caretakers impact our brain. At the same time, our surrounding environment influences our development, both in terms of the other people who surround us in our immediate family and community, and in terms of the physical space we inhabit. We carry this imprinting around with us throughout life, associating certain objects, colors, smells, sounds, and textures with a sense of safety and security. With an understanding of the importance of our environment, we can work to make our school environment a place where students and teachers feel at ease. All places of learning, in and out of the classroom, should be created as spaces of order, cooperation, and safety. What if every school was a place where students appreciated their teachers and classmates, celebrating their diversity, and everyone worked to make the classroom a place of pride, comfort, and safety?

When we think about shaping the landscape of the classroom, we need to start by paying close attention to the fundamentals: no courageous classroom can exist without a foundational sense of respect for each and every member. This semester I (Jed) am teaching a course called "Communication in a Diverse Classroom." The purpose of the course per the syllabus reads as follows:

"This course provides opportunities for students to develop effective oral, written, and listening communication skills in preparation for working in democratic, multiculturally rich learning environments. Content will address the principles of linguistics, dialects, and diverse communication styles, including communication with families."

Simply put, it is a class designed to help preservice teachers better understand the perspective and life experience of the students they will have in their future classrooms. We will focus on a variety of topics, including, but not limited to, racism, implicit bias, LGBTQ+ equality, religious diversity, sexism, ableism, and intersectionality. It is freshman level EDU class, strategically placed in their schedules so that the learning gained will follow them throughout their degree program. It is vital that educators learn early on in their careers about the varied life experiences that will accompany the students who walk through the doors of their schools. As the university was asking me to teach this class, I was told this: "Most of the teacher candidates that come through our program are straight, White, conservative, religious females, who have a very limited perspective on the world that they will encounter in the public-school setting. We need to prepare them for the diverse students that await them." Bravo to this university for making the statement and taking action to train their graduates appropriately. Knowledge and respect of students is vital to the success of teaching. When teachers strive to fully understand the lives of the students they teach and consciously have a classroom environment that is reflective of their values and desire for a peaceful, soothing classroom, the result will be a landscape of calm.

Acknowledge the School Environment

There is power in an engaging school environment. Having a school environment that is:

- dynamic,
- inspiring, and
- safe,

should be the responsibility of:

- educators,
- administrators,
- parents,
- community members, and
- school boards.

Schools can design buildings and spaces that promote creativity, curiosity, and achievement, according to the precepts of evidence-based school design which began in 1999. Based on the understanding that "a healthy indoor environment helps us make links to the outdoors," evidence-based school design was inspired by entomologist E.O. Wilson whose "Biophilia Hypothesis" explains that nature is a potent de-stresser because it promotes happiness and minimizes anxiety. Wilson formulated that because of how we evolved "out in the rough and tumble of nature," we have an innate affinity for the natural world that inspires and engages us.

Current research supports Wilson's theory. Education, health and satisfaction have been shown to improve in school buildings designed as a place where people can go to feel better (Steve Ward & Associates n.d.). For example, research has shown that "dim lighting makes schoolkids less fidgety and aggressive" (Anthes 2020, p. 6), and a "Daylighting in School Study" (Plympton, Conway, and Epstein 2020) showed that daylighting in schools – the controlled admission of natural light – significantly increased student test scores and promoted better health and physical development, and could be obtained without school construction or maintenance costs. It is more than adding windows or skylights, as it involves balancing heat loss/gain, and calibrating variations in daylight accessibility (Ander 2016).

The benefits of daylighting for students include the results of a study of more than 21,000 students in three California school districts. One school district found that students with the most daylight in their classrooms progressed 20% faster on math tests and 26% faster on reading tests compared to students in the least daylight classrooms (Plympton et al. 2020). Another study of 90 Swedish students found improved health and physical development when they were tracked by cortisol levels for more than a year. Their results indicated that "work in classrooms without daylight may upset the basic hormone pattern and this in turn may influence the children's ability to concentrate or cooperate, and eventually have an impact on annual body growth and absenteeism" (Plympton et al. 2020). Other studies show contributing factors that enhance the learning environment include reduced noises from downsized heating, ventilation, and air conditioning systems, increasing attendance of both teachers and students by enhancing well-being, and saving costs to school districts through inventive and resourceful design strategies (Plympton et al. 2020).

Acknowledge Physical Spaces

Students spend most of their day within the school environment, interacting within the building facility, with their peers, and teachers. In fact, schools should be recognized across the lifespan as having as much of an impact on "living as learning" in child development (Sanoff 1992). The school's environment can be a differentiating factor for student learning, mental health, well-being, achievement, and cognitive development. "Based on educational theory, the physical environment is a "silent curriculum" and environmental knowing is essential (Ghaziani 2012, p. 126; Healey Malinin and Parnell 2020).

When we think about the physical space of the school, there are numerous factors to consider, including classroom design. There is also growing research that links colors with student behavior. Human sensitivity to colors begins early. Infants as young as three months are able to discriminate colors. Colors play a role in emotions, with primary colors designating strong emotions. Red, orange, and yellow are colors that appear closer than we think by stimulating our nervous system and conveying warmth. Green and blue are receding colors and suggest coolness. Colors like white, black, and red are part of our earliest symbols by suggesting products of our body and are associated with life, death, wisdom, and values (Tuan 1974). The process of using colors like blue and red spaces to distinguish between high- and low-energy spaces in the classroom can promote self-awareness and choice to create effective workspaces for students to learn and thrive. Learning is not just related to what students see and hear as only 75% of students hear what is said in the average classroom (Steve Ward & Associates n.d.). What they *feel* also helps promote a learning environment.

A learning environment is an ecosystem that includes the activity and outcomes of learning with the five elements including:

- learning in innovative ways;
- education not necessarily teaching;
- content related to making connections;
- resources including digital innovations; and
- designing the use of learning spaces.

All of these elements are connected when teachers understand the powerful organization structure where learning takes place (OECD 2013). A learning environment changes core relationships by (a) regrouping teachers and educators into teams, (b) regrouping learners beyond age/fixed classes, (c) rethinking the use of learning time, and (d) innovating pedagogy and assessment. Learning environments require learning leadership where decision-makers provide information to stakeholders (teachers, students, and parents), revise strategies by highlighting what's working and fixing what's failing, and extend their capacity through partnerships.

Innovative Learning Principles

- Make learning and engagement central.
- Ensure that learning is social and collaborative.
- Are highly attuned to learner motivations and emotions.
- Are acutely sensitive to individual differences.
- Are demanding for each learner but without excessive overload.
- Promote horizontal connectedness across activities, students, teachers, and parents within the school. (OECD 2013)

School design has a 25% impact on students learning rate (Sivunen et al. 2014), highlighting the importance of learning environment facility design. According to research, better learning outcomes can be shown via student well-being and health, attainment, student engagement, attendance, affect, satisfaction, and behavior (Sivunen et al. 2014). The academic achievement of students is connected to aspects of learning that facilitate successful learning. Educational and learning spaces can create a wide range of emotions for many students. Emotions are linked to motivation, learning engagement, and achievement in learning situations (Pekrun 2002). Air quality and temperature can impact productivity in students by varying levels of carbon dioxide in the air. Prereading skills development has been associated with noise-related problems and chronic noise. A key factor for student engagement is noise. Annoying noise "affects a learner's ability to perceive visual stimuli and therefore affect a student's mental attitude" (Troussier 1999). Factors like classroom layout, arrangement, and furniture choices impact student achievement and improvement; on-task behavior has been linked to the correct installation of ergonomic furniture. Other considerations include a student's preference for privacy and the awareness that educators must maintain when correcting, evaluating, or disciplining individual students. For example, there are studies conducted in hospital emergency rooms indicating that patients feel more honest and open in individual rooms bounded by walls as opposed to flimsy curtains. Some students, no doubt, feel the same way.

A study that evaluated 262 children's voices (aged 11–12) on school design revealed that when evaluating categories such as interior, comfort and control, activity space, facilities, nature and outdoors and exterior, what was most important was usability by everyone with different abilities, ease of finding their way around, sunlight and appropriate room temperatures for the season, a space for sick students, less crowding, easy access for fire exits and drinking water, and appropriate tables, desks, lockers and a choice of cold snacks or drinks. Nature, outdoors, and the exterior layout was found as quite important, which signifies the criticalness of the landscape within learning spaces for warmth, safety, and security (Ghaziani 2012).

The design (sitting, architecture, landscape features) of a school building and environment can also influence healthy-eating outcomes, which are currently getting measurably worse. For example, children's energy intake from sweet beverages has doubled while their fruit and vegetable consumption has decreased in a very significant manner (Frerichs et al. 2015). According to the Healthy Eating Design Guidelines for School Architecture, schools have the power to positively influence healthy-eating practices and behaviors by taking into account "the interactions between spaces throughout the whole school building and its occupants" (Frerichs et al. 2015).

However, schools cannot expect to do it alone: on the one hand, they need to consider the impact of community and environmental psychology on their students; on the other hand, they need community involvement in programming and decision-making, which increases collective efficacy. Shared organizational values, school policies, and practices are important because community buy-in is necessary to improve healthy-eating attitudes.

Acknowledge Peace and Tranquility

Teaching students to be able to identify an object that instills peace and tranquility within the classroom can assist them in emotional regulation and taking control of their feelings, thoughts, and behavior. It can be modeled and encouraged.

A significant component of school and classroom culture is social and emotional learning (Greenberg et al. 2017). Competence in self-awareness and understanding your own values and goals, competence in self-management with skills and attitudes that regulate behavior, competence in social awareness with the ability to consider the perspective of others and approach difference with compassion and empathy, relationship skills and decision-making related to choice, consequences, and behavior fit nicely in a classroom or learning spaces that promote learning from a place of calm.

Aubrey Dane is a third-grade teacher at Redmond Elementary School in Redmond, Washington. She used the inspiration of a popular Danish concept of Hygge, a word that means comfort, togetherness, and well-being to create a landscape of calm within her classroom. Hygge is characterized by creating cozy spaces, where students can read and relax, otherwise known as a "hyggekrog – the cozy nook." It doesn't have to be a big space but a section to snuggle with a book and chill. Dane recommends that you start with calming colors like light blue or gray on the walls, limit wall hangings as they may distract students, dim the lights when possible, have cozy, comfortable seating, and focus on the classroom as a community "designed for their comfort" (Long 2018).

Now that we have articulated the importance of the various components of the learning landscape, take a moment to reflect on the spaces where you meet with students.

- How does the space look to those students who enter?
- How does it feel to them?
- Does it invite them to open their minds to new ideas, thoughts, and learning?
- Does it say to them, "you are safe here"?
- Does it provide them with comfort and security to be authentically themselves without fear?

Whether you are a psychologist with an office space, an educator with a classroom, or a professor who teaches online, the environment you create for your learners of any age needs to invite them to feel safe and accepted.

Acknowledge Emotions

While some of the items mentioned cost money, loving your students costs nothing. In my (Jed) travels across the country, I often encourage teachers to "love first, teach second." It is a mantra I live by in all that I do, and it is absolutely free to do so. Creating a courageous classroom is often just a matter of making sure that our students know how much they are loved and cared for. Bells and whistles are often fun, but not a requirement by any means.

While it doesn't require money or materials, loving first often comes with a cost. The emotional toll that loving your students can take on you is often overwhelming. I cannot tell you how many times I have stared at the ceiling while lying in bed at 2am worrying about a student who I know is struggling. I keep a journal by my bed for such times as those. It is often the middle of the night when an idea or thought comes to mind that will help me be better at my work. Love, regardless of the type (agape, philia, pragma, storge), is often difficult. It is laborious, tiring, and sometimes painful. But, the benefits of offering it to a fellow human far outweigh its difficulty. While I can never love a student as much as I would my own child, keeping this ideal of loving first has made my teaching so much stronger. Were all of my lessons stellar? Was my classroom always perfect? Did I always have the right tone, the right attitude, the right mindset? Of course not, I am as human as the next homo sapiens. I mess up. You will too. But, when creating the environment, crafting the lessons, cultivating the community, and confronting the misbehaviors, if we all agree that a mindset of love should drive our every decision, the humans we call students will benefit greatly from the atmosphere of safety, respect, and acceptance we provide.

A Story About the Absence of Pride, Comfort, and Safety

Almost 15 years ago, there was an incident at a school I (Jed) worked for that needs to be heard here. I heard a commotion coming from the classroom next door. The students in the next room were labeled by the state as special needs. It was common to hear students yelling or having a moment of emotional release. I don't like to call them tantrums, because some of them were merely communicating their emotions in the only way they knew how. There was a door that connected the two learning spaces so I opened it to see what was happening.

What I saw both alarmed and angered me. The assistant in the room was dragging a student, who was kicking and screaming, across the floor. In the moment my mind comprehended what was happening, the teacher's aide slid the student underneath her desk and yelled, "Stay there until you can act normal." What I had seen shook me to my core. How could an educator treat a student like that, especially one so dependent on her for basic needs such as using the restroom and eating? I had students in my classroom who heard the incident, but thankfully weren't witnesses to it. As soon as I had a break, I reported what I had seen to the principal. Sadly, I don't think she was surprised. This assistant had a reputation apparently. It wasn't long after that she was relocated to a new position in the building where she would not have as much one-on-one access with students. I honestly wish she had been fired. She should have been. Nothing about the teacher assistant promoted pride, comfort, or safety. Imagine how fearful the other students were, and no doubt the one being dragged across the floor and shoved under a desk was absolutely terrified. Where was the dignity and respect that adults in education should offer to students? This clearly wasn't a "one and done" mistake by the assistant. Sadly, it was a pattern. Imagine though . . . what if students saw respect, safety, and security in every interaction? What if they felt the excitement of learning, could smell academic excellence, tasted the great expectations of their accomplishments, and could hear their success? Thankfully, as of the writing of this book she has retired and will likely never work in education again.

Let's Chat

Jed: Dr. Janet, creating a courageous classroom for your students doesn't mean that other classrooms in the school are also safe spaces for students. How can courageous teachers help students to feel safe and valued even when they are in classrooms like the one above?

Dr. Janet: To help students feel safe when there are chaotic situations, it's really important to have spaces that are triggers for calm and safety. Before chaos breaks out, students should have established rituals that help them relax or de-stress, a corner of the classroom or even a transitional object on or around their desk that helps them relax. You can practice "what if" situations, and teach students how to feel safe when something unplanned and scary happens. We practice fire drills, why not practice drills for learned safety? Everyone feels better when there's a plan.

Jed: Could this teacher have been experiencing fear herself as a result of the student's behavior? While she didn't handle it well, what are some tips for teachers to remain calm in the face of fears created by an out-of-control student?

Dr. Janet: Look, teachers are humans and should always try to take the high road when frustrated, although I understand how the next thing can take a teacher to the brink. The reality is this, teachers have to remain in control because of their position of authority and the potential to "teach" how to be when faced with conflict or adversarial conditions. Tasks for teachers are to observe the situation and think about the end objective. Is it to quiet a student, remove them, or let them be? Have an inventory of needed resources and actions. Do you need back-up? Do students need to move out of the way? Think safety and security. Use your breath to remain calm and your frontal cortex to problem-solve. Remember stress and anxiety hijack learning and memory. Slow down, breathe, and think to resolve the situation.

Jed: As an outside observer, I was very concerned about how to intervene. I know there are teachers across the country who have been in similar situations. What is your advice for intervention to someone who witnesses this type of occurrence in a school setting?

Dr. Janet: Trauma can occur from witnessing events that cause confusion, pain, and fear to others. When in traumatic or fearful situations, many people, including teachers will freeze (think fight, flight, or freeze), but that's not optimal. Teachers who witness events like this can observe and help other students feel safe by moving them, help the teacher involved to stabilize the situation, and help the student or student(s) involved by calmly intervening with questions or standing by as a neutral, safe presence. If conflict triggers your own trauma, take care of yourself by talking about it and using your own mechanisms to feel safe.

Tips for the Courageous Classroom

Seek out student ideas and strategies for creating safe, healthy learning environments.

Learning Principle

- Teachers can teach students about the benefit of making healthy food and exercise choices.
- Incorporate fun, quick activities that incorporate a healthy diet and exercise.
- Teach students how to track their food intake and make healthy choices, share their own tips, and monitor their progress.
- Have students become buddies with accountability, supporting each other and creating fun rewards when goals are met.
- Solicit suggestions for making the classroom feel cozier with learning spaces in it.
- Make the activities fun.

Chapter 11
Health and Education

Obesity and School

According to the Center for Disease Control and Prevention (CDC 2021), almost one in five school aged children (ages 6–19) is obese. Obesity in children is defined by the CDC as having a body mass index (BMI) percentile of 95 or greater and overweight children have a BMI percentile of between 85 and 95. BMI is calculated by dividing weight in kilograms by height in meters squared. For example, a 10-year-old boy who weighs 102 pounds and is 56 inches, would have a BMI of 22.9 kg/m^2. He would be in the 95th percentile and considered obese. In other words, his BMI is more than 95% of other boys his age.

Overweight children and obesity is one of the top concerns for pediatricians and the percentage of obese children has tripled since the 1970s. Most obese children will grow up to be obese adults, which can impact their health and well-being. Children who are obese have higher rates of asthma, Type II diabetes, sleep apnea, bone and joint problems, and risk factor for heart disease. Other issues that may present as a result of childhood obesity are depression, low self-esteem, bullying, and social isolation (Elrick 2011), so prevention is imperative.

In the classroom, strategies to combat childhood overweight and obesity that teachers can use are:

- Promote and teach Health Education to your students. Begin with the basics about what a healthy diet is and how exercise is beneficial. Use your expertise as teachers to reinforce and incorporate healthy habits into your daily curriculum.
- Get kids moving with physical fitness. According to the National Institute of Health, it's recommended that kids get 60 minutes of exercise a day. Try to incorporate exercise into lesson plans. Encourage stretch breaks and simple jumping or movement activities.
- Eat snacks that are nutritious and healthy. Encourage parents to supply snacks that are healthy options like fruits, vegetables, and contain whole grains. Mindfully choose snacks for your classroom.
- Be a role model by keeping yourself healthy. Recruit your colleagues to join you in making your school aware of healthy eating and exercising while promoting health initiatives.

Physical factors contribute to supportive healthy-eating school environments but a comprehensive approach that factors in the multiple influences of building design and structure, organization attitude and practices, individual psychology, and motivation to drive change are necessary and important to reinforce positive healthy-eating behaviors.

Stress and School

Stress has been described as the "essence of uncertainty" (Peters, McEwen, and Friston (2017). Stressful situations occur when we have no information, no control, and no certainty – and a sense of threat. Sound familiar? Our brains resist disorder and when we feel threatened by changes external (i.e., social conflicts, disease, discrimination, political upheaval, financial stressors) and internal (trauma, physiologic demands, toxins, illness), neurochemicals like norepinephrine, glucocorticoids, and glucose are released in our body. These contribute to the stress response. An acute stress response can help us focus, find coping strategies, or develop a goal that helps us alleviate our stress. For example, think about how you feel when you lose your phone. Your head becomes hot, there's a sinking sensation in your belly, your breathing speeds up, you feel distracted or foggy, while worst-case scenarios play in your mind, yikes . . . and then you find your phone. Finding your phone can help your body ease into recovery mode. It is up to you as a teacher to find ways to self-manage your stress while teaching from a trauma-sensitive lens so that when your students face their own stressful experience, in or out of the classroom, they are able to move through it and allow their body to recover.

Stress isn't some nagging problem that is just an inevitable part of life. It's the factor that links 7 of the 10 leading causes of death worldwide, with cardiovascular disease the leading cause of death for both men and women (Quick and Henderson 2015). Workplace, occupational, and organizational stress is a major risk factor for cardiovascular disease. Stress enhances fear by engaging the amygdala and hippocampus, sending them both into overdrive with worsening psychological risks (anxiety and depression) and physiological consequences, including increased heart rate, higher blood pressure, and an elevated risk of diabetes. Stress also taxes the immune system, impacting well-being. It's imperative that you learn how to manage and prevent chronic stress and manage your brain health.

Being an educator is stressful, especially one who loves first, and can be taxing on your body, mind, and spirit. Sleepless nights can definitely harm our mental, physical, and emotional well-being. Stress isn't just a word. It's imperative for every educator to understand how stress presents in your body, how it makes you feel physically, and how you define stress by your thoughts and actions.

Try this exercise right now. Make yourself comfortable while you are reading these words. Reflect on the last time you felt stressed. Note the sensations that you had in your body.

- Did you feel unsettling sensations in your stomach?
- Were your hands tingly?
- Did your chest get tight or did you have trouble breathing?

Hopefully, you understand where this is going. It is imperative that you understand how YOU feel when you are stressed. Before you switch to your thoughts about being stressed or out of balance, identify your feelings. Go back to thinking about the last time you felt stressed. What were your thoughts? Our thoughts can spiral from a small wave to a tsunami quickly. By paying attention to your feelings and thoughts, you can slow down the wave by taking deep breaths, inhaling deeply for four seconds and exhale for four seconds forcefully pushing out your breath. Repeat four times and you will feel more relaxed. Using our breath to disrupt stressful thoughts and sensations is a technique that should be practiced and considered a tool in your arsenal for self-care.

Chronic stress is taxing on every organ in our body. Stress depletes our energy, challenges our immune system, can worsen every chronic medical illness, and can lead to depression and anxiety. Life can be inherently stressful, we can manage our demands by allowing our body to recover. Instead of dealing with issues that cause confusion, anger, or fear, we may try to cope with unhealthy behaviors that don't confront the problem or help our body recover from stress. Combating stress requires an active and conscious decision. To do that, we practice self-care.

Self-Care and School

Self-care is the ability of an individual to be aware of and understand their needs utilizing their own resources by balancing them against the demands they face. It's when you recognize your suffering and take care of what you need. You treat yourself as you would an old friend. The aspects of self-care are:

- **Awareness:** What is your inner dialogue? How aware are you of your suffering?

- **Take Action:** Remind yourself of your purpose. What do you want? Why? Think about your motivation, and analyze your self-efficacy. Self-efficacy is having the tools and ability to obtain what you need.
- **Confidence:** Tell yourself that "I am enough" and mean it. Be gentle and kind to yourself and bearing witness to your own ability to succeed.
- **Compassion:** Treat yourself with self-compassion, which includes mindfulness, being loving-kindness to yourself, and knowing that you are one with humanity (not suffering alone).

We need self-care to flourish. That means to live with an optimal range of human functioning, including goodness, generativity, growth, and resilience. It is estimated that only 20–30% of the population lives their lives "flourishing" (Schotanus-Dijkstra et al. 2016). The bad news is that up to 80% are languishing (feeling hollow or empty) at the cost of emotional distress, lost work days, psychosocial impairment, and limitations of daily activities. Self-care is central to happiness and well-being, health (mental and physical), meaning and purpose in life, close relationships, character and virtue, and is rooted in the pillars of family, faith, work, and education.

The primary focus of our brain is to evaluate risk and our health and safety. It comes as no surprise that most of us are on edge about some aspect of our lives. The good news is that although we can't control the trajectory of how life unfolds, our brains can be our biggest ally as we search for relief from our suffering. Any perceived threat to our existence can create fear and uncertainty. *Our brains do not like uncertainty.* Stress has been described as the "essence of uncertainty" (Peters et al. 2017)

Feeling stressed all of the time is how too many folks are. They report going to bed worried and stressed, have insomnia, and wake up feeling unsettled. Chronic stress puts us at risk for hypertension, heart attacks, strokes, anxiety, and depression. Toxic or chronic stress does not translate to great performance at home, work, or within relationships as we often feel fatigued, cranky, worried, or worse, just numb and checked out.

In times of stress, a healthy diet, mindful eating practices, good sleeping patterns, and exercise actually matter. Here's why. Our brain is the first organ in our body to receive nutrients that we ingest. Choose wisely. When stressed, our body craves things that are sweet and salty. Resist that temptation by training yourself to not reach for ice cream, cookies, or chips when stressed. Instead, drink a glass of water, have healthy snacks like fresh fruits and vegetables, or take a walk outside. It's easier to form a new habit than change an old one. Take a moment to think about a healthy habit that you can form when stressed instead of what you may usually do. A good night's sleep when feeling stressed and out of sorts is important to fight the tiredness that arises from chronic stress and allow our brain hormones like cortisol and epinephrine to get back into balance. It's also important to not use alcohol as a sleep-aid. Alcohol is a brain depressant and can worsen stress levels by prolonging cortisol in our body, which makes us feel more stressed (McEwen 2002).

Exercise can help you get back into balance and stay in balance by releasing endorphins, our bodies' natural painkillers, and increasing mental stimulation in our brain, which can help us solve our own problems. Stress can make us feel foggy and unmotivated but exercise helps turn the volume down on the stress response, providing an opportunity to perform optimally.

Another great stress buster is having an active support network. Research has shown the benefits of social support and the immune system. For example, the link between chronic stress, social support, and the immune system is evidenced by the fact that married people outlive single people (McEwen 2002). Social support helps with coping, creates resources to deal with issues, combats loneliness and isolation, and can improve a feeling of self-control. Social bonds are a critical factor in human behavior because it is how we have survived and our relationships with colleagues and students can provide you with meaning.

As humans we are hardwired to seek meaning and purpose from our work and lives. Numerous research have focused on educators' beliefs and internal motivation about teaching that reflects the importance of a sense of meaning that informs the significance and purpose of their work (Lavy and Ayuob 2019). A teacher's sense of meaning has been associated with better health, life satisfaction, job satisfaction, engagement, and decreased teacher burnout (Lavy and Ayuob 2019). The level of connectedness and collegial support plays a direct role in teacher stress and satisfaction. By promoting a healthy sharing work environment that allows new teachers to lean in and ask for help, mature teachers to feel supported by the administration as evidenced by manageable workloads, good resources and support, and high collegial support overall, healthy outcomes for educators can be attained. Taking care of yourself may be the furthest thing from your mind but is a critically important thing to do.

A Story of Teacher Self-Care

When I (Jed) began teaching in 2001, I was moderately fit and considered myself a healthy individual. By 2007, I had gained somewhere around 60 lbs. My blood pressure was often high and I developed acid reflux. Some may attribute that to the aging process, but I was only 29 years old. It wasn't time for me to start dealing with the medical issues that often come with growing older. In 2009, the school I worked for invited a local organization to come to the building to draw blood for a full report of each teacher's health. At first, I wasn't going to participate. Blood work was for old people, I thought. Reluctantly, I agreed to do it, mostly because of the nagging of the school secretary who also doubled as the mother of the staff and a yoga guru. She kept us all in line in more ways than one.

About a month after the medical Dracula had taken my blood, the results came back. The school was a bit of a buzz that day as teachers discussed their results. Who had the best cholesterol? How were your liver enzymes? What's the number of your good fat? Those were just a few questions I heard that day. As I heard the numbers my co-workers were reporting, I compared them to my own. In almost every category, my stats were much higher than my professional peers. Me . . . the 29-year-old guy, one of the youngest people in the building, was one of the least healthy people. I was floored. The highest number on my chart was something called tri-glycerides. I had no idea what those were. What 29-year-old did? I went to the mother hen secretary and sat in the rocking chair beside her desk. When I told her my triglyceride number was 692, her face told me more than her words. She was very concerned. She encour-aged me to call my doctor and share the results. During my plan-ning period, I did just that. The conversation I had with him scared me to death. He said things like, heart disease, stroke, death. I never really thought about my own mortality as a member of the 20s club. But the blood work results woke me up big time. I was not going to last forever. And, if I continued on the current trajectory my end was closer than I hoped.

What happened to get me to this unhealthy place? Teaching and a lack of self-care during the process. When I started my career in 2001, it consumed me. I arrived to work early, with a breakfast bis-cuit from a local fast-food establishment. I never packed my own lunch so the sweet cafeteria workers Ms. Gail, Ms. Sarah, Ms. Mary, and Ms. Anna always had a big tray of food ready for me. While the students received a regular burger and seven tater tots, I got a double cheeseburger with a mountain of tots and as much ketchup as I wanted. I worked until late in the evening trying to get eve-rything required of me finished. I would swing by Mickey Ds on the way home, eat it from the TV tray on the couch, and fall asleep from exhaustion, only to wake up the next day to repeat the self-destruction all in the name of education. There was no time for self-care, exercise, and healthy eating. I didn't make a lot of money either so buying the better options at the grocery store was often out of reach. Fast food and school lunch was easier, and took less of my time. All of this culminated in 2009 when I sat in that rocking chair talking to the school secretary.

After school that day I called my mom. She was shopping at a Target right near the school. I drove over to meet her so I could tell her about the results of the blood work. As soon as I saw her stand-ing in the dollar spot I completely lost it. The reality that my body was in danger, the fear of what that could mean, coupled with the presence of the one person I loved most, brought a flood of tears. Needless to say, my mother was as strong as ever. We immediately left Target and went to a grocery store across the street. We walked the aisles for three hours trying to find healthy food options for me that were both affordable and accommodating to my rather picky palate. At the end of the marathon shopping trip, I pulled up to the checkout with chicken breasts, turkey deli meat, whole wheat bread, green beans, and cucumbers. Cheerios and skim milk were also in the buggy (yep, that's what we call a shopping cart where I am from). My food future looked bleak as I walked out of the store that evening. Sadly, the next day was Halloween and candy was NOT an option.

Like smokers quit their cancer sticks cold turkey, I quit fatty foods overnight and committed to changing the course of my life. I examined my schedule and made immediate cuts to the time I spent at school. No later than 4pm for me. I would no longer eat school lunch, but prepare my own every day; a turkey sandwich on wheat with a side of cucumbers and green beans. Every morning began with an hour of exercise on the Wii Fit. Hula Hooping was my favorite, but some mornings just stepping on and off the board was the best I could do. Getting up early for fitness meant going to bed earlier. Sleep is essential to a healthy lifestyle, and it was definitely something I needed more of. Bed by 9pm, lights out by 9:30pm. Dinner was a chore for me at first. Grilled chicken could only last so long. I eventually ventured into ground turkey spaghetti and grilled shrimp, no butter of course. To drink, water . . . only water. No exceptions.

The changes I noticed were almost immediate. My mood was much more relaxed, my mind felt clearer, and my acid reflux seemed to go away overnight. Within two months, I had lost 20 lbs. My clothes started to be too big, I had more energy, and my mental health was better than it had ever been. The effect this transformation had on my teaching was noticeable as well. I remember one of my students telling me that I seemed happier lately. He was right. I was happier. The tears from Halloween Eve had been forgotten by the start of the new year as 2010 rolled in.

In March of that year, four months after I had begun the healthy journey, I got hungry. I wanted a burger and fries. I hadn't cheated one bit. Not even through Thanksgiving and Christmas. Tempted as I was by holiday goodies, I plowed ahead with my clean eating and 5am Wii Fit time. But the warming weather of spring and the long spell of no junk food made me long for a delectable treat. I caved. The fries from McDonald's tasted like manna from heaven. The salty goodness landing on my tastebuds brought tears to my eyes.

I admitted I ate the fries to the school secretary while sitting in the rocking chair as if I was talking to a priest behind the doors of the confessional. A teacher friend, Chara Hosom, overheard. She mentioned that running had helped her balance life, health, and her occasional eating of junk. She gave me some tips, empowered me with some confidence that I could do it, and challenged me to enter a local 5K race as something to keep me accountable. I had no idea that the seemingly random moment of conversation in the front office of the school would lead to a life changing habit, but that's what happened. Later that week I went for my first run. That run led to the 5K race, which led to 10Ks, half marathons, and seven full marathons. One of which took me right through Cinderella's castle at the Magic Kingdom as I completed The Dopey Challenge, a four-day race event that included all four of the aforementioned race lengths. Running led to a complete life transformation for me. I lost a total of 85 lbs. and my unhealthy blood work turned me into the poster boy for healthy living. Still to this day, I am shocked that it happened. I am equally shocked that the career I loved more than anything played a part in what almost killed me. The early mornings, the late days, the constant working to get everything done was actually keeping me from performing at my best level. It took me eight years before I realized the detrimental effects the work was having on me. Had it not been for the blood work that I was peer pressured to do, I may have died before I realized it. What good is a dead teacher?

We need healthy teachers. The great poet and author Audre Lorde, famously said, "Self-Care is not Self-indulgence, it's self-preservation and that's an act of political warfare" (Spicer 2019). For many educators and specifically women, putting yourself at the top of your To-Do list generates feelings of guilt or confusion. Women have been socialized to take care of others first. That has to stop. Remember, loving your students, providing safe spaces for them, carrying their emotional needs along with their learning needs is hard work. Loving yourself is making it easier to love them first. It is not selfish to take time for yourself, it is critically necessary to combat stress.

Let's Chat

Jed: We have mentioned the word burnout a few times. As I reread my story here, it is surprising that burnout hadn't occurred. I gather to say it was very close prior to the changes I made because my self-care habits weren't the best. In order to have a courageous classroom, teachers must avoid burnout at all costs. What are some classic signs of burnout that can alert someone to the need for more self-care?

Dr. Janet: Burnout happens when the demands of your job out-weigh the resources to do it and do it well. Signs of burnout are exhaustion, you simply feel depleted, feeling negative, emotionally distant and/or cynical, and lastly you feel like you are hopeless, and lack self-efficacy (you feel like you have the tools to succeed). Burnout is a threat to your physical, spiritual, and mental well-being.

Jed: Oftentimes, people use the term burnout a bit flippantly to reference their level of tiredness. But, naming it as a threat to our physical, spiritual, and mental well-being causes a bit more alarm to its negative effects. What happens to our brain and body when we are burned out?

Dr. Janet: Burnout is a medical condition that causes chronic stress. Stress is a contributing factor to death and worsens many major medical conditions especially cardiovascular disease. So, make no mistake, burnout can be deadly. Chronic stress causes our brain to gear up for battle, releasing blood glucose into the bloodstream, raising blood pressure, tampering down our immune system, contributes to depression and anxiety, and can lead to poor coping behaviors (overeating, drinking alcohol, smoking, and not working out). Chronic stress can lessen our brain's ability to reason and problem-solve leading to more impulsivity and in some cases isolation. Social support can be a buffer for burnout but when one feels alone, guilty or has self-blame, you may not reach out and it is necessary.

Jed: Okay, now that I read your answers here, it is clear that burnout had in fact occurred and it had definitely taken a toll on my body and mind. I took steps to correct it. What can teachers reading this book do to help themselves if they are currently experiencing the effects of burnout?

Dr. Janet: A recent study from the University of Phoenix stated that almost 77% of teachers feel stressed and 8% of the almost four million teachers leave the workforce yearly, not due to retirement (Schaffhauser 2020). It is safe to say that teachers are stressed. Burnout requires immediate attention and quite frankly a break. During that time, teachers can do a self-inventory and a work inventory. The self-inventory should focus on positive coping skills including behavioral actions (diet, exercise, sleep, support, habits) related to healthy outcomes and examine consistency and timeliness. Cognitive actions would be to cognitively re-appraise thoughts and create a mantra to help you push through to your own purpose. Having a workplace that is in alignment with goals helps. A work inventory should evaluate resources, professional support, and ways to share demand by asking for help and delegating more.

Tips for the Courageous Classroom

Be COURAGEOUS

CONSIDER where fear exists in your body, so that you can acknowledge your feelings and thoughts.

OBSERVE your stress and anxiety, and find healthy and positive ways to manage it.

UNDERSTAND your ACE score and its possible effect on your teaching.

RECOGNIZE and relay to parents about the effects that trauma on the way to school may have on learning.

ACKNOWLEDGE characteristics of bullying when you see them and act to change behaviors with a courageous mindset.

GUIDE students with a trauma-sensitive lens.

EMPOWER students to make thoughtful, courageous decisions to defuse their aggression.

OPEN your mind to evidence-based strategies to address mental health problems in students and yourself.

UTILIZE student strengths to help them overcome their fears and societal challenges.

SEEK out student ideas and strategies for creating safe learning environments.

Learning Principles

One way to actively cope with stress and fear, and manage trauma is to learn how to self-manage, cope, and adjust your thinking patterns. That all begins with self-awareness. Practice asking yourself, "How am I?" "What do I need at this moment and what can I do?" Exercising control over stressful situations strengthens the brains' ability to take control and manage your stress in the future. Practice.

Here are tips for what you can do in:

- **30 seconds to one minute** – root your feet on the floor or sink into wherever you are. Inhale and exhale deeply while thinking the word *one* with each breath.
- **Five minutes** – do a mindful walking meditation. As you move, notice all of your senses by asking what am I feeling, hearing, seeing, tasting, smelling with every breath.

    If you want more activity, start with
    - Jumping jacks 1 minute
    - Deep squats 1 minute

- High knees 1 minute
- Wall push-ups 1 minute
- Sit-ups 1 minute

Total 5 minutes

- **30 minutes** – breathe and let your thoughts flow in and out, mindfully noticing them by saying "Now I am feeling . . ." and noticing what you're feeling.
- Find a guided meditation online or use an app like `calm.com`, `insightimer.com`
- Do 30 minutes of exercise.

As Birley (1923, cited in Pury and Lopez, p. 95) states "courage, from whatever angle we approach it, whatever origin or purpose we assign to it, no matter what form it assumes, not even what motives underlie it, will always be a quality beloved of man."

Chapter 12
Talking with Parents

Approach as a Partner

Courageous classrooms partnered with guardians have the potential to influence the emotional and physical health of students by extending the knowledge about the importance of trauma-sensitive schools and the self-efficacy of educators to recognize when a mental health intervention is required beyond the school building. Trauma-informed schools:

- REALIZE the widespread impact of trauma and understand the potential paths for recovery.
- RECOGNIZE the signs/symptoms of trauma in its students, parents, and educators.
- RESPOND by fully integrating knowledge about policies, procedures, and practices.
- Avoid RE-TRAUMATIZATION. (Treleaven 2018)

As mentioned earlier in this book, one in every five children has been exposed to trauma. You have read the stories of students in Jed's classes, and these aren't his only ones. He has countless stories, as do teachers around the world. In our opinion, we should assume that many children and their families, as well as educators, have had at least one traumatic incident in their life. Trauma is one factor that can contribute to mental health issues. Trauma impacts brain functioning and learning. Schools play a significant role in identifying, diagnosing, and making referrals for the treatment of students. "Schools are the most common settings where children and youth who have mental health orders receive any services, i.e., school counseling (25%), followed by mental health specialists (24%), general medical providers (11%), human services (7%), alternative medicine (5%), and juvenile justice settings (5%) (Dikel 2014, p. 3).

Teachers play an important role in student mental health and so do their parents. Adopting a "love first" mindset is imperative at school and at home. Effective parental communication and involvement can improve student mental and physical well-being. Having a child who has a mental health issue or challenge can contribute to a range of emotions for parents leading to guilt, confusion, anger, or shame. All of those feelings can be projected onto students and teachers leading to alienation and frustration. Students may shut down, be uncooperative or angry, and parents may be as well.

Approach Without Assumptions

It is critical that educators avoid feeling as if parents are the problem and understand the underlying issues. For educators, that is the process of truly creating a courageous space. A courageous space is one where:

- openness is valued and blame is avoided;
- listening to understand is paramount; and
- clear communication leads to clear understanding.

To accomplish this, educators have to:

- focus on the issue at hand;
- avoid personal labels and assumptions; and
- be familiar with underlying risk factors for mental health vulnerability including exposure to:

- emotional, physical, and sexual trauma,
- domestic violence,
- food and housing instability,
- family history of mental illness,
- exposure to substance abuse, and
- living in at-risk neighborhoods.

Approach with Grace

The World Health Organization (2004) defines mental health as "a state of well-being in which the individual realizes his or her own abilities, can cope with the normal stress of life, can work productively and fruitfully and is able to make a contribution to the community." For students, this means being confident in their abilities to complete grade-level appropriate work, coping with the tasks required of them at school and home, and adding to the lives of their peers and family in a manner that is relevant to their age. Parents must understand the significance of household emotional stability for students; when students leave home and return to chaos or uncertainty, their school day will reflect it. Having a courageous classroom in a trauma-sensitive school can be an important buffer for them.

Three components of mental health, emotional well-being, psychological well-being, and social well-being, all apply to students and can impact their social and academic progress. Barriers to positive mental health are culture, racism, economic, educational, health status, social supports, trauma, abuse, and neglect. Within the domains of mental health and overcoming barriers, three critical aspects are (a) self-realization, which is defined as the ability to exploit your potential; (b) a sense of mastery over your environment; and (c) a sense of autonomy, so that students are able to identify, confront, and solve their problems. All of these domains can be taught and should be incorporated into the curriculum across all educational levels.

When parents are resistant to, or ignore, mental health concerns that teachers raise about their children, it may occur because of the parent's history with mental health entities. How educators characterize and explain student behaviors may trigger a parent's past history within educational systems and increase feelings of despair and guilt in the parent who passed it onto their child. Educators can prepare for parental resistance by selecting where and how a conversation will occur, the words used to explain the issue, being informed about potential resources, and being willing to get background information from parents in an attempt to understand but not castigate or label students without offering solutions.

Approach this entire section with grace. Resistant parents aren't always ignoring concerns. Their own fears and trauma are possible hindrances on the road to mental health well-being. It may take time, and that's okay.

A Story About Anne

I (Jed) once had a student named Anne. Her mother had experienced a heartbreaking event as a child that led to what could have been a career ending moment for me. Let me explain.

It was December and recess was especially cold this day. Anne was running around playing with her friends like she did every day. Happy kid, and no noticeable signs of trauma that affected her performance at school. As she rounded the corner of the playground right in front of the teacher bench, she fell and landed right on her knee. The fall ripped a big hole in her polka dotted Christmas tights and she was hysterical. She cried and cried, and the cold air of the day invited a stream of mucus from her nose. Being the ever-prepared teacher, I had tissues for that, and bandages if needed, but thankfully there was no blood. My co-teacher had a blanket due to the chill in the air, so she promptly covered the student up and snuggled her in between us on the bench to calm her down so she could continue to enjoy recess. It was a long blanket that draped the entirety of the bench. I was thankful for the moment of warmth, but in no less than one minute, Anne was back on the playground, the blanket was back on the other teacher, and the ripped tights had all but been forgotten. Incidents like that happen on a school playground every day. Kids being kids often leads to tumbles, falls, scrapes, and cuts. It never once crossed my mind to write a note home about the incident. I was confident Anne wasn't hurt, and that she could communicate to her mom about the minor incident just fine.

The next morning I found out exactly what she said to her mom as I sat in the conference room with the district personnel director, my principal, the guidance counselor, Anne's parents, and their lawyer. Did your stomach knot up as you read that? This happened 18 years ago and I still get nauseated as I retell it. Imagine how I felt as I walked into that room to see them all there. I was clueless about what I was walking into as I received no warning this meeting was happening. The personnel director spoke first and very directly as was his way. "Jed, we know you are an excellent teacher for us, but there has been an accusation made against you that we need to get to the bottom of." The following moments were a blur of fear and anxiety that I will remember forever. When her mom asked what happened, Anne told her mama that she fell at recess, but that I had got under the blanket with her and "made it all better." Any educator reading this will immediately see the implication. The parents were deeply concerned about the event and needed an explanation. I told them the events of the incident verbatim as they had happened, just as you read above. Those events were then confirmed by the other teacher on recess duty with me and the whole kerfuffle was cleared up. But it didn't happen without a very emotional moment from her mother. In the meeting, with all the adults present, Anne's mother confessed that she had been molested as a child by an adult male who was a close friend of the family. Someone she saw as an authority figure. This was something her husband didn't even know, and the moment was quite emotional. In the conference room that day, her traumatic childhood came roaring out as she feared that her own child was now a victim of the same trauma. Her own fearful memories were transferred into the moment her daughter uttered the words "under the blanket" and assumptions were made based on her personal trauma. Her own fight or flight took over and fight was the only option as she relied on her motherly instincts to protect her daughter from the harm she thought had happened.

As I look back on this moment, there are so many lessons I learned. The biggest one being . . . be careful. Be SO VERY careful. Everyone is walking around with traumatic scars we know nothing about and our actions can trigger the hurt in ways we never know. There is no way I could have known about the trauma of Anne's mother.

Approach with Care

Educators have to be skilled in difficult conversations, especially with the parents of students. Jed recounts that composure and clarity were vital as he spoke with Anne's parents. No doubt it was a terribly difficult conversation, but using the strongest of communication skills helped Jed to navigate his way through it. Most parents are challenged by their own concerns and feelings when hearing about issues concerning their child's academic performance or mental health. Imagine the challenge Anne's parents faced that evening as they worried about the events that had occurred at the school. Although their assumptions were wrong and misguided due to the childhood trauma of the mother, the anxiety and stress they experienced in their home that night as they awaited the next day's meeting was no doubt torturous. To lessen anxiety and defensiveness, educators should choose the setting appropriately. The conference room Jed mentioned, doubled as the guidance office. It was designed to be a place of safety for all who entered. Having the family lawyer in the meeting likely provided great comfort for mom and dad, knowing that he was on their side. Face-to-face meetings are always optimal. The conversation between Jed and these parents could not have taken place effectively on the phone or via email. A clear understanding of tone and emotion were a must for this meeting. Look for a neutral setting where all can feel comfortable. The guidance office was a much better choice than Jed's classroom (his turf) or the principal's office that could be perceived as the school's turf. Start with a positive statement instead of honing right in on what the concern is. The personnel director complimented Jed, then proceeded with the accusation. There was really no easy way to start this conversation, but in this case, it began as well as it could. Ask the parent or caregiver for their observations after clearing stating your own. This moment had obviously occurred prior to Jed being invited to the meeting. The administrators here did the right thing by listening to the parents' concerns, and not rushing to judgement and action. Before going to your recommendation, inquire about stressors or changes at home, by saying "Is there anything going on at home that I should be aware of?" As the meeting continued, and clarifications had been made, it is then that moments from home, albeit decades prior to the conversation at hand, came to the forefront and brought understanding to the entire reaction to the previous day's events. Be prepared to state your observations and a clear direction of what should happen next in support of a further intervention or assessment. Listen to parental concerns with a mind of collaboration not contention. Make sure that you and the parent are being heard by restating your assessment and recommendation and saying, "Are we in agreement?" Decide on next steps and a timetable.

Approach with Respect

When talking to parents where there may be a language or cultural divide, make every attempt to converse in a mutual language or have an interpreter (not the student or a family member) to assist. In many cultures, using a younger person (like a student) or even a family member may be construed as disrespectful. Understand your own biases related to "other" and differences in culture. We all have biases. Ultimately, it was the bias of the mom that influenced her perception about what her daughter told her about the ripped tights and the fall at recess. Because the mother had experienced the trauma of her own molestation, it was brought into her adult-hood as a parent. This bias was not intended to hurt Jed at all, but sadly, because of the way unchecked trauma ingrains itself into our lives, it leads to unconscious bias. According to the University of California, San Francisco definition, "Unconscious biases are social stereotypes about certain groups of people that individuals form outside their own conscious awareness. Everyone holds unconscious beliefs about various social and identity groups, and these biases stem from one's tendency to organize social worlds by categorizing" (Navarro n.d.). In the mother's case, she had unconscious bias, also known as implicit bias, towards Jed as a male in authority. Ways to mitigate bias are to use an evidenced-based approach to interacting with parents when discussing their child's need for more assistance with their mental health. Another way to mitigate bias is to connect with the parents or caregiver by learning something personal about them that goes beyond their ethnicity or cultural background. Doing that can provide for a more relatable connection. It is our opinion that every single human on the planet would benefit from an implicit bias workshop. It would strengthen every relationship we have.

Differences in the ethnicity or gender of a parent or teacher can lead to uncomfortable feelings for both. There is a long history of racism, bias, and racialized trauma in every institutional setting in the United States and schools are no exception. Racialized trauma is secondary to racial discrimination and directly impacts mental health. It can result from microaggressions or everyday discrimination. Life experiences as an "other" in the United States with disproportionate exposure to loss, the criminal justice system, witnessing violence, school suspensions, or being treated unfairly can result in internalized oppression, lowered expectations for self secondary to lowered expectations by a school system, and hyper-vigilance. Racism is a public and mental health problem resulting from 400 years of systemic racism with an emphasis on race (the color of one's skin) to wrongfully justify oppression and mistreatment.

Approach with Sensitivity

Racism is conscious, explicit, and meant to be disruptive, cause harm, limit opportunities and access, and also is costly. A study by Citigroup estimated that since 2000, the US gross domestic product secondary to discriminatory practices in education, access to business loans, and other areas has cost up to 16 trillion dollars (Akala 2020). Up to $90 billion and $113 billion dollars in lifetime income has been lost from discrimination in accessing higher education. Implicit bias or unconscious bias also plays a part. Most people are not racist, but we all have biases. If you have a brain, you are biased. Here's why. Our brain takes in 11 million bits of information per second from the external environment and cues from our senses and body awareness. We are only actively aware of 45–50 pieces of information per second. In an attempt to assist us in processing, our brain categories things/ people into categories, Black/White, good/bad, etc. This leads to stereotypes and biases that can be hurtful and flat out wrong. When we label groups and assign personality traits or behaviors to a specific group, it can lead to wrong assumptions, avoidance, and missed opportunities to clarify and understand. It is critical that teachers are aware of their own biases as they relate to their students, parents, families, and their own colleagues. A great way to mitigate bias is to ask not assume and try to learn at least one personal fact about someone else. It also helps to slow down your thinking, challenge assumptions, and always search for diverse perspectives. Changing habits may take more time, but is imperative for educators who want to have courageous classrooms. If you are serious about the work of fighting racism and bias in your teaching, we recommend the interactive workbook, *A Work of Heart, Becoming an Anti-Racist Educator*. Written by award winning educators Casey Bethel, Dr. Jemelleh Coes, Lisa Dunnigan, Kisha Mitchell, and Dr. Dwayne Wright, as well as Jed, the authors walk you through a reflective journey of your practice as an educator and provides a mirror to the habits and behaviors that are likely in need of a drastic makeover for the sake of ALL students. As of this writing, the book is exclusively available at teachyourheartoutcon.com under the social justice tab.

Racial attitudes are defined as the beliefs, stereotypes, and feelings that people have about different racial groups. They're important because beliefs impact behaviors and actions that can be perceived as discriminatory, biased, or racist. The racial attitudes of educators from PreK–12 to high school can have important consequences on the "learning and developmental outcomes of students, because teachers and administrators who are biased or racist can impact the academic growth of students, their self-perception and ultimately their life and educational opportunities" (Quinn 2007, p. 398). Teachers who report scant exposure to cultures and groups of people other than their own report feeling unprepared and uneasy. A study that compared educator to non-educator attitudes related to "worrisome" racial attitudes found that many educator/non-educator differences were explained by demographics and specifically education level (Quinn 2007). Teachers who understand how structural racism impacts equity and equality are more likely to teach their students about it through lessons that can promote fairness, teach White students about those issues, and mitigate stereotyping, bias, and prejudice. "With the right training and greater racial awareness, teachers can help students cope with the stress of racism and discrimination" (Anderson, Saleem, and Huguley 2019, p. 20).

Microaggressions are those everyday slights that occur to people of color and can happen to people based on their gender, sexual orientation, age, and immigration status. Here's an example of a microaggression. A tall Black adolescent who happens to be an honor roll student is more focused on solving algebraic equations than sports. In fact, he doesn't play a sport but is always assumed to be an athlete. A youthful looking female tenured teacher may be treated as inexperienced and asked to make coffee for a group, when in fact, she is running a seminar. Jed often tells me of the microaggressions that he faces as a gay male, sometimes from other gay men in the community. He is often viewed as not "gay enough" because he doesn't go to weekly drag shows, have the right fashion sense, or have a sculpted body. Educators may make assumptions about a student's academic capacity based on their economic background or ethnic background, leading to less expectations for a promising student.

Microaggressions may be conscious or unconscious. They are hurtful and damaging to self-esteem. Students frequently think about the meaning of race, while experiencing stress themselves from racism and implicit bias (Anderson et al. 2019). School educators and administrators cannot take a "color blind approach." When microaggressions are called out, they must be addressed, believed, and corrected. Students, educators, staff, and administrators must be trained on microaggressions and commit to eliminating them.

Students of color and their parents/caregivers feel the impact of systemic racism in and out of the school setting. What feels like hostility or disengagement may be the result of what an individual has experienced across their lifespan. Acknowledge cultural and ethnic difference by asking, not assuming the ethnicity or culture of a parent or a student. Don't ever say you don't see color. That's saying you do not see who they fully are, and ignores a large piece of their identity. Simply ask, What's your ethnic background? Allow them to tell you where they're from and their background. Inquire on what their impression of how it's been in the academic setting for them and their child. Ask if they have experienced bias or racism. Talk about your own experiences and observations with the intent of openness and incorporating your own vision of why you are an educator and the goals for your students. Be willing to listen without being defensive and the goal of shared values for the health and well-being of their child, without being condescending or feeling like you have to rescue a student or their parents. Focus on their strengths and create a plan of intervention for their student that is based on cultural humility. Cultural humility is when you are self-aware of your own experiences, biases, and knowledge, in addition to other's cultural practices, thoughts, and beliefs.

Approach with Resources

Educators should familiarize themselves with psychological resources that are available within the school setting and when a student may need to be referred out. Talk to parents about confidentiality, what happens to their students' mental health histories and be able to clearly tell a parent when they are concerned about their safety for themselves or others. Mental health disorders that may impact students will more commonly involve those of mood, attention, anxiety, behavior, thought processes, and developmental concerns. When a student's academic performance or social functioning is impacted and appears to be linked to a mental health disorder, teachers are often first in line to notice and record concern. Your role as an educator is pivotal in this regard. Courageous classrooms and educators understand that student performance is related to many factors; mental health is one important aspect.

When responding to a student who has a history of trauma and may be acting out, disruptive, or shut-down, your response should not be, "What's wrong with you?" but "What happened to you?"

As educators, students who may be experiencing trauma or a mental health disorder need a safety net composed of trauma-informed practice. They need to feel safe, empowered, feel trust, experience active collaboration, and feel respect for their history, gender, sexual orientation, and culture. When students feel unsafe, it is helpful to have them make small decisions, tell them what's coming next, and remind them of how they can be safer. If they say, "I don't trust you," it's okay for you to tell them that it's okay that they don't trust you. You don't have to have all of the answers as their teacher. If a student is angry respond in ways that are calm and non-judgmental with a focus on listening and not feeling like you have to say or do something. If a student shares a traumatic experience, remember that you don't have to be a therapist to be therapeutic. Helpful responses may be "This shouldn't happen to anyone," "It was not your fault," and "How can I help?"

How to de-escalate
- Be calm, confident, and non-confrontational.
- Create space.
- Speak slowly, gently, and clearly.
- Avoid constant direct eye contact.
- Show that you are listening.
- Explain your intent or purpose.
- Keep your own safety in mind.
- Demonstrate concern verbally and non-verbally.

Red flags requiring intervention
- Actively psychotic.
- Recent loss or death.
- Actively suicidal.
- Socially isolation.
- Violent criminal history.
- Actively threatening.

Let's Chat

Jed: Being aware of our own biases is so important to cultivating a courageous classroom where students can learn and thrive. What is the best way for educators to identify and mitigate their personal biases?

Dr. Janet: If you have a brain you're biased. We are all biased. Our brain processes 11 million bits of information per second and we're only conscious of 45 to 50. To help us, our brain creates shortcuts and labels people by groups as "others." In other words, our brain is constantly thinking "like me" or "not like me" when it is in new surroundings. To mitigate bias, slow down and avoid quick decisions or judgments because the brain is in react mode. Extend yourself and learn something about the other person. This is important because when the brain makes quick judgments about other people, it's usually wrong. Reflect on conversations and how inclusive you were. Notice who is not part of your decision-making process and be determined to invite them to your next meeting. Ask, don't assume, about your students, their parents, and your colleagues.

Jed: We all know what assuming does, and we all have made assumptions about people around us. Sometimes the assumptions can have negative effects and have very unintended consequences. From a psychological standpoint, what happens in a student's mind when they are the recipients of negative unconscious/conscious biases?

Dr. Janet: The impact on students who experience stereotyping, bias, racism, and microaggressions is tremendously damaging. It can cause teachers to have limited expectations of students related to racial bias, gender bias, and language bias to name a few. Having a limited expectation can lead to minimized demands and explorations of what's possible for students. Structural racism or explicit bias can lead to depression, anxiety, and a feeling of "why try?" All students should be seen from the lens of a growth mindset, where challenges can lead to new opportunities and there is always room to learn.

Jed: "I feel seen" is almost a cliché in some circles, especially on social media, but it is a powerful statement. What does it mean for students to feel seen?

Dr. Janet: When students are seen, they are accepted and exalted by their difference. The color of their skin, ethnic background, gender identity, and sexual orientation is honored by their presence. It's not ignored or skipped over but asked about, acknowledged, and valued as contributing factors to their very being. They don't have to downplay any aspect of themselves to fit in with others; others have to accommodate them. History lessons and references are inclusive to be reflective of an equal and just society.

Learning Principle

If you are a parent who feels disconnected from your child's educational process, find ways to connect with your child's teacher with necessity because your involvement is critical and courageous.

- Begin by reflecting on your own academic relationship and history.
- Think about the positive memories and actions; what worked? What was challenging? And construct three factors that are important to you about your child's education and future.
- Make a commitment to attend parent-teacher meetings and listen without being defensive or judgmental.
- Bring insights about your child that will help your child's teacher understand them better.
- Clarify how and when you would like to be notified about your child's academic progress and behavior.
- Volunteer, when possible, in class, as it serves as a new lens to experience your child and connects you with people in their academic setting.
- Ask teachers, don't assume without inquiring if you have questions about anything.

Chapter 13
What Now?

At the end of our introduction, we stated that *The Coura-geous Classroom* will promote creativity, communication, compassion, confidence, freedom, and connectedness, not fear. We invited you to join the movement of courageous class-rooms, and to start a conversation. As the work concludes, we hope that conversations are indeed happening. With your co-workers, with your administrators, with your district leaders, with your students and their parents, with the school board, and most importantly with yourself. When parents are involved, students get better grades, score higher on standardized tests, have better attendance records, drop out less often, have higher aspirations, and more positive attitudes towards school and homework (Bogenschneider and Johnson 2004). A child's academic achievement is largely shaped in the spaces that they spend outside the classroom, with their parents, peers, and in programs like summer school, summer camp, and out-of-school programs that promote recreational play or academic enrichment. Parents have the biggest influence on their child's development and academic success by helping their child learn at home. Parental involvement with school reform and being knowledgeable about how school works is critical to assist in children doing well.

Parents need to know how the school system works, what programs and activities are available, how legislative decisions affect their child's chances for success, what courses their child needs to prepare for the future, and what teachers expect in their courses for students to do well. Tips to navigate and become an advocate for your child are to: (1) Attend your local school board meetings; (2) Make yourself known to your school board with personal contact and be willing to discuss your family experience and story; (3) Be prepared. Educate yourself on issues that are important to you and your family around education. Write down at least three talking points; (4) Have a passionate viewpoint and be able to state it; (5) Follow-up with phone calls and handwritten letters, these stand out. The past two decades have focused on school reform within the classroom, but when parents are involved in the school and with educational policies, the benefits to school age children of parental in-school and out-of-school presence are multiplied.

The work of courageous classrooms begins with those of us on the frontlines of education and parents. Many teachers are the first people to see the effects of trauma. We are the first to take steps to provide protection and counseling. We are the first to alert parents to the negative consequences fear and trauma have on the school experience. Whether we like it or not, our role is much more than simply an educator. The role is vast and requires courage on all fronts. We must be educated on more than the traditional "reading, writing, and 'rithmetic." While our jobs may have once focused solely on the curriculum, they have evolved into essential workers, which the Covid-19 pandemic proved, that are relied upon for the mental, social, emotional, physical, and academic well-being of students. As President Barack Obama stated in his 2011 State of the Union Address, "educators are nation builders." We are indeed a crucial part of democracy, and our work requires courage on all fronts.

We shared our research and experiences in hopes that you would see the statistics regarding trauma and its effects on learning and feel called to action – to lean in, to listen, to liken the work we do to that of a lifesaving profession. We shared the heart-wrenching stories of students and ourselves in hopes that they will be heard by the universe and used as tools to educate the masses about the hurt that people all around us are carrying on a daily basis, and how our responses to that hurt can lead to healing. In the final pages of this work, we share with you a framework to help you reflect on the current structure of your own learning space and the emotional well-being of your students. Our joint experience and expertise in the field of psychology and education, while not perfect, nor the definitive voice in education, has led us to this moment. It is our desire that you all dig deep, reflect, and continue to provide safe spaces of learning for all students. We wish you all the courage as you move forward in the work of creating your own courageous classroom.

A Courageous Classroom
- Is a safe place that promotes growth and learning.
- Is a place students have areas that promote the ability to recover emotionally and recharge.
- Has a landscape of calm.

A Courageous Teacher
- Is aware of his/her own thoughts, feelings, and actions.
- Engages students and their parents with cultural humility.
- Treats colleagues with patience and humility.

A Courageous Child
- Is self-aware.
- Asks questions.
- Is creative, resilient, and whole.

A Courageous Curriculum
- Promotes emotional regulation.
- Teaches students to be aware of their emotions and teaches self-de-escalation.
- Highlights trauma-informed and culturally responsive teaching.

A Courageous School/District
- Has leadership that is trauma-informed and promotes culturally responsive teaching.

- Leads by example.
- Provides calming spaces for educators and students.

A Courageous Home
- Reinforces courageous classrooms' ethics of mindfulness, empathy, and resilience.
- Is free of emotional and physical abuse and trauma.
- Supports students, educators, and the importance of learning.

A Courageous Self
- Rests.
- Reflects.
- Renews.

Let's Chat

Jed: Dr. Janet, we hoped that our book would spur on conversations about the need for courageous classrooms so that students could learn and thrive. What do you hope is at the heart of each of those discussions?

Dr Janet: I hope that at the heart of all discussions is the incredible role of teachers as encouragers to "more courage." Fear is a part of our survival, growth, and development, but courage is also there. The same structures of the brain that are responsible for fear can provide us with a courageous mindset and the ability to reframe our thoughts and problem-solve. Our discussions should generate hope and the understanding that our brain wants us to be safe with fight, flight, and freeze but also flourish.

Jed: What does a hope-filled, flourishing brain look like to you?

Dr. Janet: A hope-filled, flourishing brain looks like a loop where negative stressors or events come in and are replaced with creativity, learning, a willingness to figure things out, acceptance of reality, and an awareness of emotion that is met with energy and a commitment to realizing one's full potential. It is also fueled by a body that sleeps well, is fed nutritious food, and is oxygenated with great blood flow from working out on a regular basis.

Jed: A human with this kind of brain would indeed be a courageous learner and thrive at life. For those who have read our work and are now feeling ready to fly, what advice can we close with that will ensure that they soar?

Dr. Janet: Our brain has evolved over millions of years to keep us safe and secure, and reproduce and learn to overcome our fears. Our brain is the best resource that we have to adapt, love, play, and connect with others. Our brain was built for us to flourish in times of conflict and thrive in times of challenges and success. Having a courageous mindset as we face obstacles and challenges is powerful because courage means perseverance through fear; our brain is equipped to mindfully self-regulate though our trauma and fears by asking the right questions and reflecting on the learning you gained throughout the book.

Learning Principle

Psychological First Aid–Listen, Protect, Connect (PFA–LPC) is a tool for teachers to help students who have experienced trauma (www.traumaawareschools.org). PFA–LPC evolved from school shootings in 1990 and is intended as a guide for teachers and staff. The main goals are to (1) stabilize the emotions and behaviors of students, and (2) to get students to optimal well-being after a disaster or crisis so that they can attend school and re-engage in learning.

The steps are as follows:

1. **Listen:** Let your students know that you are available to listen and talk. Listen to and understand their concerns and feelings.
2. **Protect:** Assist students to feel protected by listening to them. Advise them of school, home, and community resources that can help keep them safe.
3. **Connect:** Check-in with your students after a crisis or traumatic event on a regular basis. Encourage students to connect with their friends, grandparents, support networks, and school

guidance counselors or other teachers. School clubs and regular activities can be helpful for student connections.

4. **Model:** Make a commitment to your own self-care. Be honest to students about how you handled the crisis. Be aware that students watch your own behavioral cues and listen to what you say. Stay positive.

5. **Teach:** As teachers, who are experts in helping students learn new concepts and process information, encourage students to continue to reach their academic goals while managing their emotions. Acknowledge their achievements and share their courageous acts.

Appendix A:
External Stimulus of the Brain

Figure A.1 shows an example of brain circuitry responding to an external stimulus. The same pathways responsible for fear activation can cause fear extinction.

Thalamus: Acts as a relay station, taking in sensory information and sorting out where in the brain to send it

SI (Insular Cortex): Functions with emotional awareness and conscious experience of emotions

HIP (Hippocampus): Conditions contextual fear, mediates learning and memory, encoding, and retrieval of episodic memories

PFC (Prefrontal Cortex): Performs executive processing, cognitive control, and processing of emotional experience

BLA (Basolateral Amygdala): Plays a role in initial acquisition of fear and fear expression

CeA (Central Nucleus-Amygdala): Outputs processing to signal fear response and physiological reactions

Hypothalamus: Supports autonomic and neuroendocrine responses to fearful cues (i.e., fight/flight/freeze)

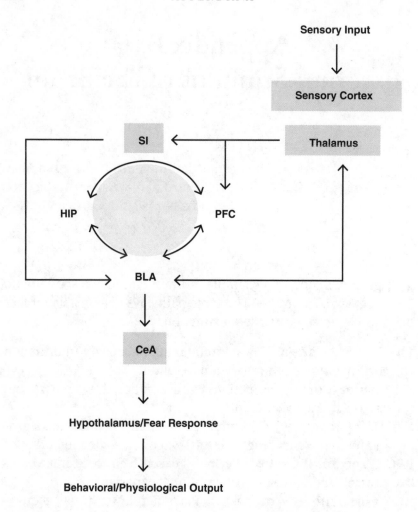

Figure A.1   Brain circuitry responding to an external stimulus
Illustrated by Tara Berg

Appendix B:
The Brain's Fear Circuit

Figure B.1 shows a fear circuit that includes the dorsomedial prefrontal cortex (dmPFC), ventromedial prefrontal cortex (vmPFC), the amygdala, hypothalamus, and hippocampus.

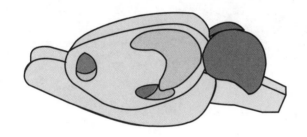

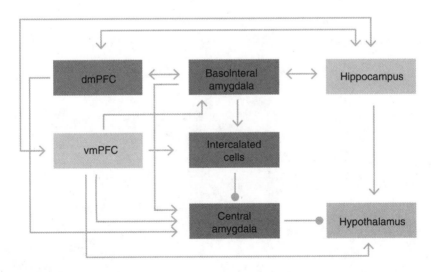

Figure B.1 Fear factor
Illustrated by Tara Berg

References

Agne, K. (1996). Fear: the teachers' teacher. *Educational Horizons* 74 (3): 130–133.

Akala, A. (2020). Cost of racism: U.S. economy lost $16 trillion because of discrimination, Bank says. *NPR*. https://www.npr.org/sections/live-updates-protests-for-racial-justice/2020/09/23/916022472/cost-of-racism-u-s-economy-lost-16-trillion-because-of-discrimination-bank-says (accessed 24 April 2021).

Allen, E.E. (1998). Keeping children safe: rhetoric and reality. *Juvenile Justice Journal* V (1): 16–23.

Allen, J.J. and Anderson, C.A. (2017). General aggression model. *The International Encyclopedia of Media Effects*. Chichester: Wiley Blackwell.

Ander, G.D. (2016). Daylighting. Whole Build Design Guide. https://www.wbdg.org/resources/daylighting (accessed 24 April 2021).

Anderson, R.E., Saleem, F.T., and Huguley, J.P. (2019). Choosing to see the racial stress that afflicts our Black students. *Phi Delta Kappan* 101 (3): 20–25.

Anthes, E. (2020). *The Great Indoors*. New York: Scientific American.

Anxiety and Depression Association of America (ADAA) (2017). Alleviating anxiety, stress and depression with the pet effect. https://adaa.org/node/2792 (accessed 22 April 2021).

APA (American Psychological Association) (2016). A silent national crisis, violence against teachers. https://www.apa.org/education/k12/teacher-victimization (accessed 23 April 2021).

APA (American Psychological Association) (2017). Bullying and school climate. www.apa/org/advocacy/interpersonal-violence/bullying-school-climate (accessed 23 April 2021).

Auwarter, A.E. and Aruguete, M.S. (2008). Effects of student gender and socioeconomic status on teacher perceptions. *The Journal of Educational Research* 101 (4): 242–246.

Baker, M.R., and Wong, R.Y. (2019). Contextual fear learning and memory differ between stress coping styles in zebrafish. Scientific reports 9 (9935). https://www.nature.com/articles/s41598-019-46319-0 (accessed 22 April 2021).

Bateson, M., Desire, S., Gartside, S.E., and Wright, G.A. (2011). Agitated honeybees exhibit pessimistic cognitive biases. *Current Biology* 21 (12): 1070–1073.

Birley (1923). The psychology of courage. *Lancet* 204 (2): 778–784.

Bishop, G. (2019). "Active shooter!" How life put Keanon Lowe where he was supposed to be. *Sports Illustrated*, August 29, p. 6.

Bland, A.G. (1979). The teacher in a therapeutic role: a historical perspective. *Peabody Journal of Education* 56 (4): 279–287.

Bogenschneider, K., and Johnson, C. (2004). Family involvement in education: How important is it? What can legislators do? In: *A Policymaker's Guide to School Finance: Approaches to Use and Questions to Ask* (eds. K. Bogenschneider and E. Gross), 19–29. Madison: University of Wisconsin Center for Excellence in Family Studies. https://www.purdue.edu/hhs/hdfs/fii/wp-content/uploads/2015/06/fia_brchapter_20c02.pdf (accessed 24 April 2021).

Breit, S., Kupferberg, A., Rogler, G., and Hasler, G. (2018). Vagal nerve as modulator of the brain–gut axis in psychiatric and inflammatory disorders. *Frontiers in Psychiatry* 9, article 44.

Brown, B. (2018). *Dare to Lead*. London: Random House.

Brown, B. (2019). Teachers: our most daring leaders. www.brenebrown.com/blog/05/07/teachers-our-most-daring-leaders (accessed 29 April 2021).

Brunzell, T., Waters, L., and Stokes, H. (2015). Teaching with strengths in trauma-affected students: a new approach to healing and growth in the classroom. *American Journal of Orthopsychiatry* 85 (1): 3–9.

Bucher, K.T., and Manning, M.L. (2005). Creating safe schools. *The Clearing House: A Journal of Educational Strategies, Issues and Ideas* 79 (1): 55–60.

Burke Harris, N. (2018). *The Deepest Well*. London: Pan Macmillan.

CDC (Center for Disease Control) (2019a). Preventing Adverse Childhood Experiences (ACEs): leveraging the best available evidence. https://www.cdc.gov/violenceprevention/pdf/preventingACES.pdf (accessed 22 April 2021).

CDC (Center for Disease Control) (2019b). Preventing bullying. https://www.cdc.gov/violenceprevention/youthviolence/bullyingresearch/fastfact.html (accessed 23 April 2021).

CDC (Center for Disease Control) (2021). Childhood obesity facts. https://www.cdc.gov/obesity/data/childhood.html (accessed 29 April 2021).

Chandra, S., Chang, A., Day, L., et al. (2020). Closing the K–12 digital divide in the age of distance learning. San Francisco, CA: Common Sense Media. Boston, Massachusetts, Boston Consulting Group. https://www.commonsensemedia.org/sites/default/files/uploads/pdfs/common_sense_media_report_final_7_1_3pm_web.pdf (accessed 29 April 2021).

Chen, G. (2019). The dramatic link between sleep and student performance. *Public School Review*, 25 February. https://www.publicschoolreview.com/blog/the-dramatic-link-between-sleep-and-student-performance#:~:text=According%20to%20the%20American%20Sleep, sleep%20habits%20to%20allow%20their (accessed 23 April 2021).

Copeland, W.E., Keeler G., Angold, A., and Costello, E.J. (2007). Traumatic events and posttraumatic stress in childhood. *Archives of General Psychiatry*. 64 (5): 577–584.

Cops, D. (2010). Socializing into fear. The impact of socializing institutions on adolescent's fear of crime. *Nordic Journal of Youth Research*. Doi: 10.1177/110330881001800402.

Darwin, C. (1871). *The Descent of Man and Selection in Relation to Sex*. London: John Murrey.

De Cordova, F., Berland, S., Pedrazza, M., and Fraizzoli, M. (2019). Violence at school and the well-being of teachers: the importance of positive relationships. *Frontiers in Psychology* 10: article 1807.

Deans for Impact (2015). The science of learning. https://deansforimpact.org/resources/the-science-of-learning/ (accessed 23 April 2021).

Debiec, J., and Sullivan, R. (2017). The neurobiology of safety and threat learning in infancy. *Neurobiology Learning and Memory* 143: 49–58.

DeSaulnier, M. (n.d.). By the numbers: America's gun problem. https://desaulnier.house.gov/legislation/numbers-climate-change (accessed 23 April 2021).

Dikel, W. (2014). *The Teacher's Guide to Student Mental Health*. New York: W.W. Norton & Company, Inc.

Donahoe, E. (2018). Teaching with trauma. https://www.edutopia.org/article/teaching-trauma (accessed 23 April 2021).

Duffy, K.A., Mclaughlin, K.A., and Green, P.A. (2018). Early life adversity and health-risk behaviors: proposed psychological and neural mechanisms. *Annals of the New York Academy of Sciences* 1428 (1): 151–169.

Dutro, E. and Bien, A.C. (2014). Listening to the speaking wound: a trauma studies perspective on student positioning in schools. *American Educational Research Journal* 151 (1): 7–35.

Dweck, C. (2007). *Mindset: The New Psychology of Success*. New York: Ballantine Books.

Dweck, C. (2014/2015). Teacher's mindsets: "Every student has something to teach me." *Educational Horizons* 93 (2): 10–14.

Elrick, L. (2011). A teacher's guide to childhood obesity prevention in the classroom. Rasmussen University, 12 February. https://www.rasmussen.edu/degrees/education/blog/obesity-prevention-in-the-classroom/ (accessed 24 April 2021).

Espelage, D., Anderman, E.M., Brown, V.E. et al. (2013). Understanding and preventing violence directed against teachers: recommendations for a national research, practice, and policy agenda. *American Psychologist* 58 (2): 75–87.

EveryTown Research and Policy (n.d.). Gunfire on school grounds in the UnitedStates.https://everytownresearch.org/gunfire-in-school/#16842 (accessed 23 April 2021).

Farran, J.C., Miller, H.B., Kaufman, E.J., and Davis, L. (1997). Race, finding meaning, and caregiver distress. *Journal of Aging and Health* 9 (3): 316–333.

French, R.A. (1997). The teacher as a container of anxiety: psychoanalysis and the role of teacher. *Journal of Management Education* 21 (4): 483–495.

Frerichs, L., Brittin, J., Sorensen, D. et al. (2015). Influence of school architecture and design on healthy eating: a review of the evidence. *American Journal of Public Health* 105 (4): e46–e57.

Garcia-Moya, I., Brooks, F.M., and Spencer, N.H. (2018). School-level factors associated with teacher connectedness: a multilevel analysis of the structural and relational school determinants of young people's health. *Journal of Public Health* 40 (2): 366–374.

Garrett, L. (2020). America's schools are a moral and medical catastrophe. https://foreignpolicy.com/2020/07/24/americas-schools-are-a-moral-and-medical-catastrophe/ (accessed 22 April 2021).

Ghaziani, R. (2012). An emerging framework for school design based on children's voices. *Children Youth and Environments* 22 (1): 125–144.

GLAAD (2013). Facts. https://www.glaad.org/spiritday/about/facts (accessed 23 April 2021).

GLSEN® (2013). The 2013 National School Climate Survey. https://www.glsen.org/research/2013-national-school-climate-survey (accessed 23 April 2021).

Goud, N.H. (2005). Courage: its nature and development. *Journal of Humanistic Counseling, Education and Development* 44 (1): 102–116.

Government Accountability Office (GAO) (2020). GAO: shootings at K-12 schools more commonly resulted from disputes or grievances. *Security* 10 August. https://www.securitymagazine.com/articles/92802-gao-shootings-at-k-12-schools-most-commonly-resulted-from-disputes-or-grievances (accessed 23 April 2021).

Gozzi, A., Jain, A., Giovanelli, A. et al. (2010). Neural switch for active and passive fear. *Neuron*: 67: 656–666.

Graff, N. (2018). A majority of U.S. teens fear a shooting could happen at their school, and most parents share their concern. *FacT Tank News in the Numbers*, April 18. https://www.pewresearch.org/fact-tank/2018/04/18/a-majority-of-u-s-teens-fear-a-shooting-could-happen-at-their-school-and-most-parents-share-their-concern/ (accessed 22 April 2021).

Greenberg, M.T., Domitrovich, C.E., Weissberg, R.P., and Durlak, J.A. (2017). Social and emotional learning as a public health approach to education, the future of children. *Social and Emotional Learning* 27 (1): 13–32.

Hall, P. and Souers, K. (2015). *Fostering Resilient Learners Strategies for Creating a Trauma-Sensitive Classroom*. Alexandria, VA: ASCD.

Hasan, M.T., Althammer, F., Silva da Gouveia, M. et al. (2019). A fear memory engram and its plasticity in the hypothalamic oxytocin systems. *Neuron* 103: 133–146.

Healey Malinin, L., and Parnell, R. (2020). Reconceptualizing school design: learning environments for children and youth. *Children Youth and Environments* 22 (1): 11–22.

Herringa, R.J. (2017). Trauma, PTSD and the developing brain. *Current Psychiatry Reports* 19 (10): 1–9.

Holdaway, A.S., and Becker, S.P. (2018). Children's sleep problems are associated with poorer student-teacher relationship quality. *Sleep Medicine* 47: 100–105.

Huberman, A. (2018). Scientists find fear, courage switches in brain. *Stanford Medicine.* https://med.stanford.edu/news/all-news/2018/05/scientists-find-fear-courage-switches-in-brain.html (accessed 22 April 2021).

Johns Hopkins Medicine (n.d.). The friend who keeps you young. https://www.hopkinsmedicine.org/health/wellness-and-prevention/the-friend-who-keeps-you-young (accessed 22 April 2021).

Jones, E.A. and Borgers, S. (1986). Parent perceptions of children's fears. *Elementary School Guidance & Counseling* 23 (1): 10–15.

Karatekin, C., and Hill, M. (2019). Expanding the original definition of adverse childhood experiences (ACEs). *Journal of Child & Adolescent Trauma* 12: 289–306.

Karpov, Y.V. (2014). *Vygotsky for Educators*. New York, Cambridge University Press.

Kottwitz, M.U., Gerhardt, C., Pereira, D. et al. (2018). Teacher's sleep quality: linked to social job characteristics? *Industrial Health* 56: 53–61.

Lankes, T. (2014). How Bronx's Eagle Academy helps inner-city kids soar. *Buffalo News*, June 22.

Lavy, S., and Ayuob, W. (2019). Teachers' sense of meaning associations with teacher performance and graduates resilience: a study of schools serving students of low socio-economic status. *Frontiers in Psychology* 10: 823.

Lebel, C. and Deoni, S. (2018). The development of brain white matter microstructure. *Neuroimage* 182: 207–218.

LeDoux, J. (2019). *The Deep History of Ourselves*. New York: Viking Press.

Lerner, R.M. and Steinberg, L., eds. (2009). *Handbook of Adolescent Psychology*, vol. 1: *Individual Bases of Adolescent Development*. Hoboken: John Wiley & Sons.

Lewis, S. (2020). March 2020 was the first March without a school shooting in the U.S. since 2002. https://www.cbsnews.com/news/coronavirus-first-march-without-school-shooting-since-2002-united-states/ (accessed 23 April 2021).

Long, C. (2018). Hygge: the classroom design word that means calm. *NEA News*, 17 July, https://www.nea.org/advocating-for-change/new-from-nea/hygge-classroom-design-word-means-calm (accessed 24 April 2021).

McCullough, A., Ruehrdanz, A., and Garthe, R. (2019). Measuring the social, behavioral, and academic effects of classroom pets on third and fourth-grade students. *Human Animal Interaction Bulletin* 9 (1): x–xx.

McEwen, B. (2002). *The End of Stress as We Know It*. Washington, DC: Joseph Henry Press.

Mclaughlin, K.A., and Lambert, H.K. (2017). Child trauma exposure and psychopathology: mechanisms of risk and resilience. *Current Opinion in Psychology* 14 (April): 29–34.

Melgar, L. (2019). Are school shootings becoming more frequent? Center for Homeland Defense and Security, 21 May. chds.us/ssdb/are-school-shootings-becoming-more-frequent-we-ran-the-numbers/ (accessed 23 April 2021).

Merriam-Webster (n.d.). Courage. https://www.merriam-webster.com/dictionary/courage (accessed 22 April 2021).

Merrick, M.T., Ports, K.A., Ford, D.C. et al. (2017). Unpacking the impact of adverse childhood experiences on adult mental health. *Child Abuse Neglect* 69 (7): 10–19.

Minke, K.M., Sheridan, S.M., Moorman Kim, E. et al. (2014). Congruence in parent–teacher relationships: the role of shared perceptions. *The Elementary School Journal* 114 (4): 527–546.

Morocco, J.C. and Camilleri, J. (1983). A study of fears in elementary school children. *Elementary School Guidance & Counseling* 18 (2): 82–87.

Muris, P. (2009). Fear and courage in children: two sides of the same coin? *Journal of Child and Family Studies* 18 (1): 486–490.

National Bullying Prevention Center (2020). Bullying statistics. https://www.pacer.org/bullying/info/stats.asp (accessed 23 April 2021).

National Center on Safe Supportive Learning Environments (n.d.). Safety. https://safesupportivelearning.ed.gov/topic-research/safety (accessed 23 April 2021).

National Child Traumatic Stress Network (n.d.). Essential elements. https://www.nctsn.org/trauma-informed-care/trauma-informed-systems/schools/essential-elements (accessed 23 April 2021).

Navarro, J.R. (n.d.). Unconscious bias. https://diversity.ucsf.edu/resources/unconscious-bias (accessed 24 April 2019).

New York City Comptroller (2016). Diploma disparities: high school graduation rates in New York City, 22 September. https://comptroller.nyc.gov/reports/diploma-disparities-high-school-graduation-rates-in-new-york-city/ (accessed 23 April 2021).

Newman, T. (2017). White matter: the brain's flexible but underrated super-highway. *Medical News Today*, 16 August. https://www.medicalnewstoday.com/articles/318966#:~:text=This%20neural%20information%20highway%20is,of%20far%2Dflung%20brain%20center (accessed 22 April 2021).

Noble, G.V. and Torsten Lund, S.E. (1951). High school pupils report their fear. *The Journal of Educational Sociology* 25 (2): 97–101.

OECD (2013). *Innovative Learning Environments*. Paris: OECD. http://dx.doi.org/10.1787/9789264203488-en (accessed 24 April 2021).

Ortiz, J.L. (2014). Sandy Hook school shooter had "scorn for humanity," according to newly released documents. *USA Today News*. https://eu.usatoday.com/story/news/2018/12/09/sandy-hook-shooter-adam-lanza-had-scorn-humanity/2259413002/ (accessed 23 April 2021).

Ouellette, R.R., Frazier, S.L., Shernof, E.S. et al. (2018). Teacher job stress and satisfaction in urban schools: disentangling individual, classroom, and organizational level influences. *Behavior Therapy* 49 (4): 494–508.

Pearce Stevens, A. (2014). Learning rewires the brain. https://www.sciencenewsforstudents.org/article/learning-rewires-brain (accessed 23 April 2021).

Pekrun, R., Goetz, T., Titz, W., and Perry, R.P. (2002). Academic emotions in students' self-regulated learning and achievement: a program of qualitative and quantitative research. *Educational Psychologist* 37 (2): 91–105.

Peters, A., McEwen, B.S., and Friston, K. (2017).Uncertainty and stress: why it causes diseases and how it is mastered by the brain. *Progress in Neurobiology* 156: 164–188.

Pinker, S. (1999). *How the Mind Works*. New York: Penguin.

Pinkser, J. (2019). When was the last time American children were so afraid? *The Atlantic*. 9 May. https://www.theatlantic.com/education/archive/2019/05/lockdown-drill-fear/589090/ (accessed 23 April 2021)

Platt, J.M., McLaughlin, K.A., Luedtke, A.R. et al. (2018). Targeted estimation of the relationship between childhood adversity and fluid intelligence in a US population sample of adolescents. *American Journal of Epidemiology* 187 (7): 1456–1466.

Plympton, P., Conway, C, and Epstein K. (2020). Daylighting in schools: improving student performance and health at a price schools can afford. National Renewable Energy Laboratory, August, NREL/CP-550-28049.

Pury, C.L.S., and Lopez, S.J. (2010). *The Psychology of Courage: Modern Research on an Ancient Virtue*. Washington, DC: American Psychological Association.

Quick, J.C. and Henderson, D.F. (2015). Occupational stress: preventing suffering, enhancing wellbeing. *International Journal of Environmental Research and Public Health* 13 (5): 459.

Quinn, D.M. (2017). Racial attitudes of preK-12 and postsecondary educators: descriptive evidence from nationally representative data. *Educational Researcher* 46 (7): 397–341.

Rachman, S.J. (2010). Courage: a psychological perspective. In: *The Psychology of Courage Modern Research on An Ancient Virtue* (eds. C.L.S. Pury and S.J. Lopez), 91–107. Washington, DC: American Psychological Association.

Reuters Staff (2019). Kidnapped children make headlines, but abduction is rare in the US (Reuters), 11 January. https://www.reuters.com/article/us-wisconsin-missinggirl-data-idUSKCN1P52BJ (accessed 22 April 2021).

Rivara, F., and Le Mensestrel, S. (2016). *Preventing Bullying through Science, Policy and Practice.* Washington, DC: The National Academies Press.

Robinson III, E.H., Rotter, J.C., Fey, M.A., and Robinson, S.L. (1991). Children's fears: toward a preventive model. *The School Counselor* 38 (3): 187–202.

Rubie-Davies, C.M., Flint, A., and McDonald, L.G. (2011). Teacher beliefs, teacher characteristics, and school contextual factors: what are the relationships? *British Journal of Educational Psychology* 82 (2): 270–288.

SAMHSA (Substance Abuse Mental Health Administration) (2012). SAMHSA's concept of trauma and guidance from a trauma-informed perspective. https://ncsacw.samhsa.gov/userfiles/files/SAMHSA_Trauma.pdf (accessed 29 April 2021).

Sandy Hook Promise (n.d.). 16 facts about gun violence and school shootings. https://www.sandyhookpromise.org/gun-violence/16-facts-about-gun-violence-and-school-shootings/ (accessed 23 April 2021).

Sanoff, H. (1992). *School Design.* New York: Van Nostrand Reinhold.

Schaffhauser, D. (2020). Educators feeling stressed, anxious, overwhelmed and capable. https://thejournal.com/articles/2020/06/02/survey-teachers-feeling-stressed-anxious-overwhelmed-and-capable.aspx (accessed 29 April 2021).

Schiller, D., Levy, I., Niv, Y. et al. (2008). From fear to safety and back: reversal of fear in the human brain. *The Journal of Neuroscience*, 28 (45): 11517–11525.

Schneider, K. (2016). How kids around the world get to school, *The Urbanist*, 9 September. https://nymag.com/intelligencer/2016/09/how-kids-around-the-world-get-to-school.html (accessed 23 April 2021).

Schotanus-Dijkstra, M., Pieterse, M.E., Drossaert, C.H.C. et al. (2016). What factors are associated with flourishing? Results from a large representative sample. *Journal of Happiness Studies* 17 (4): 1351–1370.

Schott Foundation (2004). Public education and Black male students. http://schottfoundation.org/tags/black-boys-report (accessed 23 April 2021).

Sege, R.D., and Harper Browne, C. (2017). Responding to ACEs with HOPE: Health Outcomes from Positive Experiences. *Academics Pediatrics* 17 (7): S79–S85.

Seligman, D. (n.d.). Positive Psychology Center. https://ppc.sas.upenn.edu/

Serrato, G. (2017). The young and courageous: Ruby Bridges. https://stmuhistorymedia.org/the-young-and-courageous-ruby-bridges/ (accessed 24 April 2021).

Simon, S. (2020). Ruby Bridges 60 years later, Ruby Bridges tells her story in "This Is Your Time." *NPR* 7 November. https://www.npr .org/2020/11/07/932091148/60-years-later-ruby-bridges-tells-her-story-in-this-is-your-time (accessed 24 April 2021).

Singh, M. (2018). Gratitude journaling is good for your mental health and maybe physical health. *Shots Health News from NPR.* https://www .npr.org/sections/health-shots/2018/12/24/678232331/ if-you-feel-thankful-write-it-down-its-good-for-your-health?t=1619193402405 (accessed 23 April 2021).

Sinha, R., Lacadie, C.M., Constable, R.T., and Seo, D. (2016). Dynamic neural activity during stress signals resilient coping. https://www.pnas.org/ content/113/31/8837 (accessed 29 April 2021).

Sivunen, M., Viljanen, J., Nenonen, S., and Kajander, J-K. (2014). Evidence-based design in learning environments: a practical framework for project briefing. *International Journal of Facilities Management*: 162–174.

Soleimanpour, S. (2017). Adverse childhood experiences and resilience: addressing the unique needs of adolescents. *Academics Pediatrics* 17 (7): S108–S114.

Sparks, S.D. (2019). "Nobody learns it in a day" creating trauma-sensitive schools. *Education Week*, 20 August. https://www.acesconnection .com/blog/nobody-learns-it-in-a-day-creating-trauma-sensitive-schools-edweek-org (accessed 23 April 2021).

Spicer, A. (2019). "Self-care": how a radical feminist idea was stripped of politics for the mass market. *The Guardian*, 21 August. https://www .theguardian.com/commentisfree/2019/aug/21/self-care-radical-feminist-idea-mass-market (accessed 24 April 2021).

Steve Ward & Associates, (n.d.). www.swain.com/edu (accessed 24 April 2021).

Sweeney II, P.J. (2020). *Fear is Fuel*. Lanham, MD: Rowan & Littlefield.

Tabibnia, G., and Radecki, D. (2018). Resilience training that can change the brain. *Consulting Psychology Journal* 70 (1): 59–88.

Treleaven, D.A. (2018). *Trauma-Sensitive Mindfulness*. New York: W.W. Norton & Company.

Troussier, G. (1999). Comparative study of two different kinds of school furniture among children. *Ergonomics* 42 (3): 516–526.

Tuan, Y-F. (1974). *Topophilia: A Study of Environmental Perception, Attitudes and Values*. New York: Columbia University Press.

Tuan, Y-F. (1979). *Landscapes of Fear*. Minneapolis: University of Minnesota Press.

Turnbull, C. (1962). *The Forest People*. New York: Simon & Schuster.

van der Kolk, B. (2015). *The Body Keeps the Score: Brain, Mind and Body in the Healing of Trauma*. New York: Penguin.

Voss, P., Thomas, M.E., Cisneros-Franco, J.M., and de Villers-Sidani, É. (2017). Dynamic brains and the changing rules of neuroplasticity: implications for learning and recovery. *Frontiers in Psychology* 8.

Watson, A.J. (1994). The teacher as encourager. *Journal of Christian Education* 37 (1): 5–14.

Whalen, P.J. (2007). The uncertainty of it all. *Trends in Cognitive Sciences* 11 (12): 499.

Wood, L., Martin, K., Christian, H. et al. (n.d.). The pet factor – companion animals as a conduit for getting to know people, friendship formation and social support. *PLOS ONE* 10 (4). http://journals.plos.org/plosone/article?id=10.1371/journal.pone.0122085 (accessed 22 April 2021).

Woods, N.I., and Khierbeck, M.A. (2017). The small world of a fear memory. *Neuron* 94 (2): 226–227.

Woodward, C.R. (2010). The courage to be authentic: empirical and existential perspectives. In *The New Psychology of Courage Modern Research on An Ancient Virtue* (eds. C.L.S. Pury and S.L. Lopez). Washington, DC: APA.

World Health Organization (2004). *Promoting Mental Health: Concepts, Emerging Evidence, Practice (Summary Report)*. Geneva: World Health Organization.

Zalewski, M., Goodman, S.H., Cole, P.M., and McLaughlin, K.A. (2017). Clinical considerations when treating adults who are parents. *Clinical Psychology: Science and Practice* 24 (4): 370–388.

Ziv, Y., Sofri, I., Capps Umphlet, K.L. et al. (2018). Children and caregivers' exposure to Adverse Childhood Experiences (ACEs): association with children's and caregivers' psychological outcomes in a therapeutic preschool program. *International Journal of Environmental Research and Public Health* 15 (4): 646.

Index